NEMESIS AT POTSDAM

NEMESIS AT POTSDAM

THE ANGLO-AMERICANS AND THE EXPULSION OF THE GERMANS
BACKGROUND, EXECUTION, CONSEQUENCES

ALFRED M. de ZAYAS

Foreword by
ROBERT MURPHY

ROUTLEDGE & KEGAN PAUL
London, Henley and Boston

First published in 1977
by Routledge & Kegan Paul Ltd
39 Store Street,
London WC1E 7DD and
Broadway House,
Newtown Road,
Henley-on-Thames,
Oxon RG9 1EN and
9 Park Street
Boston, Mass., 02108, USA
Set in Monotype Plantin 110
by Kelly, Selwyn & Co.,
Inter-City Trading Estate, Melksham, Wiltshire
and printed in Great Britain by
Unwin Brothers Ltd

ISBN 0 7100 8468 4

Years ago I read a short but provocative book entitled *Our Threatened Values*. The author, Victor Gollancz, was a distinguished English publisher and humanitarian. I never met him. He died in 1967 in London after a long and fruitful life.

To the memory of this courageous man and to the principles of human dignity for which he stood I wish to dedicate this book.

CONTENTS

ILLUSTRATIONS

MAPS

FOREWORD

Fortunately, Mr Alfred de Zayas undertook to write a vivid account of *Nemesis at Potsdam: The Anglo-Americans and the Expulsion of the Germans*. It is a revealing account which is timely, and it accurately portrays the tragic fate of the dramatic transfer of millions of Germans from Eastern Europe to the West, as the Second World War ground to a halt. It deals especially with the fate of millions of women and children whose male relatives had disappeared in the maelstrom of the war. Many in the West gave very little, if any, thought to the tragedy of that massive transfer of human beings involving harshest punishment in various forms, including the loss of their possessions, and even their living space, as they were driven from their homes.

I remember the discussion of the problem at the Potsdam meeting, and Generalissimo Stalin's answers to the question regarding the exodus. He was of course completely unsympathetic which is understandable, no doubt, in the light of the horrendous suffering of the Russian population at the hands of the German invaders in the Second World War. At the same time, that did not obscure the cruelty of the treatment of many millions of innocent persons who were swept along in the massive expulsion.

There is no doubt that many of us in the West were indifferent, or actually uninformed and casual about the flight of these millions of Germans.

It was advertised that the transfers should be made under 'humane' conditions. There were no controls or authoritative supervision, so that the individual refugee had no recourse or protection. It is true that the United States State Department voiced proper regard for the humanities, but its voice was not vigorous or even heard in Eastern Europe at the time of the expulsion. Few Americans dreamt of a brutal expulsion affecting perhaps 16 million persons!

New York   February 1976   Robert Murphy

ACKNOWLEDGMENTS

The idea of writing this book first came to me in the year 1969, when I was a student at Harvard Law School. 1969 was a year of fierce fighting in Vietnam, of free-fire zones and tens of thousands of war refugees. That year I became acquainted with the works of Victor Gollancz particularly with *Our Threatened Values* and *In Darkest Germany*, two deeply disturbing books focusing on the refugee problems of an earlier generation in Europe. For the first time I realized the immensity of the human tragedy that struck so many millions of human beings at the end of the Second World War, victims, as they were, of politics and of politicians.

Two of my Harvard professors deserve my special thanks for their guidance and encouragement. They are Richard Baxter of the Law School and Dean Richard Hunt of the Graduate School of Arts and Sciences.

After graduating in 1970, I became a member of the Bar in the States of New York and Florida and practised law in a Wall Street law firm until October of 1971. A Fulbright Fellowship to Germany then allowed me to commence serious research on the German expellee question. I am particularly indebted to Professors Thomas Oppermann and Hans Rothfels of the University of Tübingen and to Joachim and Freda von Loesch of Bonn for their manifold assistance during my Fulbright year. Returning to the practice of law in New York, I continued working on the unfinished manuscript. One year later a fellowship at the Institute of International Law of the University of Göttingen provided me with the opportunity of interviewing hundreds of German expellees and many of the functionaries of the Landsmannschaften. For their expert guidance I am indebted to Professors Dietrich Rauschning, Richard Nürnberger and Gottfried Zieger of the University of Göttingen, to Professor Hans Booms, President of the Bundesarchiv in Koblenz, to Dr Johannes Hopf, archivist of the Ost-Dokumente at the Bundesarchiv, and to the directors and staff of the many archives and institutes that facilitated my research.

Many people have helped in the making of this book. To name them all would make a very long list. I express my gratitude to all who so freely gave of their time and whose perceptive criticism and encouragement accompanied my research into this sad chapter of twentieth-century history.

For whatever mistakes I may have made in this study, I take full responsibility. In so far as some of the facts contained in these pages encourage more gifted authors to help fill the gap of information and thus contribute to a re-evaluation of this period of history and to a reaffirmation of the humanist commitment to charity for all and malice toward none, my effort shall have been justified.

New York
December 1975

INTRODUCTION

The most grievous violation of the right based on historical evolution and of any human right in general is to deprive populations of the right to occupy the country where they live by compelling them to settle elsewhere. The fact that the victorious Powers decided at the end of the Second World War to impose this fate on hundreds of thousands of human beings and, what is more, in a most cruel manner, shows how little they were aware of the challenge facing them, namely, to re-establish prosperity and, as far as possible, the rule of law.

Albert Schweitzer in his speech when receiving the Nobel Peace Prize in Oslo on 4 November 1954. *Das Problem des Friedens in der heutigen Welt*, 1954, p. 6.

There are events in the history of mankind that become pedestrian knowledge and form part of the consciousness of a people. The Babylonian captivity of the Jews, the fall of the Roman Empire, the great crusades of the Middle Ages, the discovery and colonization of the New World, the French Revolution . . . these are but a few of the ingredients that have contributed to our common historical awareness.

One of these epoch-making events was, of course, the Second World War. Many good studies have been published on various aspects of this war – on German aggression, the extermination of the Jews, the Nuremberg Trials, the emergence of the Soviet Union as a Super-Power, etc. A very important outcome of the war, however, has somehow escaped the attention which it deserves: the displacement of 16 million Germans[1] from their homes in Central and Eastern Europe. This movement radically altered the economic, political and demographic map of Europe. Over 2 million Germans did not survive their involuntary migration; the other millions were crowded into the truncated Reich, a country with an area smaller than that of the State of California and a population density of 600 persons per square mile.[2] The human misery that accompanied this movement, especially in the years 1945–8, makes up one of the most distressing chapters of twentieth-century history. It is in a sense astonishing that thirty years after the war so little has become known outside Germany about this unhappy sequel. Even less has been discussed about the role that the United States and Great Britain played in authorizing the expulsion. How did this extraordinary event come about? Was it necessary for the peace of Europe? To what extent did the Western democracies share in the responsibility? Was their involvement compatible with democratic and humanitarian principles? American and British historians have largely neglected to come to grips with these questions.

Let us briefly review what happened. In October 1944 the Soviet Army advanced into East Prussia and triggered a massive flight of German civilians to the West. Four to 5 million persons fled by land and by sea from East Prussia, Pomerania, Silesia and Eastern Brandenburg. Over 4 million were not evacuated in time or refused to abandon their homes in spite of the dangers of the front and enemy occupation. Millions of Germans also remained in the Sudetenland, which had been annexed to the Reich by virtue of the Munich Agreement of 1938. Large German enclaves, some dating back to the Middle Ages, remained in other areas of pre-war Poland, in Hungary, Romania and Yugoslavia. In the last two years of the war, however, a far-reaching Allied policy had been taking form, which aimed at substantial territorial amputations from the Reich and at the radical removal of all Germans from Eastern and Central Europe. At the conclusion of the Potsdam Conference (17 July–2 August 1945) a Protocol was announced, Article XIII of which authorized the transfer of the Eastern Germans to what was left of the Reich.

Was there an historical parallel or precedent for such an enormous displacement? In ancient times mass deportation of vanquished populations had already been practised, even as a matter of routine procedure in the Neo-Assyrian Empire, which forcibly resettled 4·5 million persons between the reigns of Assurnasirpal II (883–859 BC) and Assurbanipal (669–627 BC).[3] This practice of physically removing vanquished peoples from conquered territories was later abandoned in the Christian era; the territory of vanquished enemies could be partitioned and annexed, but the native populations would be allowed to remain on their lands, automatically becoming subjects of the new sovereign. An exception to this general rule arose in the New World, where the American policy of 'manifest destiny' resulted in the gradual displacement of the American Indian and in the deportation during the nineteenth century of the remaining tribes to special government 'reservations'.[4] After the First World War the principle of compulsory population transfers gained in international acceptance. The population exchange treaty between Turkey and Greece,[5] involving some 2 million persons, acquired unique historical significance because it was approved and supervised by the League of Nations; it was an ominous prelude to what was yet to come. Hitler gave further impetus to the transfer syndrome by transplanting several hundred thousand Germans from the Baltic States and Bessarabia to Western Poland[6] and by forcibly resettling the Poles of these areas in Eastern Poland. The intense hatred generated by these and other Nazi crimes in the occupied countries of Eastern Europe finally set the stage for the momentous decisions at Yalta and Potsdam with respect to the fate of the Eastern Germans.

But what did it mean in human terms to transfer 16 million Germans at the end of the war?[7] Were they all *Parteibonzen* or were the great majority of them plain people – farmers, industrial workers, men and women of all trades and professions? It may not shock the conscience of every reader to be confronted with such a statistic, with a mere number of uprooted people somewhere in the world. To understand its import it would be necessary to visualize the statistical record as concrete persons suffering the very real misfortune of losing the native soil, the soil where they had grown and where their predecessors had lived and prospered for many generations. It is not possible to perceive existentially a statistic of '16,000,000 expellees' except by visualizing the half-starved mother and child, the broken old man with vacant eyes and bundles holding his last belongings – and not just once, but millions of times over. It is this picture of human misery, the sum total of individual tragedies that should have been balanced against the political expediency of shifting these Germans to the West. Indeed, if the Allies fought against the Nazi enemy because of his inhuman methods, could they then adopt some of those same methods in retribution? Who was it then, who succeeded in imposing his methods on the other? Whose outlook triumphed?

But even assuming *arguendo* that the principle of compulsory population transfers was an acceptable policy according to the standards of a civilized world, the actual execution of the transfers still required close supervision to minimize suffering and death. The text of Article XIII of the Potsdam Protocol imposed on the Signatory Powers the obligation to see that the terms of the agreement were in fact observed, to ensure that transfers were carried out gradually and in an 'orderly and humane' manner. In so far as the Signatory Powers failed to take the necessary steps to prevent the transfers from degenerating into wild expulsions, they were co-responsible for the abuses that accompanied the implementation of the transfer agreement.

And how were the transfers actually carried out? Were the Germans merely transported west or were they also massacred in the process? For an American who only knows about the abhorrent crimes of the Nazis, it is an excruciating experience to learn of the excesses of the expulsion. The study of expulsion reports and affidavits is not a pleasant assignment.[8] Personal interviews with non German witnesses[9] and also with hundreds of German survivors of the flight and expulsion confirm this grim chronicle of inhumanity. The revenge taken upon the simple German peasant of East Prussia or the Sudetenland was no less abominable than the Nazi crimes that had provoked it. Acts of incredible cruelty and sadism were committed. Helpless civilians were evicted from their homes with clubs, women were raped, men were conscripted into slave labour, thousands were interned in camps awaiting expulsion . . . appalled, one asks whether the western democracies fought a war against Hitler in order to permit the erection of more Buchenwalds and more Belsens, to authorize an expulsion policy that would claim hundreds of thousands of innocent victims. What was left of humanism, of what President Wilson had called the 'enlightened conscience of mankind'?

It is beyond the scope of this study to examine why the facts of the expulsion of the Germans have remained largely unknown in the Anglo-American world. It appears that after the war had been won, the victors did not feel called upon to reexamine the principles for which the war had been fought or to test whether these principles were being observed in the peace. Only a few public figures in the United States and Great Britain raised their voices in protest. Their words have been long forgotten.

On the other hand, the German people, having survived the trauma of unconditional surrender, dismemberment and expulsion, could not escape the necessity to reassess their history. They had lost in total war and had to chew upon the cud of defeat. It is difficult to convey to people unfamiliar with German traditions and attachment to the soil the emotional meaning of the loss of the ancient German provinces east of the Oder-Neisse Line, the native provinces of Immanuel Kant (East Prussia), Johann Gottfried Herder (East Prussia), Joseph Freiherr von Eichendorff (Silesia), Gerhart Hauptmann (Silesia), Ewald von Kleist (Pomerania) and Arthur Schopenhauer (Danzig), to name but a few. The loss of these historic provinces, which constituted one fourth of the territory of the old Reich, appears today to be irreversible, but many Germans have not ceased to experience the pain of their loss. It is to their credit that they have renounced violence and irredentism. While many of the expellees and their children would want to return to their homes in the East, they would do so only in peace and friendship, and very few would ever go back to a communist Silesia or Pomerania. For this reason the German expellees have fully integrated in the free West, and what could have proved to be a dangerous time-bomb, a cause for a war of revenge as feared by Churchill[10] and many other Western statesmen, has been neutralized. This recognition of political realities as manifested in the *Ostpolitik* initiated by Chancellor Willy Brandt, however, does not imply retroactive consent to the expulsion or to the German partition. It is rather a manifestation of a genuine desire for good neighbourly relations. Still, if unforeseeable political developments should make a peaceful revision of the Oder-Neisse frontier possible, the German government would no doubt negotiate for a return of at least a portion of the old eastern provinces. Preliminary to any such negotiations would have to be the development of genuine détente in Europe and the reunification of Germany.

Thirty years after the Potsdam Conference Europe remains divided by an iron curtain which Anglo-American wartime decisions unwittingly helped to ring down. Although it would be desirable to alter many things in today's Europe, inertia weighs heavily against changing the *status quo*. Moreover, the cause of securing world peace clearly takes precedence over that of achieving local justice. It is in this sense that the Conference on Security and Co-operation in Europe, labelled a 'second Potsdam' by some over-zealous observers, should be understood. With respect to post-Second World War borders in Eastern Europe, the final protocol signed at Helsinki on 1 August 1975 effected a quasi-ratification of the *status quo*, which was indeed the central objective of the Soviet Union and its highest priority in seeking the conference. By achieving this general recognition of the iron curtain, the Soviet Union further reduced the probability of German reunification and of revision of the Oder-Neisse frontier, notwithstanding the fact that the Helsinki protocol also includes an endorsement of the principle that borders can be changed by peaceful means. Some critics consider Helsinki a betrayal of all the peoples on the other side of the iron curtain and see distinct parallels to the Munich Conference of 1938. Alexander Solzhenitsyn has been especially outspoken in deploring the air of 'appeasement' that characterized the meetings at Geneva and Helsinki. Yet, what viable alternatives did the European power constellation offer for the last quarter of the twentieth century? Politicians will now have to come to grips with the issues and ambiguities left open at Helsinki.

This study does not pretend to forecast solutions. It essays to fill a gap on an important chapter of contemporary history and beyond that to contribute to a reassessment of the policy of compulsory population transfers on the basis of the German experience. While some may be tempted to say that the Germans lost the war and have to accept the consequences, this rather inhuman axiom surely does not exhaust the problem. It is true that Germany lost the war, but does that necessarily justify the amputation of a fourth of its territory and the brutal expulsion of millions of its people? Does it justify the further partition of rump Germany into East and West Germany? Does it justify the extraordinary fact that thirty years after the war no peace treaty has been signed with Germany? A commitment to humanism requires that these injustices be faced, injustices which are incompatible with the Atlantic Charter and with the Anglo-American Credo. The present study is dedicated to the idea of the *dignitas humana*, which is at the base of our civilization. Let us hope that in the coming decades this idea of the dignity of the individual and the principle of equity to all, even to former enemies, shall be vindicated not only by words but also by deeds.

THE GERMAN POPULATION IN THE AREAS OF EXPULSION *

BEFORE EXPULSION

GERMAN POPULATION IN 1939

Eastern Areas of Germany		9,575,000
East Prussia	2,473,000	
Eastern Pomerania	1,884,000	
Eastern Brandenburg	642,000	
Silesia	4,577,000	
Czechoslovakia		3,477,000
Baltic States and District of Memel		250,000
Danzig		380,000
Poland		1,371,000
Hungary		623,000
Yugoslavia		537,000
Roumania		786,000
(total*)		16,999,000

EXCESS OF BIRTHS OVER DEATHS 1939–45	+659,000
	17,658,000
WAR LOSSES 1939–45	—1,100,000
GERMAN POPULATION AT THE END OF THE WAR	16,588,000

* In addition in the Soviet Union 1½ to 2 million

WAR LOSSES	1,100,000
EXPULSION LOSSES	2,111,000
TOTAL LOSSES	3,211,000

AFTER EXPULSION (1945—1950)

SURVIVED THE FLIGHT AND EXPULSION

from the Eastern areas of Germany	6,944,000	
from Czechoslovakia	2,921,000	
from other countries	1,865,000	
		11,730,000

REMAINED IN THE HOME AREA

in the Eastern areas of Germany	1,101,000	
in Czechoslovakia	250,000	
in other countries	1,294,000	
		2,645,000

PRESUMED STILL ALIVE AS PRISONERS	72,000
	14,447,000

DEAD AND MISSING DURING THE FLIGHT AND EXPULSION

in the Eastern areas of Germany	1,225,000	
in Czechoslovakia	267,000	
in other countries	619,000	
		2,111,000
		16,558,000

TOTAL NUMBER OF GERMAN EXPELLEES IN 1966 (ESTIMATED):

in the Federal Republic of Germany	10,6 million
in the German Democratic Republic	3,5 million
in Austria and other western countries	0,5 million

Source: German Federal Ministry for Expellees. Bonn, 1967.
*The German Bureau of Statistics gives a higher figure for losses due to the flight and expulsion in *Die Deutschen Vertreibungsverluste*, 1958.

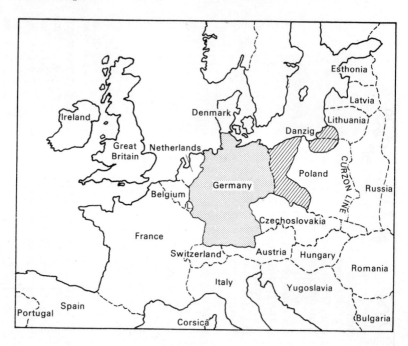

Map I.   Germany in its frontiers of 31 December 1937

Map 2   xxvii

District of Memel
separated 1920,
occupied by
Lithuania 1923

Danzig
1920 Free State

*UNDER
SOVIET
ADMINISTRATION*

Königsberg

EAST   PRUSSIA

Danzig

POMERANIA

*POLISH
ADMINISTRATION*

West Prussia
1920
to Poland

Allenstein

UNDER

Stettin

Bromberg

Plebiscite 1920
Result: 96.7 per cent
for Germany

GDR

Posen 1920
to Poland

GERMAN FRONTIER OF 1914

POLISH

Warsaw

*EAST
BRANDENBURG*

Posen

POLAND

ADMINISTRATION

GERMANY

SILESIA

R. Oder

Breslau

R. Neisse

Although the 1921
plebiscite in the whole of
Upper Silesia resulted in
59.6 per cent for Germany
eastern Upper Silesia had
to be ceded to
Poland in 1922

CZECHOSLOVAKIA

Kattowitz

District of Hultschin
1920 to Czechoslovakia

Map 2.   The Oder-Neisse territories

CHAPTER ONE

THE PRINCIPLE OF POPULATION TRANSFERS

expulsion is the method which, so far as we have been able to see, will be the most satisfactory and lasting. There will be no mixture of populations to cause endless trouble. . . . A clean sweep will be made. I am not alarmed by these large transferences, which are more possible in modern conditions than they ever were before.

Winston Churchill, 15 December 1944. *Parliamentary Debates*, House of Commons, vol. 406, col. 1484.

The twentieth century is a new era of mass migrations. Vast nations have been displaced. Millions of refugees have perished.

Of all these involuntary population movements by far the most momentous from the point of view of historical consequences – and also the best documented – was the flight and expulsion of the Germans from Eastern and Central Europe at the end of the Second World War. Had there been no Hitler and no war, 16 million German men and women would still live in their 700-year-old homelands of East Prussia, Pomerania, Eastern Brandenburg and Silesia, in the Hanseatic cities of Danzig and Memel, in the Bohemian Sudetenland and in hundreds of settlements throughout Eastern Europe. The physical and psychological suffering of the uprooted millions can hardly be estimated. To this day the wounds have not completely healed.

How did this displacement take place, and why? Thirty years after the events it may astonish some to learn that the removal of the Germans from Central and Eastern Europe was advocated and carried out in the name of peace, by nations publicly committed to democratic and humanitarian values. The main protagonists in this tragedy were, of course, the expelling States and the conquered Germans. Yet, probably no expulsions would have taken place – or at least no expulsions of this magnitude – if the Western Powers had not given an early approval to the principle of compulsory population transfers.

What led the Western Powers to authorize a policy that could bring them no direct advantage? Indeed, the sole beneficiaries of the expulsion policy were the expelling States, which confiscated billions of dollars worth of German property and annexed over a fourth of the territory of the old Reich. But not only did the Western Powers fail to derive material gain from the expulsion policy; in their role as Occupying Powers they ultimately bore a considerable financial burden because, deprived of substantial sources of food and fuel in the East of Germany, they were left to face the gargantuan task of housing and feeding the millions of expellees dumped into their zones by the Polish, Czechoslovak and Hungarian governments.

What factors, then, motivated the leaders of the United States and Great Britain to assent to the displacement of the Germans? There were many factors and complex reasons of which the following were the most important:

1 the hope of securing a more lasting peace by eliminating the problem of German minorities in Europe;

2 the need to compensate Poland in the West at the expense of Germany, without thereby leaving a potential German 'fifth column' within the new Poland;

3 the belief that transfers could be carried out in an orderly and humane manner; and

4 the desire to punish the conquered Germans.

HISTORICAL BACKGROUND

Before examining more closely the factors that influenced the Western Allies to authorize the transfer of the Germans we ought to review the history of the distinct groups of persons who were affected by these measures, paying especial attention to the different problems associated with pre-Second World War German minorities (*Volksdeutsche*), with the so-called *Lebensraum* colonizers, and lastly with the largest group of expellees, the Germans of the eastern Provinces (*Reichsdeutsche*).

VOLKSDEUTSCHE The problem of 'German minorities' in Europe dates back to the territorial settlements made at the Paris Peace Conference of 1919.

Before the First World War there had been no troublesome German minorities in Europe, since most Germans lived either within Bismarck's Reich or within the Austro-Hungarian Empire. 'Splinters of German nationality' in tsarist Russia, Romania and Serbia were mainly engaged in agriculture and lived at peace with their rulers.[1]

Large and discontented German minorities were the result of the Treaties of Versailles and St Germain, which too often failed to apply the principle of nationality[2] in redrawing post-war European frontiers. At St Germain the Austrian Empire was dismantled and new Slavic and Magyar States were set up. A German-Austrian Republic was also allowed to emerge after the war, but its frontiers were so shrunken (Austria was reduced to an area approximately that of the State of South Carolina) that 5 million German-Austrians were left as irredenta within Czechoslovakia, Poland, Italy, Yugoslavia and Hungary.

To a lesser extent the Treaty of Versailles also reduced the frontiers of the German Reich, taking from it 27,000 square miles and allocating these territories to France, Belgium, Denmark and Poland. The separation without plebiscite of the provinces of Posen and West Prussia and the allocation to Poland of parts of Upper Silesia by decision of the League of Nations following the mixed Upper-Silesian plebiscite of 1921 (60 per cent for Germany, 40 per cent for Poland) left a German minority numbering some 2 million inside the newly established Polish State.[3]

Having left so many ethnic Germans outside the new frontiers of Germany and Austria, the Paris Peace Conference attempted to salvage the wreckage of the principle of nationality by creating the minority system of the League of Nations and requiring the countries receiving large German minorities to sign a treaty guaranteeing them a measure of cultural autonomy as well as equality of treatment with the majority. Poland and Czechoslovakia, however, soon found the minority treaties to be burdensome and increasingly characterized the League of Nations minority system as an unbearable imposition on their national sovereignty. For this reason evasion gradually became more the rule than the exception. On the other hand, the German minorities, unaccustomed to foreign rule, did not make things easier. On the contrary, encouraged by their paper rights, they became restless and angry. During the 1920s they proved to be somewhat of a headache for the international community and constantly bombarded the offices of the League of Nations with petitions and protests against their host countries. During the 1930s Hitler's rise to power in Germany poured oil on the fire and through infiltration of cultural organizations succeeded in turning some discontented Volksdeutsche into disloyal elements who endangered their host countries and later played a role in preparing the way for the Nazi expansionist thrust.

FIFTH COLUMNS AND DISLOYAL MINORITIES The idea of a Nazi 'fifth column' made up primarily of German minorities is one which has gained general acceptance.[4] Indeed, the participation of persons of German ethnic origin in fifth-column activities in pre-war Poland and Czechoslovakia, as well as during the war in Yugoslavia and other countries is a matter of public record. It was therefore altogether predictable that after Hitler's defeat some form of retaliation would strike the German minorities in Eastern Europe. Certainly, a State must have the right to defend itself against disloyal elements by excluding these persons from its territory.[5]

However, it is important to know precisely what is meant by a 'fifth column' and who may be considered to be a member of it. This term of art was originally coined during the Spanish Civil War by the nationalist General Emilio Mola who, upon approaching Republican-held Madrid with four columns, referred to the nationalist-inclined elements there as his 'fifth column'. Yet, this term did not necessarily mean 'spies' or 'saboteurs'; more concretely, it referred to civilian persons who without choice or connivance happened to find themselves within enemy territory, and who could, perhaps, be turned into useful agents. For this reason the term 'fifth column' soon developed into an equivalent for 'traitor' and was conveniently used as a defamatory label against all minorities, many of whom were in no way responsible for their unenviable status as minorities, having been placed against their will under a foreign ruler, without a plebiscite or any right of option.

Were the German minorities in Eastern Europe genuine 'fifth columns'? Did they rise in a mass to betray their host countries? Opinions differ widely.

The German minorities most frequently accused of having betrayed their host countries were those of Czechoslovakia and Poland.[6]

History may still pronounce them guilty. It remains the task of post-war scholarship to analyse the complex historical background that determined their relations to the host countries, without losing sight of the fact that an ethnic minority is not necessarily disloyal merely because it demands the observance of minority treaties or because it demonstrates against second-rate citizenship. In the case of Poland, for instance, the violations of the Minorities Treaty of 28 July 1919 are documented in several thousand petitions which were submitted to the League of Nations in the years 1919 to 1934.[7] There were two areas of frequent conflict between the German minorities and Polish authorities, one being the question of obtaining Polish citizenship and the other the widespread confiscation of German farms and eviction of the German owners through discriminatory Polish legislation. A typical eviction case came before the Permanent Court of Justice in the Hague, which on 10 September 1923, delivered an advisory opinion on the merits.[8] The Court unanimously held[9]

> that the measures complained of were a virtual annulment
> of legal rights possessed by the farmers under their
> contracts, and, being directed in fact against a minority and
> subjecting it to discriminating and injurious treatment to
> which other citizens holding contracts of sale or lease were
> not subject, were a breach of Poland's obligations under the
> Minorities Treaty.

This sort of case frequently reappeared in court[10] and in other petitions submitted to the League of Nations through the year 1934, when the Polish government finally repudiated the League's minority system.

The violations of the Minority Treaty by Czechoslovakia were certainly not quite as numerous,[11] but the Germans in that country were none the less aggrieved by discriminatory treatment. Chapter 2 of this study explores in greater depth the sources of Sudeten German dissatisfaction and their struggle for equal treatment with the Czechs.

It seems, moreover, that the disloyalty of German minorities and their discrimination in treatment formed a sort of vicious circle. While the German minorities argued that loyalty could be expected only as a consequence of just treatment, the States under which they lived claimed that the enjoyment of rights was contingent on prior demonstrations of loyalty. This vicious circle ultimately shattered the League's system of minority protection.

In seeking to understand why the League's system failed so miserably, one should not look for scapegoats but merely focus on those obstacles that made success practically impossible from the outset. Perhaps the greatest obstacle was one of sheer numbers. Two million Germans in Poland and $3\frac{1}{2}$ million in Czechoslovakia could only prove indigestible to their host countries; concerted efforts to de-Germanize them, especially in Poland, could hardly increase their loyalty. With roots sometimes dating as far back as the Middle Ages, the German minorities of Poland and Czechoslovakia resented being treated as intruders or as undesirable aliens. Disappointed during the 1920s, many saw their only hope in the protection offered by the German neighbour across the border.[12] It was a situation not unlike that of many Alsatians who after the Franco-Prussian war of 1870–1 longed to see Alsace-Lorraine back in France and who did all they could to thwart Berlin's efforts to Germanize them. It is indeed ironic that the same delegates who solved the Alsatian problem at the Paris Peace Conference created another source of international friction by forcing millions of nationality-conscious Germans under Czech and Polish rule.

Later, during the Second World War, the leaders of Czechoslovakia and Poland looked decidedly upon their German minorities as collectively responsible for the Nazi invasion and for the oppressive occupation policies that followed. Most of the *Volksdeutsche* had indeed welcomed the Nazi invaders, but in point of fact they had done little to bring about the invasion, which was but the fulfilment of Hitler's fundamental policy of gaining *Lebensraum* in the East. Where the German minorities sinned more broadly was in their adoption of the racial hybris of the invaders and in their condescending treatment of Slavic peoples during the years of Nazi occupation. Out of the bitterness against the *Volksdeutsche* in Czechoslovakia and Poland arose a powerful impulse to settle the score once and for all.

EXPULSION FOR PEACE: PANACEA AND FINAL
SOLUTION OF THE MINORITY PROBLEM

In the years immediately before and during the Second World War the idea of compulsory transfer of populations was rapidly gaining in popularity – first with the leaders of the minority countries and later with the planners of post-war Europe. This relatively new idea was welcomed by a radicalized Europe as a means of permanently eliminating the hated minority problem.

With the fresh memory of the failure of the League's minority system in their minds, the planners of post-war Europe proposed to solve the problem of minorities not by redrawing frontiers nor by attempting another guarantee of minority rights, but rather by eradicating the minorities themselves. Of course, any such programme would necessarily raise additional problems from the humanitarian point of view, but it was thought that temporary discomfort and dislocation were not too high a price to pay for future peace and stability.

The earliest serious proposal that large numbers of Germans should be uprooted at the end of the war originated with President Eduard Benes of the Czechoslovak government-in-exile.

In September 1941 Dr Benes disclosed his population policy for post-war Czechoslovakia in the following words:[13]

> I accept the principle of the transfer of populations. . . . If the problem is carefully considered and wide measures are adopted in good time, the transfer can be made amicably under decent human conditions, under international control and with international support.

He further emphasized that he did 'not recommend any method which involves brutality or violence'.[14]

On the basis of these rather utopian representations British Foreign Minister Anthony Eden informed Benes as early as July 1942 that 'his colleagues agree with the principle of transfer.'[15] A decision of the British Cabinet that it had no objection to the transfer of the Sudeten Germans was shortly afterwards communicated to Benes.[16] Soviet[17] and American[18] approval followed in June 1943.

As originally proposed, the idea of population transfers was directed only against *Volksdeutsche*. In so far as persons of German ethnic origin had participated in 'fifth-column' activities in pre-war Poland and Czechoslovakia, it appeared justified for the sake of peace to remove the troublemakers. It was also generally agreed that the so-called *Lebensraum* colonizers would be expelled. These were approximately one million *Volksdeutsche* and *Reichsdeutsche* whom Hitler had sent to settle certain areas of Poland and Yugoslavia which had been purportedly annexed to the Reich. Most of these colonizers would be later evacuated by the retreating German armies and were no longer in Poland or Yugoslavia when the large-scale expulsions began. Having no roots in their *Lebensraum* parcels, these colonizers found it easier to move out when the fortunes of war turned against the Reich.

The population-transfer syndrome, however, would not remain limited in its application with respect to disloyal minorities and Lebensraum colonizers. The German minorities of Transylvania (Romania), which were loyally fighting with their country on the side of the Axis, were also singled out for expulsion. Upon concluding talks with President Roosevelt in Washington in July 1943, Dr Benes cabled to the Czechoslovak government-in-exile reporting: [President Roosevelt] 'agrees to the transfer of the minority populations from Eastern Prussia [sic!] Transylvania and Czechoslovakia. . . .'[19] The ominous extension of the principle of population transfers would still claim a larger group. Indeed, the great bulk of the expellees would be made up by the Reichsdeutsche, that is, by the indigenous population of purely German territories such as East Prussia, Pomerania, Brandenburg and Silesia.

In a conversation between President Roosevelt and British Foreign Minister Eden at Washington in March 1943, both agreed that Poland should have East Prussia.[20] With respect to the native German population, Harry Hopkins noted in a memorandum:[21]

> The President said he thought we should make some arrangements to move the Prussians out of East Prussia the same way the Greeks were moved out of Turkey after the last war; while this is a harsh procedure, it is the only way to maintain peace and that, in any circumstances, the Prussians cannot be trusted.

Thus, there was no longer any talk about 'the necessary transfer of German minorities back to where they came from'. The Germans of East Prussia were not a minority in any sense of the word. Their ancestors had lived in East Prussia centuries before the English had colonized North America. To suggest, then, that East Prussians should go back to the Rhine should have sounded as nonsensical to Roosevelt and Eden as any half-baked proposal to resettle Americans in Great Britain or Britons in Denmark and Lower Saxony. Yet, it did not appear nonsensical to the leaders of the West, for the principle of population transfer 'for the sake of peace' had become a respectable corollary to territorial settlements.

From the practical point of view alone it should have been further considered that the transfer of *Volksdeutsche* to Germany would present very great problems because there were several million *Volksdeutsche* in Eastern Europe. Still, their transfer might have been technically feasible, although even granting a gradual and orderly movement it would have indubitably compounded the misery in post-war Europe. What was hardly feasible or for that matter justifiable in the light of humanitarian principles was a transfer of populations other than 'minorities'. There were, indeed, other less radical solutions. Retrospectively this may appear too obvious, but in the midst of the great war the idea of transferring *Reichsdeutsche* somehow failed to arouse sufficient alarm on the policy-making level. How could such a plan be carried out without necessarily unleashing a vast human catastrophe? Even if the desired end were a more lasting peace, could the means be considered legitimate? A well-meaning but dilettantish answer was formulated by Viscount Cranborne in the British House of Lords:[22]

> The humanitarian case must be considered in relation to the causes of war. It can fairly be said, I think, that the suffering caused by a week's war would be more than the suffering caused by the efficient resettlement of these populations whose present situation is liable to endanger future peace.

COMPENSATION OF POLAND AT THE EXPENSE OF GERMANY

Once the principle of population transfers had been accepted by the Allied Powers as shown above, the door was wide open to the extension of the application of the principle. Thus, every proposal to revise frontiers at the expense of Germany brought with it a proposal to expel the native populations.

While the expulsion of the Germans from Czechoslovakia and the Sudetenland was advocated by the Allies as a form of collective punishment for their 'disloyalty' to the Czechoslovak State, the expulsion of the Germans from the German provinces east of the Oder-Neisse was simply a by-product of redrawing Poland's frontiers.

The frontier changes proposed by the Polish provisional government entailed the separation of enormous numbers of Germans from the Reich by placing extensive and homogeneous German territories under Polish rule. The natives of these territories would thereby be converted into 'minorities', which, it was feared, would develop tendencies 'subversive' to Poland. Anticipating these subversive tendencies, Poland claimed the right to expel its new made-to-order minorities.

These proposals were so patently in violation of the principles of the Atlantic Charter, that it is hard to believe that the Western Allies had anything to do with them. However, the problem had become one of compensating Poland, the first victim of the war, for territories lost by her in the East. Already at the Tehran Conference Marshal Stalin had made it clear that the Soviet Union would keep that half of Poland which it had swallowed pursuant to the Ribbentrop-Molotov Pact in September 1939. The Western Allies were at first opposed to this illegal annexation, but they soon realized that Stalin was not going to change his mind. At the same time most American and British political leaders felt themselves bound as a matter of honour to give some sort of a fair deal to Poland. Thus, Poland was offered territorial accessions in the north (East Prussia and Danzig) and in the west (Upper Silesia) at the expense of Germany. In order to avoid creating a large German minority by leaving them within the new frontiers of Poland, the Western Allies agreed in principle that the native Germans would have to be transferred out.[23]

In a letter to Mr Mikolajczyk, the Polish President-in-exile, dated 17 November 1944, President Roosevelt stated:[24]

If the Polish Government and people desire in connection with the new frontiers of the Polish state to bring about the transfer to and from territory of Poland of national minorities, the United States Government will raise no objection, and as far as practicable, will facilitate such transfer.

One month later the same policy was repeated by Secretary of State Stettinius in a public statement on US policy toward Poland:[25]

If . . . the Government and people of Poland decide that it would be in the interests of the Polish state to transfer national groups, the United States Government in

cooperation with other governments will assist Poland, in
so far as practicable, in such transfers.

The British government took the same position with respect to
the necessity of compensating Poland in the West and of transferring the Germans out. However, a far smaller compensation for
Poland had been contemplated than Poland in the end took.[26]
The Western Allies had been prepared to consent to the transference of 2 to 4 million *Reichsdeutsche*, but never to the expulsion of over 9 million.

'ORDERLY AND HUMANE' TRANSFERS: THE PRECEDENT OF THE TREATY OF LAUSANNE

The very wide adherence to the principle of population transfers
among the leaders of the Western democracies was attributable
in part to a rather optimistic appraisal of the results of the Greek-
Turkish population exchange, which was carried out after the
First World War pursuant to the Lausanne Treaty.[27] While a
few leading politicians deplored the transfers, a majority gradually
exhibited a peculiar euphoria over the conceptual simplicity of the
solution.

In his widely quoted speech before the House of Commons
on 5 December 1944, Prime Minister Churchill said of the
proposed expulsion of the Germans:[28]

> A clean sweep will be made. I am not alarmed by the
> prospect of the disentanglement of populations, nor even by
> these large transferences, which are more possible in modern
> conditions than they ever were before.
> The disentanglement of populations which took place
> between Greece and Turkey after the last war – my noble
> Friend opposite may remember – was in many ways a success,
> and has produced friendly relations between Greece and
> Turkey ever since. . . .

Churchill's expressed enthusiasm for the precedent of the
Lausanne Treaty sharply contrasts with the denunciation of the
principle of compulsory population transfers by Lord Curzon,
British Foreign Minister from 1919 to 1924 and participant at the
Lausanne Conference, who at that time warned of the dire
consequences that would follow such a 'thoroughly bad and

vicious solution, for which the world will pay a heavy penalty for a hundred years to come.'[29]

Similarly, the Lord Bishop of Chichester condemned the principle of population transfers in an address before the House of Lords and expressed a judgment on the Lausanne Treaty substantially different from that which Prime Minister Churchill had hailed:[30]

> There was a Turco-Greek exchange of populations after the
> first world war which made perhaps the best of a bad job;
> but it was not a model of either humanity or wisdom, and its
> repercussions, economic and political, are still with us.
> Only just over 1,000,000 Greeks were transferred from
> Turkish territory and, as Sir John Hope-Simpson, who was
> intimately concerned, has remarked, it involved an appalling
> amount of misery and hardship.

Still, a crucial factor in the consent of the Western Allies to the transfer of the Germans after the Second World War was their sanguine belief that the transfer would be carried out in an orderly and humane manner and that the expelling countries would co-operate with them and observe the timing and methods prescribed by the Control Council to assure a transfer with a minimum of complications.

The Western Allies had even planned to provide compensation for the transferees, an idea expressly adhered to by the Czech government-in-exile[31] but not by the Polish. A memorandum prepared in the US State Department and dated 31 May 1944 recommended, for instance, that the American government should oppose the mass transfer of Germans immediately upon the cessation of hostilities, so that arrangements for an orderly transfer could be made. It further observed that 'serious economic injury would be done if these people should be summarily uprooted from their homes and thrown into Germany without compensation for their possessions and without provision for livelihood.'[32]

The story of the consternation of the Western Allies at their later inability to control the expulsions is the subject of Chapters 5 and 6 of this study. Suffice it to say for now that the Western Allies would have never given their authorization to the transfer of the Germans if they had realistically foreseen the chaos that would unfold before their eyes. They had deluded themselves with the comforting idea of an internationally supervised transfer that would function as smoothly as a business transaction. It had been easy to plan orderly transfers on paper. Later, when these stampeded into grotesque expulsions, it was too late to stop them, and the Western Allies found themselves sharing in the responsibility for a catastrophe they had never intended.[33]

THE PREVALENT DESIRE TO PUNISH THE GERMANS COLLECTIVELY

Although it is true that the Western Allies had foreseen a different kind of displacement, one which would have been less harsh on those affected, the desire to punish the Germans collectively for the misery brought to the world by the war played a not unimportant role in inducing the Allies to authorize the removal of millions of Germans from the East and to offer some of their lands to the Poles and the Czechs in compensation for what these peoples had suffered in the years of Nazi occupation.

Yet, in September 1939 few persons in Britain or in the United States would have advocated the idea of punishing the Germans collectively, even though Hitler had just invaded Poland. Cool heads still differentiated between Hitler and the Germans, realizing that Hitler had launched his war without consulting the people and even against the cautious advice of many of the military. After all, dictators usually decide on their own authority without first asking the approval of a parliament or of the people. But as the European conflict escalated to 'total war'[34] the German enemy was increasingly identified with Hitler and Nemesis was invoked upon the entire German race. Fantastic theories that militarism and nihilism were innate in the German character were developed and even professed by persons on the policy-making level. These ultra-rational manifestations, however, were but a reaction to the ideological cold-bloodness of the National Socialist leadership and especially to the genocidal implications of the *Herrenvolk Weltanschauung*. Thus, conventional hatred of the enemy evolved into an intense and pervasive Germanophobia, making no distinction between Nazis and non-Nazis in Germany, between the guilty and the innocent.

With respect to population transfers as a form of collective punishment, the Nazi leadership had already set the precedent in 1939–41 by expelling over one million Poles[35] from the annexed

voivodeships of Posen and Pomerellen into the so-called Government General of Poland. With this background it is not at all
surprising that after the defeat of the German Reich the *lex
talionis* found many adherents among the Poles, who did not
merely propose to clear Posen and Pomerellen of Germans, but
beyond that intended to annex entire provinces of pre-war
Germany and to expel the indigenous population, so as to make
room for Polish colonizers from the East. The German *Drang
nach Osten*, which for centuries had been feared by Germany's
Eastern neighbours, was suddenly reversed and supplanted by a
revival of the old slavic *Drang nach Westen*, this time supported
by the victorious Red Army and authorized in part by the Western
Powers.

The United States and Great Britain, of course, did not have
any historic stake in promoting the westward push of the Slavic
nations. It was simply the unspeakable inhumanity of Hitler's
regime that made Roosevelt and Churchill morally insensitive
to what might happen to millions of Germans in the East. The
odour of Belsen and Buchenwald was in the air and the dominant
thought among many Western politicians was that the Germans
had not suffered nearly enough, although Germany lay in ruins
and 4 million German soldiers were dead (as compared with about
300,000 US casualties). The Germans could not repay the
enormous suffering they had caused.[36]

It was in this spirit that President Roosevelt had written to
Secretary of War Stimson: 'The German people as a whole must
have it driven home to them that the whole nation has been
engaged in a lawless conspiracy against the decencies of modern
civilization.'[37] The whole German nation? In this communication
dated 26 August 1944, President Roosevelt completely disregarded the existence of a German opposition to National
Socialism[38] which not infrequently had manifested itself during
the twelve short but fateful years of Nazi rule. Student dissidents
like the brothers Hans and Sophie Scholl had been executed for
distributing anti-Nazi propaganda at the University of Munich.[39]
The Bishop of Munich Johann Neuhäusler[40] had been interned
in Dachau, the Lutheran Pastor Martin Niemöller[41] in
Sachsenhausen, the Theologian Dietrich Bonhoeffer had been
executed. Several attempts on the life of Adolf Hitler had been
made, culminating in the unsuccessful conspiracy of 20 July 1944,
which counted among the conspirators thousands of prominent

Germans including Claus Graf von Stauffenberg, Intelligence-Chief Admiral Canaris, Carl Goerdeler, Generaloberst Ludwig Beck and even the 'Desert Fox' Fieldmarshal Erwin Rommel. Despite these facts most politicians in the West saw Germany as a Nazi monolith and considered all Germans to be equally guilty. Evidence of the prevailing mood was given in the 1943 annual meeting of the British Labour Party which adopted a resolution making the entire German people responsible for Hitler.[42]

Somehow very few politicians remembered the fact that in the German election of 20 May 1928 only 2·8 per cent of the Germans had voted for the Nazis.[43] It had not been until the great depression that Hitler's party had gained in popularity by offering *Arbeit und Brot* at a time when there were 6·6 million workers unemployed. And even then the party had only mustered 33 per cent of the vote in the November 1932 election. Later, in the first election *after* Hitler's appointment as Chancellor in January 1933, after the *Reichstag*'s fire and the banning of the large German Communist Party, the National Socialists again failed to win over a majority of the Germans, reaching only 44 per cent of the vote in the election of 5 March 1933. Yet, the Minister of Propaganda, Dr Joseph Goebbels, knew well how to manipulate the masses and how to further the growth of totalitarian society through the so-called *Gleichschaltung*, implemented, of course, on a 'like it or not' basis.

Overreaction to something evil is hardly a rare occurrence, especially when that evil threatens essentials of one's civilization or way of life. In this sense overreaction to the Nazi threat in the form of extreme Germanophobia is not at all surprising. However, the historical record also reveals that in the midst of the anti-German chorus some voices were raised in Great Britain and America that pleaded for moderation at a time when moderation was definitely out of fashion.[44]

Robert Hutchings, President of the University of Chicago, was one of those dissenters who rejected the popular thesis of collective guilt and expressed grave concern over the callousness shown by American and British leaders with respect to the future of Germany and the Germans. In a speech before 2,000 of his students he observed shortly after the signing of the German unconditional surrender:[45]

The most distressing aspect of present discussions of the

future of Germany is the glee with which the most
inhuman proposals are brought forward and the evident
pleasure with which they are received by our fellow citizens. . . .

Surely one of the most inhuman proposals brought forward was
the uprooting of millions from their homelands. But, advocated
by many respected political leaders, this extraordinarily severe
measure had gained social acceptability. In the British House of
Lords on 8 March 1944, the Earl of Mansfield had already stated
the essence of the new doctrine of impassiveness to human
suffering:[46]

The Atlantic Charter will not apply to Germany, and
therefore there is no reason whatever why we should not
contemplate, if not with equanimity, at least without undue
consternation, any unavoidable sufferings that may be
inflicted on German minorities in the course of their
transference.

One year later, shortly before the end of hostilities, Clement
Attlee echoed the popular doctrine of collective guilt in an
address in the House of Commons:[47]

They have broken down the old barriers, and therefore I
say that they cannot appeal to the old Europe. If they have
to yield, to make restitution, they are not entitled to appeal
on the basis of the moral laws that they have disregarded or
the pity and mercy that they have never extended to any
others.

But who were 'they'? The expulsion would affect guilty and
innocent with equal severity. Nothing would protect the Social
Democrats or the moderates of Brüning's[48] Zentrum Party from
Nemesis's fury. Nemesis was free to smite the East Prussians,
the Pomeranians, the Silesians, the Sudetenlanders. 'They' had
no rights.

CHAPTER TWO

THE GERMANS
OF CZECHOSLOVAKIA

We must get rid of all those Germans who plunged a
dagger in the back of the Czechoslovak State in 1938.

Benes in a broadcast from London, 1944. Holborn,
War and Peace Aims of the United Nations, vol. 2, p. 1036.

THE TREATY OF ST GERMAIN-EN-LAYE

Of all the expulsions that followed the Second World War, the
expulsion of the Sudeten Germans was the most popular and
the first one to be approved by the Western Allies. Dr Benes, the
Czechoslovak President-in-exile, persuasively presented the Czech
case for expulsion. Everyone seemed to agree that the Sudeten
Germans had betrayed the Czechs and should therefore be
punished. But what precisely was the nature of the Sudeten
German betrayal?

All discussion about the Czech-German controversy must
begin somewhere. The Munich Agreement is a popular starting
point. Indeed, mere mention of the Sudeten problem immediately
evokes memories of the Munich Conference and of Neville
Chamberlain's famous umbrella. Whatever the underlying facts,
'appeasement' is the first word one associates with Munich; the
'sell-out' of the Czechoslovak cause is the second. Yet, as shown
in the preceding chapter, Munich had a long history, and only in
this perspective can it be understood. Approaching the problem
in this way, one becomes aware of the reality of close Slavic-
German co-operation but also of the unhappier confrontations
that flared up periodically over a period of 700 years of joint
history. Particularly relevant to an understanding of Munich are
the emergence of nationalism in the nineteenth century and the
events leading to the outbreak of the First World War and to the
Treaty of St Germain-en-Laye, which set up Czechoslovakia as a
free state. In a very real sense, the errors of the Paris Peace

Conference made the adjustments of the Munich Conference inevitable sooner or later, and thus any re-evaluation of Munich necessarily entails also a re-evaluation of Paris.

Central to the Czech-German controversy was the desire of both peoples to achieve self-determination, even at the expense and to the detriment of the other. A vigorous and creative people, the Czechs had never wanted to live as subordinates of the Germans and had in fact enjoyed a liberal degree of autonomy throughout their history, both within the Holy Roman (German) Empire and later as part of the Austro-Hungarian Monarchy. Upon the collapse of the Dual Monarchy after the First World War, Czech and Slovak nationalists succeeded in their goal of establishing a wholly independent Czechoslovak republic. Born upon the dismemberment of the Austro-Hungarian Monarchy and yet not a natural product of its disintegration, this new State emerged as an improbable amalgam of different ethnic groups and languages which two able statesmen, often against the will of the peoples involved, were determined to forge into a new nation, a new Switzerland.

Thomas Masaryk and Eduard Benes, while undoubtedly patriots and capable statesmen à la Cavour, were not universal idealists like President Woodrow Wilson, who genuinely advocated the noble ideal of self-determination for all peoples. Masaryk and Benes were above all nationalists pledged to the difficult endeavour of setting up an independent Czechoslovakia that would be able to survive both culturally and economically in the sea of nationalities that live in Central Europe. As nation-builders they set out to procure the most advantageous conditions for their new nation. Needing both land and people, they persuaded the Allies to approve their proposal of a state of nationalities which would include Czechs, Slovaks, Poles, Hungarians, Romanians, Ukrainians, Serbs, Croats, Slovenes and $3\frac{1}{2}$ million Austrians, better known as 'Sudeten' Germans.[1]

At the Paris Peace Conference Masaryk and Benes were not required to put their programme to the acid test of national plebiscites. As history was to prove, however, the amalgam would not hold together for long, and the circumstances of its collapse would contribute to the outbreak of a new war.

The world would probably have been spared much misery if politicians in 1919 had recognized the fact that in the same degree that Czechs did not want to live as a minority in a preponderantly

German State, Germans did not want to be a minority in a predominantly Slavic State. Given this state of affairs, the logical solution at the end of the First World War should have been to redraw frontiers along clearly definable ethnic lines, as repeatedly proposed by President Woodrow Wilson.[2] If necessary, this frontier based on ethnic and language considerations could have been adjusted in certain areas to accommodate important economic and military interests. Of course, drawing frontiers does not always lend itself to such a simple solution, since ethnic lines may be mixed, and in some areas intermixture may be so advanced that the different ethnic groups cannot be disentangled. This was the case in Slovakia, where some 150,000 Germans lived intermingled with Slovaks and Ruthenes. Quite a different situation prevailed in Bohemia and Moravia, where the 3·3 million Germans could have been easily segregated from the Czechs, since they lived in frontier communities bordering Upper Austria, Bavaria, Saxony and Prussian-Silesia. Rejecting all proposals to effect this reasonable and, indeed, natural solution which would have incorporated the Sudeten territories into those contiguous States with which the Sudetens were united by race and language, the Peace Conference at Paris collected the old Habsburg provinces of Bohemia, Moravia and Austrian Silesia, and joined them with the former Hungarian provinces of Slovakia and Ruthenia to form the new Czechoslovak nation, without making any territorial adjustments for the non-Czechoslovak population groups.

Contrary to President Wilson's efforts, it was not the principle of equity and self-determination which reigned at this conference, but the old-fashioned play of power politics and, of course, the necessity of repaying political debts to wartime allies. Prime Minister Orlando of Italy, for instance, was awarded the Austrian Southern Tyrol, although this mountainous region was not populated by Italians but rather by 250,000 German-Austrians, who strongly protested against being forced under alien rule. Their appeals went unheard. The parallel case was that of Masaryk and Benes, who had also fought on the side of the Allies[3] and whose services for the cause had to be honoured in some way. Apparently the only reward available entailed the allocation of Habsburg Sudetenland to the new Czechoslovak State.

Although a harsh reality was soon to dispel such illusions, it is none the less true that the international atmosphere preceding the armistice was swept by winds of democratic change, by the idea of building a just world in which the principle of self-determination and the equality of sovereign nations would play a central role. Point 10 of President Wilson's Fourteen Points, proclaimed on 8 January 1918, had provided with respect to the Austrian Empire: 'The peoples of Austria-Hungary, whose place among nations we wish to see safeguarded and assured, should be accorded the freest opportunity of autonomous development.'[4]

In the course of the summer of 1818 events outdistanced this moderate programme for self-determination. Mere autonomy for the Slavic peoples of the Austrian Empire ceased to be the Allied goal. Instead, complete independence of the Czechs, the Slovaks, the Slovenes, etc. became a requirement of the peace. Thus, when the Austrians asked for an armistice with the Allies in October 1818 they well knew that it necessarily meant the end of the empire, but they understood that the principle of self-determination would be equally applied to *all* of the various peoples making up the empire, including the Germans. On 6 October 1818, the German members of the Austrian parliament made the following statement:[5]

> We recognize the right of self-determination of the slavic and romanic peoples of Austria and claim the same right for the German-Austrians. . . .
> We declare that the German people of the Austrian Empire will oppose a dictated determination of the status of any of its parts. Against any such attempt the German-Austrians will defend their right to self-determination by all means at their disposal.

On 21 October 1918 the members of the provisional Austrian National Assembly passed a resolution in which the Austrian State claimed authority over all German settlements of the empire, in particular over the Sudetenland, and pledged itself to oppose any attempt by other States to annex territories which were predominantly populated by Germans.[6]

On the same date the Sudeten-German members of the Austrian parliament passed resolutions declaring the Bohemian and Moravian districts which they represented to be part of the German-Austrian State.[7]

Yet, the German-Austrians had lost the war and were at the mercy of the Allies. As the Czech politician Rašin said on 4 November 1918: 'The right of self-determination is a nice phrase – but now that the Entente has won force will decide.'[8]

The Czech and Slovak militia accordingly began to occupy the German Sudetenland, even before receiving official authorization from the Entente.

Appalled at what they considered a betrayal of trust, the German-Austrian government[9] sent a note to President Wilson via the Swedish Foreign Office on 12 December 1918:[10]

It appears from a communication from the Czecho-Slovak Government that the Allied Powers intend to incorporate with the Czecho-Slovak State those large, coherent territories of Bohemia and Moravia, which are populated by more than three million Germans. This measure, it is said, will be taken without awaiting the results of the peace conference. Notwithstanding that the Austro-German Government supposes that this is due to incorrect information from the Czecho-Slovak Government, it feels obliged to call this fact to everybody's attention and to insist upon that tendencies of this kind are not practically carried out. There can be no doubt as to the German character of the territories in question. Their population has on several occasions manifested their ardent desire to maintain their liberty and their independence of the Czecho-Slovak state. This desire of the people has been expressed especially by the unanimous vote of its representatives, elected on basis of equal suffrage. If, however, the Allied Powers have any doubts in this regard, the Austro-German Government proposes to make clear without delay the situation by plebiscite superintended and guided by neutral authorities and to give every guarantee besides, as to the liberty of vote. In such a case, the Austro-German Government asks the Allied Powers not to decide upon the fate of the people in question except upon basis of the results of this plebiscite. This way of procedure seems to be the only one in conformity with the principles recently proclaimed by the Entente itself as expressed in President Wilson's message of the 8th of January, 1918, in articles 2 and 4 of his speech of the 11th of February, 1918, and in his speech of the 4th of July, 1918; that is to say, in conformity with the principles of justice, of the world's peace and the nations' rights of self-determination.

The government of France rejected the Austrian appeal on 20 December 1918. Italy and Great Britain considered it and finally rejected the idea of a plebiscite in January 1919. Austria's direct demand to the new Czechoslovak government at Prague that the question of the $3\frac{1}{2}$ million Sudeten Germans be taken before an international tribunal for adjudication was rejected out of hand.

Only the United States government continued to entertain other ideas with respect to the Austrian settlement.

In the report of Professor Archibald Cary Coolidge to the American commission to negotiate peace, dated 10 March 1919, Professor Coolidge foresaw that the Germans would prove to be indigestible and warned against forcing them under foreign rule:[11]

> To grant to the Czechoslovaks all the territory they demand would be not only an injustice to millions of people unwilling to come under Czech rule, but it would also be dangerous and perhaps fatal to the future of the new state. . . . The blood shed on March 3rd when Czech soldiers in several towns fired on German crowds . . . was shed in a manner that is not easily forgiven. . . .
> For the Bohemia of the future to contain within its limits great numbers of deeply discontented inhabitants who will have behind them across the border tens of millions of sympathizers of their own race will be a perilous experiment and one which can hardly promise success in the long run.

Because of these dangers Professor Coolidge went on to propose that the Austrian frontier 'in the south, Lower and Upper Austria should be extended as nearly as possible to the existing ethnic line' while in the west 'the Eger District which is not part of the original Bohemia should be allowed to go to Bavaria if it wants to', and the industrial German districts in Northern Bohemia should be allowed to join Saxony, giving the Czechs the preference in doubtful districts, or if not allowed to join Saxony, then compensation should be given to the Germans by extending the territory of Eger; the so-called Sudetenland (Coolidge is referring here only to the area of the Sudeten mountains, not to the whole area popularly known as Sudetenland), which could be 'easily cut from Bohemia and Moravia' should be allowed to 'exist as a small state in the new German republic or be united to Prussian Silesia'; and Austrian Silesia, which was the subject of the Inter-Allied Teschen Commission, should be attributed or divided according to the judgment of the Commission, taking into account that 'the Czechs and the Poles are not the only people to be considered, but that the Germans have some rights, and that much of this territory forms a natural portion of the Sudetenland mentioned above.'[12]

These proposals would have still left a few hundred thousand Germans under Czech rule, but it would have been as fair a settlement as could have been expected. Yet, the recommendations of the Coolidge Mission and the repeated protests of the Austro-German government were completely disregarded in the final drawing of the Czechoslovak frontiers, which awarded without plebiscite all the disputed areas to Czechoslovakia.

In Article XXVII of the Treaty of St Germain Austria was required to recognize the new frontiers of Czechoslovakia, including all German-Austrian settlements. In Article LIV Austria renounced her rights over former territories and in Article XCI undertook to accept all territorial settlements made by the principal Allied and Associated Powers, 'particularly in so far as concerns the nationality of the inhabitants.'[13] In Article LXXXI of the Treaty of Versailles the German Weimar government was similarly required to recognize the independence of Czechoslovakia and in Article LXXXII to accept the frontier between Germany and Czechoslovakia, even though the entire frontier region separating the two countries was populated by Germans, not Czechs, which for centuries had maintained close cultural and economic contacts with the Germans of Bavaria, Saxony and Silesia. Only a frivolous person would today fail to experience a certain visceral discomfort with these decisions. Only a blind person would fail to appreciate their unsalutary consequences.

On the eve of the signing of the Treaty of St Germain, the National Assembly of the Austro-German Republic issued a statement condemning the violation of the right of self-determination of the Sudeten Germans:[14]

In painful disappointment the National Assembly protests against the alas irrevocable decision of the Allied and

Associated Powers to force a separation between three and a half million Sudeten Germans from the Alpine Germans with whom they had formed a political and economic community for centuries, and to rob these Sudeten Germans of their national freedom and to subject them to foreign rule under a people who in this very Peace Treaty declare themselves to be their enemy. . . .

Less than one year after the signing of the Treaty of St Germain, Princeton University Professor, Philip Marshall Brown (member of the Board of Editors of the *American Journal of International Law*), expressed the following opinion with respect to the Austrian settlement:[15]

In the case of Austria-Hungary, not only is it evident that the Peace Conference failed to define the right of self-determination, or to provide rules for its practical application, but, worse still, it is evident that there was no united purpose to mete out 'a justice that knows no standard but the equal rights of the several peoples concerned.' The dominant motives of the Peace Conference would seem to have been: first, to gratify faithful allies; secondly, to show severity to the conquered foe; and, thirdly, to establish a new balance of power.

Thus, the Treaty of St Germain artificially created a large and discontented minority, which, as the Coolidge Mission to the American Peace Delegation had predicted, would handicap the orderly development of the experimental Czechoslovak State. Nor was this German 'minority' a minority in the pedestrian sense of the word, constituting, as it did, the second largest ethnic group in Czechoslovakia, and numbering over 1 million more members than the third largest ethnic group – the Slovaks, who spoke a Slavic language similar to Czech, but had had a separate cultural development (as a former Hungarian province). It is interesting to note that the Slovaks were promised a liberal measure of autonomous development in the new State. On the other hand, the Sudeten Germans, who made up approximately one fourth of the population of the new State, were neither granted autonomy nor given a voice in Czechoslovak affairs proportionate to their numbers. Even the name of the State seemed to discriminate against them: according to German numerical strength the new country could have been named Czecho-Germania. But, of course, the Germans would not have been interested in a Czecho-German State, since they aspired to complete self-determination, in the same sense that the Czechs had aspired to it during the Habsburg Empire. The delegates at the Peace Conference thus lost an admirable opportunity to do justice to both sides and to vindicate the universal validity of the principle of self-determination.[16]

As a result of the adverse settlement some 300,000 Sudeten Germans emigrated to Austria and Germany.[17] Over 3 million, however, chose not to abandon the lands where their ancestors had lived for centuries. They intensely resented having been turned into a 'minority' overnight but persevered in their determination to wrest at least some degree of autonomy from the new Czechoslovak majority.

On 1 June 1920, on the occasion of the opening of the Czechoslovak parliament in Prague, the Union of German Parliamentarians delivered a sharp statement condemning the Treaty of St Germain and repeating the will of the Sudeten Germans to determine their own affairs. They continued:[18]

> The Czechoslovak Republic is . . . the outcome of a
> unilateral act of Czech volition which included an illegal
> military occupation of German territory. The Sudeten
> Germans were . . . never asked for their consent and the
> Treaty of Peace for this reason constitutes the approval
> of a condition of force but never of a condition of Law. . . .
> Injustice will not become justice even if it is practiced for a
> thousand years, as long as those affected do not freely
> accept the imposed condition as legitimate, and we hereby
> solemnly declare, that we shall never cease to demand the
> self-determination of our people. . . .

Agitation for self-determination continued for eighteen more years until the Sudeten German claims were recognized, at sword's point, in the Munich Agreement of 1938. This Treaty is objectionable inasmuch as it was obtained by the threat of the use of force; on the other hand, the subjugation of the Sudeten Germans by the Czechs in 1918–19 had been accomplished by the actual use of force involving the shedding of blood. Alone at the demonstrations in favour of German self-determination on 3/4 March 1919 fifty-four unarmed German civilians had been

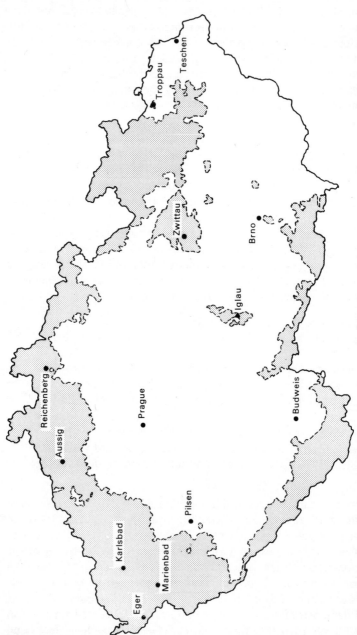

Map 3.   Language map of the Sudeten territories according to the official Czechoslovak census of 1 December 1930

killed by Czech militia and eighty-four had been seriously wounded.[19] The lives of many more Sudeten Germans were claimed until it became evident that resistance to Czech rule had no likelihood of succeeding. The only hope of achieving self-determination remained assistance from Big Brother across the border.

It has been suggested that this painful process might have been avoided by the expulsion of all the Germans out of the Sudetenland immediately after the First World War. Yet, President Masaryk himself opposed this idea because he did not want to launch his new nation by embarking upon a policy of mass deportation of indigenous populations.[20] Nor did he want to handicap his country by depriving it of German manpower.

THE NEW SWITZERLAND

Having forced the Sudeten Germans into an unwanted union, the Prague government could have prevented unnecessary friction by taking the Germans into full partnership in the Czechoslovak State, on a footing of absolute equality, both practical and theoretical. More concretely, the Prague government should have assured the Germans the same privileges and opportunities enjoyed by the Czechs and the Slovaks. Unfortunately, the model of a new Switzerland – so solemnly proclaimed by Dr Benes at the Paris Peace Conference – was never to be realized. While on the one hand the Czech government's policy toward the very small Polish minority justifiably drew widespread praise,[21] its policy toward the German minority never went as far as it could and should have gone to meet their manifold grievances.

What were the most frequent German grievances? Were these grievances legitimate? The Sudeten Germans complained bitterly, for instance, that their share in State service was not representative. It is a sad fact that the Czech government largely ignored these complaints until 1937 when world attention was focused on Czechoslovakia and the government belatedly admitted that German representation in public service was, in fact, inadequate.[22] The fact that most public service jobs in predominantly German areas were occupied by Czechs, who for the most part spoke little or no German, further exacerbated the Germans, as did the fact that the majority of State contracts for public works in German areas were placed with Czech and not with German contractors. Moreover, the official and exclusive use of the Czech language in the central ministries was seen as a form of discrimination which showed that members of the Czech majority enjoyed advantages disproportionate to their numbers.[23]

Upon returning from a trip to Czechoslovakia in 1937, Professor Arnold Toynbee observed in a widely discussed article for *The Economist*:[24]

> The truth is that even the most genuine and old-established democratic way of life is exceedingly difficult to apply when you are dealing with a minority that does not want to live under your rule. We know very well that we ourselves were never able to apply our own British brand of democracy to our attempt to govern the Irish. And in Czechoslovakia to-day the methods by which the Czechs are keeping the upper hand over the Sudetendeutsch are not democratic. . . .

But by the time of Toynbee's Czechoslovak visit events were moving very fast. The Sudeten Germans had become a potent political force and were pressing their demands in the Czech Parliament. Both the Social Democrats under the leadership of Wenzel Jaksch and Ernst Paul and the Nationalists under the leadership of Konrad Henlein (Sudetendeutsche Partei, SdP) were determined to gain political and social equality with the Czechs as well as some degree of autonomy in the German-populated districts. The SdP had even grown to be the largest single party in the Czech parliament, a position it did not fail to use to articulate the grievances of the German minority.

It has been frequently suggested that Henlein was a sinister schemer and his SdP nothing more than a subversive Nazi organization bent on the destruction of Czechoslovak independence. It is easy to understand how these notions arose, yet neither Henlein at the outset of his political career nor the SdP for many years of its development had anything to do with the National Socialist movement in Germany. Both were originally dedicated to a democratic settlement of the Sudeten German question, which was to be achieved by peaceful negotiations in the Czech parliament. All attempts to reach an acceptable settlement, however, failed, and the gradual escalation of the Czech-Sudeten confrontation resulted in forcing Henlein into the arms of Adolf Hitler, who promised to provide an international sounding board for the Sudeten case. If a Social Democratic Chancellor in

Germany had offered to publicize the Sudeten case so as to bring international pressure on the Czechoslovak government, Henlein would have just as readily turned to him as he turned to a National Socialist – not out of political conviction, but simply out of practical necessity. Hitler, of course, more than welcomed the opportunity of making the Sudeten case his own and did not hesitate to misuse the principle of self-determination as a weapon to further his own *Lebensraum* policy.

On 24 April 1938, Henlein announced his so-called 'Carlsbad Programme' during the annual congress of the SdP in Carlsbad. This programme consisted of eight points intended to serve as a basis for a settlement of the German grievances within the Czechoslovak State: full equality with the Czech people; recognition of the German ethnic group as a legal personality entitled to safeguard this equality; delimitation of the Sudeten German districts; German self-government in German districts; legal protection for those Germans living outside the predominantly German areas; removal of injustices inflicted upon the Germans since 1918; recognition of the principle 'German civil servants in German districts'; and complete freedom to profess the 'deutsche Weltanschauung'.[25]

Predictably, President Benes rejected the Carlsbad programme because he regarded several points as inadmissible. Only in the last weeks before the Munich Conference would Benes offer those concessions which might have been accepted in April, but which in August proved to be 'too little, too late'.

On 3 August 1938 Viscount Walter Runciman arrived in Prague on a peace mission.[26] Neither the Germans nor the Czechs had asked Great Britain to act as arbitrator, but a genuine concern to preserve the peace in Europe led Britain to attempt this initiative. Lord Runciman's mission remained six weeks in Czechoslovakia, conferring with representatives of the Czechoslovak government, of the SdP and of the German Social Democratic Party. After returning to Great Britain, having failed as a mediator, Lord Runciman sent a sad letter to President Benes, in which he recognized that responsibility for the final break would rest upon Henlein, whose connection with the government of the Reich had become a dominant factor, but he continued:[27]

I have much sympathy, however, with the Sudeten case. It

is a hard thing to be ruled by an alien race, and I have been left with the impression that Czechoslovak rule in the Sudeten areas for the last twenty years, though not actively oppressive, and certainly not 'terroristic', has been marked by tactlessness, lack of understanding, petty intolerance and discrimination, to a point where the resentment of the German population was inevitably moving in the direction of revolt. . . . Czech officials and Czech police, speaking little (or no)* German, were appointed in large numbers to purely German districts; Czech agricultural colonists were encouraged to settle on land transferred (confiscated) under the Land Reform in the middle of German populations; for the children of these Czech invaders Czech schools were said to have been built (were built) on a large scale; there is a very general belief that Czech firms were favoured as against German firms in the allocation of State contracts and that the State provided work and relief for Czechs more readily than for Germans. I believe these complaints to be in the main justified. Even as late as the time of my Mission, I could find no readiness on the part of the Czechoslovak Government to remedy them on anything like an adequate scale. . . .

For many reasons, therefore, including the above, the feeling among the Sudeten Germans until about three or four years ago was one of hopelessness. But the rise of Nazi Germany gave them new hope. I regard their turning for help towards their kinsmen and their eventual desire to join the Reich as a natural development in the circumstances.

With the failure of Lord Runciman's mission it was clear that the Czechoslovak powder keg would explode unless the leading European statesmen would take immediate action. Hitler was standing by with a match in his hand. The European democracies only had two rather unpalatable alternatives – to call Hitler's bluff by unequivocally threatening war if Czechoslovakia were attacked, or to appease Hitler by persuading the Czechs to let the Sudeten Germans secede.

Although with the perspective of the Second World War it is evident that the Western democracies gained nothing by appeasing

---

* The words in parenthesis were used in the less diplomatic letter Lord Runciman sent to Mr Chamberlain.

Hitler in 1938, most European statesmen at that time were genuinely ambivalent about taking a hard line on the Sudeten question. For most of them it was simply not sufficient cause to risk a European war. Thus, diplomatic activity in September 1938 turned feverish in an attempt to avert the catastrophe that would descend upon Europe but one year later.

In a letter to the American Secretary of State, Cordell Hull, dated 14 September 1938, Ambassador to France, William Bullit, reported:[28]

> during the past few days the French newspapers have published many maps showing the racial divisions in Czechoslovakia . . . public opinion has begun to develop the attitude, 'Why should we annihilate all the youth of France and destroy the continent of Europe in order to maintain the domination of 7,000,000 Czechs over 3,200,000 Germans?'

Bullit concluded his letter sarcastically:[29]

> In view of the growing belief among the French and the British that Benes in his heart of hearts has decided to provoke general European war rather than accept complete autonomy for the subject nationalities of Czechoslovakia, intense pressure will unquestionably be brought on Praha. . . .

A similar message was sent by Joseph Kennedy, the American Ambassador to Great Britain, to Secretary Hull, in which Kennedy quoted Prime Minister Chamberlain as saying: 'I can see no rhyme nor reason in fighting for a cause which, if I went to war for it, I would have to settle after it was over in about the same way I suggest settling it now.'[30] In the same sense Arnold Toynbee spoke of a prevailing 'feeling of acute moral discomfort' at the prospect of 'fighting for the balance of power in defiance of the principle of nationality'.[31] For him and for many others it was a genuine 'moral impasse'.[32]

The Munich Agreement thus seemed in September of 1938 to provide if not the best at least a tenable solution, which was welcomed with relief by a majority of the Press both in France and in Great Britain. By its terms 3 million Germans living in the affected districts were allowed to secede from Czechoslovakia and be united with Germany, while half a million Germans still remained within the borders of the reduced Czechoslovak State.[33] This entailed, of course, an economic loss for Czechoslovakia, but the new ethnic frontier rendered the state more homogeneous by eliminating a large and discontented minority. It was a division not unlike that which the Coolidge Mission had recommended in 1919.

What was unpleasant about the Munich Agreement was not the settlement itself, but the fact that it had been extorted. Moreover, any gain Hitler made, even the application of the principle of national self-determination for his benefit, was seen with concern by the European democracies.

Unfortunately for all concerned, the Munich crisis did not end with the separation of the Sudetenland from Czechoslovakia, but soon triggered the progressive disintegration of the amalgam of St Germain. On 30 September 1938, the Polish government followed suit by delivering an ultimatum to Prague and unilaterally annexing the rich industrial district of Teschen,[34] which, admittedly, had a large Polish population. Poland even went on to expel to rump Czechoslovakia some 40,000 Czechs and Germans formerly resident in the Teschen area.[35] Hungary was the next country to employ force to take a large slice from Czechoslovakia, this time annexing the mostly Magyar half of Southern Slovakia. Thereupon the Slovaks declared their independence from the Czechs and, afraid of being completely swallowed up by Hungary, made a 'friendship' treaty with Germany. The old and confused Czech President Hacha, not knowing what else to do, turned on 14 March 1939 to the German dictator, who promptly directed him to sign away the freedom of his people. Hitler's occupation of Bohemia and Moravia on 15 March would turn out to be one of his major political miscalculations. To paraphrase Talleyrand, this was more than a crime – it was a fatal mistake[36] – for here Hitler dropped the mask of pursuing 'national self-determination' and for the first time practised his announced *Lebensraum* policy upon a non-German State.

This turn of events gave rise to justified indignation on the part of England and France. Both countries had committed their honour to the frontiers of post-Munich Czechoslovakia. A few short months after the Munich Agreement Czechoslovakia had fallen apart and Hitler had taken the lion's share in the partition. Yet, in the few remaining months of European peace both England and France came to accept the new order and the Bank of England went as far as to transfer Czech gold assets to the Protectorate.[37]

THE SECOND WORLD WAR AND THE EXPULSION

The outbreak of the Second World War set the stage for the complete cancellation of the effects of the Munich Agreement. The extraordinary bitterness of the war even made talk of the expulsion of the Sudeten Germans sound reasonable.

In December 1938, hardly two months after the Munich Agreement, Dr Benes had already started reflecting upon the eventual employment of a transfer of population as the solution of the German 'minority' problem in Czechoslovakia.[38] But before any expulsion could take place, the 'humiliation' of the Munich Agreement had to be repudiated. From the moment of the outbreak of the Second World War, the Czechoslovak government-in-exile devoted itself to this goal.

Retrospectively, it is easy to recognize the fact that the Munich crisis and the Munich Agreement were a response to genuine problems arising out of the Treaty of St Germain and therefore a matter that cannot be considered in a vacuum as a moment of national humiliation for the Czechs or as *the* classical example of unjustified appeasement at the expense of the Czechs. Yet, Dr Benes was obsessed with this very idea of Munich. A Czech patriot whose nation owed its existence to the Wilsonian ideal of self-determination, Benes was never capable of accepting the exercise of this same right by the Sudeten Germans. He considered those Germans who were not happy to live under Czech rule to be 'traitors' to the Czech State – to a state that had existed not quite twenty years! In a broadcast from London he stated: 'We must get rid of all those Germans who plunged a dagger in the back of the Czechoslovak State in 1938.'[39] For Minister Dr Ripka the number of dagger-plunging Germans was 'about two million'.[40] More than 3 million were later to be expelled.

To understand how British public opinion came to accept the expulsion programme it is necessary to observe that the proposed plan envisaged a transfer that would be carried out gradually and under international supervision.

In a lecture at Manchester University in 1942 Benes argued, 'Transfers are a painful operation. They involve many secondary injustices. The framers of the peace settlement could not give their consent unless the transfers were humanely organized and internationally financed.'[41] Two years later, after the principle of transfer had been approved by the Great Powers, Benes again wrote:[42]

> If a solution of the minority problem is impossible
> in any other manner, I am prepared for the grim necessity
> of population transfers. . . . Such transfers can
> create many hardships and even injustices. But I am
> bound to say that they may be worth while if they help
> to establish a more permanent equilibrium and a
> lasting peace.

Dr Benes's presentation of his case sounds rather persuasive until the reader reflects and discovers that the proposed transfers were wholly unnecessary provided that national frontiers remained where they had been set at the Munich Agreement, drawn along ethnic lines. Only by repeating the injustice of the Treaty of St Germain would large numbers of Germans find themselves again under Czech rule. It should be remembered that during the Munich crisis the British Prime Minister clearly informed Benes that in the event of a conflict Czechoslovakia 'could not be reconstructed in her frontiers, whatever the result of the conflict may be'.[43] Even after Hitler's violation of the Munich Agreement by the illegal occupation of Bohemia and Moravia in March 1939, Neville Chamberlain repeated in a speech at Birmingham on 17 March 1939 that the frontiers drawn at St Germain had been wrong. Yet, on 5 August 1942, the new British Foreign Minister, Anthony Eden, reversed that British pronouncement: 'At the final settlement of Czechoslovak frontiers to be reached at the end of the war, they [the British Government] will not be influenced by any changes effected since 1938.'[44]

Having secured the repudiation of the Munich Agreement, President Benes again approached the Allied Powers who would be occupying the Reich in order to seek their approval for his expulsion programme. As early as 7 July 1942, Eden informed Benes that 'his colleagues agree with the principle of transfer'.[45] A decision of the British Cabinet, that it had no objection to the transfer of the Sudeten Germans, was shortly thereafter communicated to Benes.[46] This was the first official approval of the anti-humanitarian concept of uprooting a people from their homeland. United States and Soviet approval followed in the summer of 1943.[47]

Upon Dr Benes therefore rests the historical responsibility for inaugurating an expulsion syndrome that was to affect not only the Sudeten Germans but also all Germans living east of the Oder and Lusatian Neisse rivers. In 1943 it was announced that the population of East Prussia would be 'transferred' to the West. In 1944 the announced victims of the expulsion epidemic included the Germans of Pomerania, East Brandenburg and Silesia. In 1945 the expulsions became grotesque reality.

It is a sad phenomenon that world public opinion has to a large extent condoned the expulsion of the Sudeten Germans with the easy explanation that they were all 'Nazis' and had 'betrayed' the Czechs. In fact, while much sympathy and regret would later be expressed for the expelled Germans of East Prussia, Pomerania and Silesia, the expulsion of the Sudeten Germans has been justified in a sense as a reprisal for the crime of Lidice,[48] where the Nazis avenged the assassination of Reinhard Heydrich, Deputy 'Protector' of Bohemia and Moravia, by shooting the entire male population numbering 186, deporting their women to concentration camps and spreading their children throughout German homes or internment camps in the Reich. Lidice was indubitably a horrendous Nazi crime, but it was a crime for which the Sudeten Germans were in no way responsible, neither individually nor collectively.

The Nazis committed many more crimes in the Protectorate, and the last months of the war witnessed fanatical acts of incredible cruelty.[49] It has been estimated that the Czechoslovak people suffered as many as 250,000 losses[50] during the war, although other Czech estimates give a lower figure of 75,000,[51] including the Czechs and Slovaks who fell fighting the Nazis, executed partisans, Jews deported to concentration camps, and other victims of Nazi terror. These crimes and inhumanities committed upon the Czech people, however, were for the most part committed by members of the SS, the majority of whom were not Sudeten Germans. The simple German farmer living in the Sudetenland had little contact with Czechs and could not be held responsible for any abuses committed by the NSDAP in the Protectorate. Yet, he was left to pay the bill for the crimes of the Nazi regime.

On 22 October 1945 *Time* provided its readers with a rather questionable report on the expulsion of the Sudeten Germans: 'Toward its disloyal minorities the once tolerant Czechoslovak heart has hardened. Dr Benes and his Government are adamantly determined to rid the state of almost all of its 3,000,000 Sudeten Germans. . . .'[52] Again, on 5 November 1945, another article openly partial to the idea of expelling the Germans as collective punishment for Nazi crimes observed: 'The 3,000,000 Sudeten Germans, now joining Europe's miserable displaced millions, had risen in a mass to betray the Czechs. . . .'[53] Even the British Foreign Minister, Ernest Bevin, in explaining the expulsion of the Sudeten Germans stated before the British parliament that the Sudeten Germans and the Czechs had lived together in harmony until Hitler's stooges 'broke up what was a great effort to create and build a democratic state'.[54]

Statements like these were quite common in 1945, and could be attributed to the charged atmosphere that lingered after the war. Yet, in spite of the distortions of history necessitated by wartime propaganda and the thorough moral defamation of the enemy, there were independent voices trying to disabuse the public of their wartime prejudices. On 30 January 1946 the Lord Bishop of Chichester, Dr George Bell, publicly condemned the expulsion of the Sudeten Germans and reminded the British House of Lords of the actual background of the Czech-German conflict:[55]

> that the conditions under which the Sudeten Germans were incorporated in the Czech State were quite different from the conditions under which Slovakia was incorporated . . . that there are many people in high authority who in the period between the wars maintained that the Sudeten Germans were not getting their economic and political rights in the same way as the other minorities in Czechoslovakia. . . .

Indeed, contrary to Bevin's classical simplification of the facts, the truth is that since the Treaty of St Germain-en-Laye the Sudeten Germans had not been given a fair deal in Czechoslovakia and accordingly had not lived in harmony with the Czechs, but in a state of constant striving for self-determination. Nor was their nationalism an invention of Hitler or the Nazis. Hitler was merely the opportunist who promised the means to the desired end. Even Konrad Henlein, the head of the SdP, only gravitated to Hitler because all efforts of the Sudeten Germans to gain a measure of autonomy from the Czechs had failed at Prague and at the

League of Nations. The Sudeten marriage to Hitler was therefore as much a marriage of necessity as the later alliance between Finland and the Axis during the Second World War. Finland was not Nazi, but only with Hitler's military assistance could it defend itself from the aggression of the Soviet Union, which in the end robbed it of 18,000 square miles of its territory and forced 450,000 Finns to resettle elsewhere in Finland.[56] Similarly, a majority of the Sudeten Germans were not Nazis, but they knew that liberation from Czech rule could not be attained without Nazi help.

Thirty years after the end of the Second World War there appears to be little justification to perpetuate the inveterate legend that the Germans stabbed the Czechs in the back, for if the German minority had been 'disloyal' to the Czechs, they were 'disloyal' in the sense that every colonial people is disloyal to the foreign ruler;[57] if they demanded their right of self-determination, that does not mean *eo ipso* that they 'had risen in a mass to betray the Czechs'. Surely the German minority had been no more disloyal to Prague than the Czech minority had been disloyal to Vienna before (and during!) the First World War. If Henlein was a traitor to Czechoslovakia, then by the same token Masaryk and Benes had been traitors to the Austrian Empire. Yet, each only sought the realization of the right of self-determination for his own people. The only difference lies in the fact that the Germans lost both the First and the Second World War, and that the Sudeten German striving for self-determination, which had logically led them to Munich, also delivered them to the disaster of 1945 which, with the approval of the Western democracies, extinguished 700 years of German presence in Bohemia, Moravia and (Austrian) Silesia, a history that had produced such great names as the geneticist Gregor Mendel, the poet Rainer Rilke, the industrialist Emil von Skoda and the automobile pioneer Ferdinand Porsche.

CHAPTER THREE

THE GENESIS
OF THE ODER-NEISSE LINE:
THE CONFERENCES OF TEHRAN
AND YALTA

> Eden said that what Poland lost in the East she might gain
> in the West. . . . I then demonstrated with the help of three
> matches my idea of Poland moving westward. This pleased
> Stalin, and on this note our group parted for the moment.

Churchill, *Closing the Ring*, 1953, p. 362.

THE ATLANTIC CHARTER

Territorial amputations of Germany did not initially constitute a
war aim of the Western Allies. First and foremost they fought to
eliminate Hitler and National Socialism from the European
political scene; they formulated no plans to reduce the size of
pre-war Germany because any reduction would aggravate the
chronic *Volk ohne Raum*[1] syndrome in Germany and lead to
further instability in Central Europe. Indeed, Germany was
already about twice as densely populated as her neighbours
Poland and France – in actual size it did not even reach the area
of the American State of Texas.

On 9 February 1940 Churchill had stated:[2]

> We are opposed to any attempt from outside to break up
> Germany. We do not seek the humiliation or dismemberment
> of your country. We wholeheartedly desire to welcome you
> without delay into the peaceful collaboration of civilized
> nations.

Such was the dominant opinion in the West during the first
months of the war. Even one year later, after the Battle of Britain,
the Allies still adhered to a moderate and humane peace programme. On 14 August 1941, at the conclusion of the Atlantic
Conference, Prime Minister Churchill and President Roosevelt
proclaimed the Atlantic Charter[3] in which they renounced
'aggrandizement, territorial or other' and undertook a commitment to oppose 'territorial changes that do not accord with the

freely expressed wishes of the peoples concerned'. This widely praised declaration represented an attempt to set a higher standard of international morality based on the principle of equal rights and self-determination of peoples. The escalation of the war, however, led to a progressive abandonment of the ideals of the Atlantic Charter. Indeed, it was the brutality of the Axis enemy that gradually drove the Allies to deny them the benefits of the charter. Before long Churchill stated that the charter had no 'legal' validity and that in any case it would not be applied to enemy countries.[4] Yet, recalling the historical context in which the charter was proclaimed, it would be difficult to imagine to what other than enemy countries the pledge of no territorial aggrandizement was meant to apply[5] – certainly the charter would have been superfluous if it had only meant that the Allies would not recognize Hitler's territorial gains in Europe. The very fact that the Allies were at war with the Axis sufficed to prove their intention to restore Nazi-occupied countries to their pre-war frontiers.

This chapter traces the evolution of Allied war aims and the emergence of new Soviet-Polish and Polish-German frontiers, which were to effect extensive territorial changes in contravention to the wishes of the populations involved. To understand this considerable departure from the principles of the Atlantic Charter it is important to note the development of a new power constellation in Europe and the rise of an undemocratic and ruthless dictatorship to a position of preponderant power. Representatives of this new totalitarian power adhered *pro forma* to the charter at the inter-Allied meeting at St James's Palace in London on 24 September 1941 and even a second time at the Joint Declaration of the United Nations in Washington on 1 January 1942, but Marshal Stalin never intended to and never did take obligations under the Charter seriously and thus frustrated observance by the other parties. Moreover, as indicated above, the struggle against the Axis assumed the character of a crusade with the unmistakable trappings of punitive expeditions. In the eyes of the leaders of the anti-Hitler coalition, post-war Germany would have to pay for the war, even if payment was territorial in nature. Lastly, the argument of securing the future peace of Europe was frequently strained to defeat the pledges of the charter. As Prime Minister Churchill summed up for the parliament on 24 May 1944:[6] 'There is no question of Germany enjoying any guarantee that she will not undergo territorial changes if it should seem that the making of such changes renders more secure and more lasting the peace in Europe.'

STRATEGIC AMPUTATIONS: EAST PRUSSIA

The first proposals of depriving Germany of parts of her pre-war territories were strategic in nature. It was thought that by reducing Germany's frontiers she would have less opportunity to invade her neighbours. Indeed, the case for separating East Prussia from Germany was precisely that Poland's pre-war frontier was strategically untenable, as the disastrous campaign of 1939 had shown.

Not long after the catastrophe of September 1939 the Polish government-in-exile set out to impress upon London and Washington the necessity of incorporating East Prussia into post-war Poland.[7] After the German attack upon the Soviet Union in the summer of 1941, Marshal Stalin became an enthusiastic supporter of the proposal of taking East Prussia away from Germany,[8] although as history was to show, he coveted the northern half including Königsberg for himself. Meanwhile, the leaders of the West were not at all unsympathetic to the Polish demand for East Prussia. At a dinner with President Roosevelt and Harry Hopkins in Washington on 15 March 1943, British Foreign Minister Eden candidly discussed the problem of Poland's post-war frontiers. In a memorandum Hopkins noted:[9]

> Poland wants East Prussia and both the President and Eden agree that Poland should have it. Eden said that the Russians agree privately with this but are not willing to tell this to the Poles because they want to use it as a bargaining instrument at the Peace Conference.

On the following day Hopkins called on Soviet Ambassador Litvinov in order to confirm Eden's statement. Ambassador Litvinov advised Hopkins that 'Russia would agree to Poland having East Prussia but that Russia would insist on what he called "her territorial rights" on the Polish frontier.'[10] What this quite obviously meant was that the Soviets were intent on keeping that part of Poland which they had seized pursuant to the Ribbentrop-Molotov Pact of 1939,[11] basing their claim on the purely ethnic argument that a majority of the population of that area was Ukrainian. Although this was true, it did not necessarily follow that the religious Ukrainians would have preferred union with militantly anti-religious Soviets than with their equally Slavic brothers, the Poles, with whom they also had long historical and cultural ties. Moreover, several million ethnic Poles lived intermingled with the Ukrainians in the area in question and vigorously opposed annexation by the Soviet Union.

TERRITORIAL ADJUSTMENTS AS COMPENSATION

When the London Poles learned that the Soviet Union was planning to retain after the war 70,000 square miles of pre-war Poland, they appealed to the Western Allies for help and at the same time intensified claims to German territory in the West.[12] A genuine dilemma had arisen for the Western Allies. Great Britain had gone to war on account of her guarantee of Poland's territorial integrity against German attack. It was more than awkward for Britain later to advocate a peace settlement that would sanction the annexation of half of Poland's pre-war territory in the East, including Poland's timberlands, the Galician oil fields and the old Polish cities of Wilno and Lvov (Lemberg). In the light of the pledges of the Atlantic Charter it seemed grotesque to deliver Eastern Poland to the mighty Russian neighbour, the age-old enemy that had seized a third of Poland in the infamous partitions of the eighteenth century and subjugated much of the rest in the nineteenth century. It was not until the end of the First World War that Poland had regained her independence and succeeded in establishing her eastern frontier slightly to the east of the line of the second partition, thus leaving Russia most of her gains of 1772 and 1793. Now Marshal Stalin was claiming more than the tsars had carved out of Poland in the third partition of 1795; even that frontier, obtained, as it was, through aggression, had not included Lvov or Galicia, which had been incorporated by Maria Theresa into the Austrian Empire in the course of the first partition in 1772. If the Soviet Union was to be allowed to improve on the third partition of Poland, then Hitler could have just as well been permitted to keep Warsaw, which had been part of the Prussian booty in the 1795 partition – and the ghastly blood-letting of the Second World War might have been averted!

This, however, would have meant Western capitulation to force and abandonment of democratic principles.

THE CONFERENCE OF TEHRAN

The Tehran Conference (28 November to 1 December 1943), which was devoted primarily to discussion of military matters, also focused on the question of Poland's post-war frontiers, even though Churchill had no power from Parliament nor Roosevelt from Congress to define post-war frontiers. Unfortunately, instead of reminding Stalin of his obligations under the Atlantic Charter, neither Churchill nor Roosevelt offered much resistance to the proposed land-grab. 'Personally,' Churchill recollected, 'I thought Poland might move westward, like soldiers taking two steps "left close". If Poland trod on some German toes, that could not be helped, but there must be a strong Poland. . . .'[13]

In spite of this lip-service to the sentiments of the Poles, no Polish representatives were called in to participate in the discussions on the future frontiers of their country. The Big Three intended to reach an informal agreement among themselves and go to the Poles later. Marshal Stalin was calculatingly generous in proposing that the Poles should go as far west as the Oder – in 1943 a rather revolutionary proposal, to say the least. Indeed, before Tehran the talk among the Allies had been limited to the possible detachment of East Prussia, Danzig and Upper Silesia; nothing more had been seriously considered. Entirely new vistas were thus opened by Stalin. Not without relief, Foreign Minister Eden observed succinctly 'what Poland lost in the East she might gain in the West.'[14] A solution had been found for saving face with the Poles. Weary of war and unwilling to fight against the Soviet Union over the fate of Eastern Poland, the Western Allies preferred to compensate Poland at the expense of the common enemy – Germany. Principle was thus sacrificed to political expediency and a quasi-Hitlerian settlement, totally disregarding the rights of the millions of persons affected, emerged from this conference. In a familiar and thoroughly characteristic episode Churchill then illustrated the westward displacement of Poland with the help of three matches representing Russia, Poland and Germany. By pushing the Russian match westwards, the Polish and German matches were similarly displaced. 'This pleased Stalin, and on this note our group parted for the moment.'[15]

One aspect of this displacement – deliberately ignored by the Big Three – was the conceptual possibility of a resulting westward displacement of Germany, for, indeed, if Poland could be placed on wheels and moved 150 miles west into the more densely populated German State, the latter could in turn be pushed to the Atlantic.[16] What would have happened if Germany had gained 150 miles along its western frontier to 'compensate' it for its loss in the East? Holland and Belgium would have disappeared as well as parts of France, including Alsace-Lorraine. Such an unwelcome consequence would have meant a partial re-establishment of the frontiers of the First German Reich, that is, the (Hohenstaufen/Habsburg) Holy Roman Empire, which for centuries had included not only all of Holland and most of modern Belgium, but also Alsace-Lorraine, the Rhone Valley, Savoy, Lombardy, Tuscany, etc. Of course, no such theoretical consequences were ever contemplated at Tehran! On the agenda were solely the practical problems of giving Stalin what he wanted and seeking suitable compensation for Poland elsewhere.

Yet, would Poland agree to being placed on wheels and pushed *ad libitum* by the Great Powers? No one at Tehran seemed to perceive the meaning of land as something more than an article that could be sold or bartered. No one gave much thought to the fact that inseparable from land is its history and the human response, the deep and ineffable sentiments that it evokes.[17] There is no doubt that the Poles would have preferred to keep their own eastern provinces rather than be forced to exchange them for German lands in the West. The Poles had a very special attachment to the cities of Lvov and Wilno and wanted to keep them at all costs within Poland. On the other hand, the value of the German lands east of the Oder, especially Upper Silesia, was acknowledged to be greater than that of Eastern Poland.[18] As Churchill frequently pointed out:[19]

It was industrial and it would make a much better Poland. We should like to be able to say to the Poles that the Russians were right, and to tell the Poles that they must agree that they had a fair deal. If the Poles did not accept, we could not help it.

The spirit of President Woodrow Wilson had been chased out. Hardly a quarter of a century had elapsed since Wilson had pronounced the moral principles that should govern peace-making. At his memorable address of 11 February 1918, before the joint Houses of Congress, he had insisted that 'peoples and provinces are not to be bartered about from sovereignty to sovereignty as if they were mere chattels and pawns in a game, even the great game, now forever discarded, of the balance of power.'[20] How laudable, how eminently humane – and how majestically naïve!

Summing up the results of the Tehran Conference, Prime Minister Churchill proposed a tentative formula on the frontiers of post-war Poland:

> It is thought in principle that the home of the Polish state
> and nation should be between the so-called Curzon Line
> and the line of the Oder[21] including for Poland East Prussia
> and Oppeln; but the actual tracing of the frontier line
> requires careful study, and possibly disentanglement of
> population at some points.[22]

This formulation, however, exceeded the compensation favoured by the United States. Half a year after the Tehran Conference, in May 1944, the Committee on Post-War Programs in the State Department prepared a memorandum containing policy recommendations with respect to the treatment of Germany in the light of long-term United States interests. On the matter of the German-Polish frontier it recommended:[23]

> This Government should not oppose the annexation by
> Poland of East Prussia, Danzig and in German Upper
> Silesia the industrial district and a rural hinterland to be
> determined primarily by ethnic considerations. *The United
> States, however, would not be disposed to encourage the
> acquisition by Poland of additional German-populated
> territory in the trans-Oder region.* [emphasis added]

Yet, regardless of the size of the territorial compensation actually contemplated by the Allies at Tehran, the Polish government-in-exile would vigorously oppose all efforts to force it into a surrender of any part of Eastern Poland.

For the endeavour of persuading Poland to accept the Tehran plan the Allies availed themselves of the services of Dr Eduard Benes, President of the Czechoslovak government-in-exile. Clad as mediator, Benes tried to 'make the Poles see reason', that is, to convince them of the political necessity of ceding half of their country to the Soviet Union.[24]

THE PROBLEM OF KATYN

It is conceivable – although not likely – that Dr Benes's efforts at mediation might have had some measure of success if at least no other obstacle had blocked the way to a Polish-Soviet understanding. The major obstacle was, of course, the unpalatable Katyn affair.[25]

In the summer of 1940, one year before the German attack on the Soviet Union, Soviet authorities had murdered more than 10,000 Polish officers, the cream of Poland's military and professional class. Since the discovery of the graves by the Germans in the spring of 1943 at Katyn Forest near Smolensk, Polish-Soviet relations had rapidly deteriorated. General Sikorski, President of the Polish government-in-exile, promptly requested an investigation by the International Red Cross, which was, in fact, the least he could have done under the circumstances. Acutely embarrassed by this discovery and aware that no adequate or respectable excuse could ever be found for Katyn, the Soviet government feigned indignation, accused Sikorski of working for Hitler's propaganda and broke diplomatic relations with the Polish government-in-exile at London.[26] Under pressure from Churchill and Roosevelt, General Sikorski let the request to the International Committee of the Red Cross lapse, but the break with the Soviet government was permanent. With one stroke Stalin had shoved aside the non-Communist Poles and gained a free hand to shape a rival Polish government in Moscow.[27] While neither Sikorski[28] nor later Mikolajczyk were disposed to approve the Soviet landgrab in Eastern Poland, the vassal Polish-Communist Committee which Stalin allowed to blossom out into a 'Committee of National Liberation' would gladly comply.

Notwithstanding the very charged atmosphere in 1943-4, Dr Benes did go about his mission to attempt to induce the London Poles to go along with the Russian plan. If his efforts had succeeded Czech prestige would have further increased in the eyes of Moscow, London and Washington – good will which Benes was eager to tap for his plans for post-war Czechoslovakia. Thus, on 10 January 1944, Benes discussed with Mikolajczyk the Soviet attitude with respect to Poland's post-war frontiers:[29]

Moscow could not give way about the Curzon Line but was ready to consent to territorial compensations for Poland at the expense of Germany in full agreement with Poland, Great

Britain and America – Moscow would accept any western line upon which they agreed even if it were the Oder Line.

But, alas, because of Katyn and more generally because of older Polish resentments against their eastern neighbour, Mikolajczyk knew that he could not persuade the Polish people to accept the proposed Polish-Soviet frontier. If at least Lvov and Wilno could be saved for Poland! Time, of course, kept working against Mikolajczyk and the London Poles, for in the summer of 1944 Poland was being liberated from the Germans and occupied by the Red Army, in the wake of which communist Poles were coming from Moscow and assuming positions of real – not only paper – authority. Meanwhile the legitimate Polish government-in-exile could only watch from far-off London.

MOSCOW: JULY AND OCTOBER 1944

On 27 July 1944 Mikolajczyk left for Moscow in order to confer with Stalin and Molotov. On the same day Soviet newspapers announced the conclusion of an agreement between the Soviet government and the Polish-Communist Committee of National Liberation, permitting the latter to assume 'full direction of all the affairs of civil administration' in those areas of Poland which Soviet military authorities saw fit to give them. The London Poles were doomed, but they did not know it yet. At the very best all that Mikolajczyk could have realistically expected to get was a post in a Polish government composed largely of the members of the Communist Committee of National Liberation, together with certain pro-Soviet Poles from abroad.

Very much aware of the unfavourable position of his protégé London Poles, Churchill decided that it would be better for them to forget Katyn and start co-operating with the Russians – even if they did not like them. Otherwise they would be completely out of the picture in post-war Poland.

Prerequisite for working with the Russians was capitulation on the question of Poland's eastern frontier. At the meeting held on 14 October 1944 at the British Embassy in Moscow, both Churchill and Eden applied massive pressure on Mikolajczyk to induce him to give his consent to the Curzon Line without Lvov or Galicia. The encounter is so revealing of the realities of power politics, that one can hardly help thinking back to the infamous Berlin meeting in March 1939 between President Hacha of Czechoslovakia and the German dictator, who, after receiving Hacha with the honours due a Head of State, proceeded to instruct him to sign away the independence of his people. The Churchill-Mikolajczyk encounter at Moscow is well worth reproducing in excerpt, because it vividly and succinctly displays the great political tensions that produced not only the Polish-Soviet frontier, but also the Oder-Neisse Line:

Mikolajczyk. I know that our fate was sealed in Tehran.
Churchill. It was saved in Tehran.
M. I am not a person completely devoid of patriotic feeling, to give away half of Poland.
C. What do you mean by saying 'you are not devoid of patriotic feeling'? Twenty-five years ago we reconstituted Poland although in the last war more Poles fought against us than for us. Now again we are preserving you from disappearance, but you will not play ball. You are absolutely crazy.
M. But this solution does not change anything.
C. Unless you accept the frontier you are out of business forever. The Russians will sweep through your country and your people will be liquidated. You are on the verge of annihilation.
Eden. Supposing that we get an understanding on the Curzon Line, we will get agreement on all the other things from the Russians. You will get a guarantee from us.
C. Poland will be guaranteed by the three Great Powers and certainly by us. The American Constitution makes it difficult for the President to commit the United States. In any case you are not giving up anything because the Russians are there already.
M. We are losing everything.
C. The Pripet marshes and five million people. The Ukrainians are not your people. You are saving your own people and enabling us to act with vigor.
M. Must we sign this if we are going to lose our independence?
C. You have only one thing to do. It would make the greatest difference if you agreed.
M. Would it not be possible to proclaim that the three

Great Powers have decided about the frontiers of Poland
without our presence?

C. We will be sick and tired of you if you go on arguing.

Eden. You could say that in view of the declaration made
by the British and Soviet Governments, you accept a *de
facto* formula, under protest if you like, and put the blame on
us. I quite see the difficulty of saying it of your own volition.

. . .

M. We lose all authority in Poland if we accept the
Curzon Line, and furthermore nothing is said about what we
could get from the Germans.

Eden. I think we could do this, we could take this risk.
We could say what you are going to get.

At this point Churchill came back with the draft of a declaration
and explained to Mikolajczyk that:

Publication at present of what it is intended to take away
from the Germans in the East would arouse the German
fury and this would cost many human lives. On the other
hand if the agreement between Poland and Russia is not
reached now, it would also cause victims in human beings.

Churchill then read the draft declaration which provided for a
Polish acceptance of the Curzon Line. Mikolajczyk repeated his
objections and the morning meeting ended. A second conference
took place in the afternoon. Churchill was in an angry and im-
patient mood. Mikolajczyk informed Churchill that after renewed
consideration he could not consent to the Curzon Line and
continued: 'The Polish Government cannot determine the loss of
nearly half of the Polish territory in the east without hearing the
opinion of the Polish People, which is decisive for the Government.'[30]

C. You are no Government if you are incapable of taking
any decision. You are callous people who want to wreck
Europe. I shall leave you to your own troubles. You have
no sense of responsibility when you want to abandon your
people at home, to whose sufferings you are indifferent.
You do not care about the future of Europe, you have only
your own miserable selfish interest in mind. I will have to
call on the other Poles and this Lublin Government may
function very well. It will be *the Government*. It is a criminal

attempt on your part to wreck, by your 'Liberum Veto,'
agreement between the Allies. It is cowardice on your part.[31]

This duel of words was interrupted because Churchill had an
appointment to see Marshal Stalin that same afternoon.

On 15 October Mikolajczyk again conferred with Churchill
and after painful deliberation finally offered to accept the Curzon
Line as Poland's eastern frontier, on condition that the more
favourable version of the Curzon Line were adopted, thus securing
at least Lvov and the Galician oil fields for Poland. This offer
constituted in fact a very substantial concession from the Polish
standpoint, but the reality of the situation was that Poland was
not in a position to bargain, but could only accept what was
determined for her by the Great Powers. In an outburst of
impatience and bad temper, Churchill shouted to Mikolajczyk
that 'everything between us is finished' and left the room banging
the door behind him. The Great Powers had decided that Poland
would have to accept the Curzon Line without Lvov or the
Galician oil fields. The Soviet Union, which already possessed so
much land and had a population density of barely twenty-five
persons per square mile, insisted on annexing half of Poland.
Stalin would have his way without any concessions or comprom-
ises. The Western Allies, who could have said 'no' and made their
opposition more emphatic by threatening to deny Stalin further
military aid, did nothing. Churchill took the easier path of
bullying Mikolajczyk and then offering to repay him at the
expense of Germany. A bitter Mikolajczyk left the conference
room after refusing to shake Foreign Minister Eden's hand.[32]

After this ugly encounter Mikolajczyk continued his verbal
campaign against the Curzon Line, not only because he considered
it a flagrant violation of solemn pledges, but also because he
genuinely believed that a hard position might still salvage some
of Eastern Poland. Meanwhile, British pressure intensified
because the Lublin Poles, who had already recognized the Curzon
Line, were rapidly consolidating their power in Poland with the
help of the Soviet Union. It was not compatible with the interests
of the Western Allies to permit Poland to fall completely within
the Soviet sphere. Only gradually, in the painful months following
the fiasco of the Moscow negotiations, did Mikolajczyk realize
that there was absolutely no hope of salvaging any part of Eastern
Poland. The best deal remained to try to wrest as much

compensation as possible in the West at the expense of Germany. On this point Stalin showed himself generous. Indeed, he had already offered Mikolajczyk not only the Oder frontier but even an extension westward as far as the Neisse River.[33]

On 18 December 1944 *Pravda* published a long article by Dr Stefan Jedrichowski, propaganda chief of the Lublin Committee and an important representative of that Committee in Moscow. In this article Jedrichowski recommended that the western frontier of Poland should run from Stettin south along the Oder and Western or Lusatian Neisse to the Czechoslovak border. No one had publicly claimed this much territory before. Poland's official bid for compensation now comprised not only all of Germany east of the Oder, but also very substantial German territories west of the Oder, affecting an additional 3 million

Map 4. The agricultural territory between the two Neisse Rivers had a German population of approximately 2·8 million

Germans. Stettin, the capital of Pomerania, which lay on the western bank of the Oder, was to become a Polish port, and all of lower Silesia west of the Oder River including the city of Breslau. The Western Allies were unequivocally opposed to this proposal, but the appearance of the Jedrichowski article in *Pravda* was a palpable indication that the Soviet Government sponsored the claim – that this was, in effect, the new Soviet position as to where the future border should be.

Having read this ominous article in Moscow, where he was stationed at the time, George F. Kennan immediately reported to the American Ambassador Averell Harrimann on the far-reaching implications of the new arrangement. First and foremost he noted that Poland's dependence on the Soviet Union would be immeasurably increased. In a memorandum written a full six weeks before the Yalta Conference, Kennan expressed his misgivings with a frontier arrangement which[34]

> makes unrealistic the idea of a free and independent Poland. It establishes a border in Central Europe which can be defended only by the permanent maintenance of strong armed forces along its entire extent. Despite Churchill's unconvincing optimism as to the ease with which new homes can be found in Germany for six million people (I believe the figure is too low) it renders the economic and social problems of the remainder of Germany . . . highly difficult of solution, and reduces radically the possibilities for stability in that area. . . .
>
> We may not be able to prevent the realization of this project. . . . But I think we are being unrealistic if we fail to recognize it for what it is and give it its proper place in our thinking about the future of Europe. Above all, I see no reason why we should have to share responsibility for the complications to which it is bound to lead.

The majority of American and British politicians, however, did not see the situation with Kennan's pessimistic eyes and still made an attempt to reach a friendly agreement with the Soviet Union. Marshal Stalin was a comrade-at-arms in the titanic struggle against Hitler, and this joint endeavour did not fail to engender more than just a modicum of friendship and good will.

Today every political amateur knows that Stalin was far more adept at the game of power politics than the leaders of the Western democracies, who during the years of co-operation never imagined the extent to which many of their war aims would be frustrated. Particularly on the matter of Poland's frontiers and Poland's future as a free State much confidence was wasted on Stalin. It had been the consistent policy of President Roosevelt, for instance, to postpone clear decisions on boundaries until after the termination of hostilities.[35] This failure to impose a limit on Stalin's ambitions at an early date resulted in the Polish-Soviet frontier being shifted west and this in turn gave rise to the dispute over the new Polish-German frontier. Western failure to exact a definite commitment from Stalin left him, of course, free to encourage the Soviet-dominated Polish government to take a much bigger bite out of Germany than either the Americans or the British would have been willing to concede.

THE CONFERENCE OF MALTA

On the eve of the Crimea Conference the frontier settlements envisaged by the Western Allies with respect to Germany included the acquisition by Poland of East Prussia (except for the Koenigsberg area), the Free City of Danzig, German Upper Silesia, and the eastern tip of Pomerania, involving a total addition to Poland of an area of about 21,000 square miles – or roughly half of what Poland later took.[36]

At the meeting of Foreign Minister Eden with Secretary of State Stettinius in Malta on 1 February 1945, both Ministers expressed their disapproval of the territorial demands of the provisional Polish government as announced by Dr Jedrichowski in *Pravda*. Eden and Stettinius agreed to oppose the western Neisse, but 'even the Oder line frontier would severely tax the Polish capacity for absorption and would increase the formidable difficulties involved in the transfer of millions of Germans.'[37]

A United States Delegation Memorandum containing concrete proposals on the Polish question recommended: 'We should resist vigorously efforts to extend the Polish frontier to the Oder Line or to the Oder-Neisse Line.'[38] Yet, as Yalta and Potsdam would show, these efforts were not resisted vigorously enough.

THE CONFERENCE OF YALTA

As feared by Eden and Stettinius, Marshal Stalin pressed at

Yalta for the Oder and the Western Neisse.[39] Molotov further clarified the Soviet position by claiming the town of Stettin on the western bank of the Oder River.[40] At this point Prime Minister Churchill objected because 'a considerable body of British public opinion . . . would be shocked if it were proposed to move large numbers of Germans.'[41] To this objection Marshal Stalin replied that most of the Germans in the proposed areas, including the Germans between the two Neisse Rivers, had run away from the Red Army. This statement, made during the fourth plenary session on 7 February 1945, was patently false. At least 5 million Germans still resided in these areas, even though nearly 4 million had already fled from the advancing Red Army. Notwithstanding the Soviet attempt to make the problem appear a trifle, Churchill insisted that any transfer of populations should be 'proportioned to the capacity of the Poles to handle it and the capability of the Germans to receive them.'[42] Moreover, 'it would be a pity to stuff the Polish goose so full of German food that it died of indigestion.'[43] Unimpressed by Churchill's objections, Molotov again pressed for the Western Neisse, adding that the Polish provisional government (the puppet government set up by the Soviets themselves) also wanted the Western Neisse.

In the fifth plenary session on 8 February, President Roosevelt submitted a new proposal which, while not representing a binding commitment on the part of the United States government did manifest a readiness to soften the American position on Poland's western frontier, granting for the time being an extension up to the line of the Oder. President Roosevelt, however, drew the line there, stating that 'there would appear to be little justification to the extension of the western boundary of Poland up to the western Neisse River.'[44] This considerable concession to Stalin was, however, part of an American 'package-deal' which aimed primarily at setting up a democratic Poland and at securing free elections. The United States would thus agree to consider the Oder frontier on condition that the Soviets would make corresponding political concessions.

Also on 8 February Churchill submitted a revised formula for Poland, in which he conceded 'the lands desired by Poland to the east of the line of the Oder'.[45] Polish wishes would thus be consulted, but the western Neisse as proposed by the Soviets was shown to be quite out of the question. As Churchill informed the other conferees, he had received a telegram from the War Cabinet

Population 1939 census	Percentage of Germans	Area in sq. ml.
2,104,553	100	10,473
2,721,512	100	8,106

PROPOSED CESSION OF
TERRITORY BY GERMANY

Territory east of Line D

Territory added by Line
Total east of Line

Territory added by Line
Total east of Line

Territory added by Line
Total east of Line

NOTE: The former Free City o
        above tables

Map 5.   Germany – Poland: proposed territorial changes

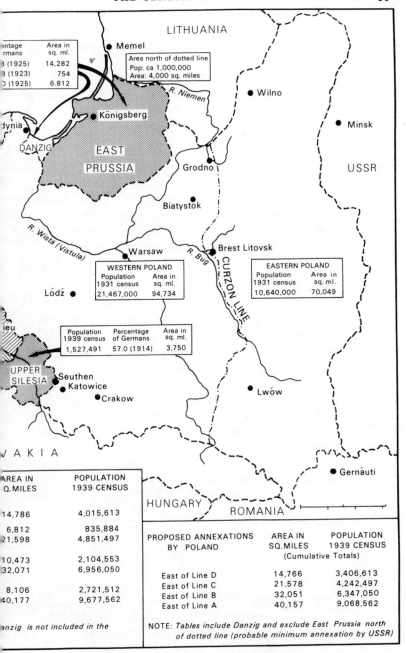

LITHUANIA

Memel

entage rmans	Area in sq. ml.
3 (1925)	14,282
3 (1923)	754
0 (1925)	6.812

Area north of dotted line
Pop: ca 1,000,000
Area: 4,000 sq. miles

R. Niemen

Wilno

Königsberg

Minsk

dynia

DANZIG

EAST
PRUSSIA

Grodno

USSR

Biatystok

R. Wista (Vistula)

Warsaw

R. Bug

Brest Litovsk

CURZON LINE

WESTERN POLAND

Population 1931 census	Area in sq. ml.
21,467,000	94,734

EASTERN POLAND

Population 1931 census	Area in sq. ml.
10,640,000	70,049

Lódź

ieu

Population 1939 census	Percentage of Germans	Area in sq. ml.
1,527,491	57.0 (1914)	3,750

UPPER
SILESIA

Seuthen
Katowice

Crakow

Lwów

VAKIA

Gernäuti

AREA IN Q.MILES	POPULATION 1939 CENSUS
14,786	4,015,613
6,812	835,884
21,598	4,851,497
10,473	2,104,553
32,071	6,956,050
8,106	2,721,512
40,177	9,677,562

anzig is not included in the

HUNGARY   ROMANIA

PROPOSED ANNEXATIONS BY POLAND	AREA IN SQ.MILES	POPULATION 1939 CENSUS (Cumulative Totals)
East of Line D	14,766	3,406,613
East of Line C	21,578	4,242,497
East of Line B	32,051	6,347,050
East of Line A	40,157	9,068,562

NOTE: Tables include Danzig and exclude East Prussia north
of dotted line (probable minimum annexation by USSR)

in London deprecating any frontier going as far west as the Neisse. 'They feel that the population problem is too large to handle.'[46]

Thus, even though tentative concessions were made by the Western Allies, no final commitments were entered into. It is significant that the text approved in the seventh plenary session on 10 February was deliberately vague on the question of Poland's western frontier:[47]

> It is recognized that Poland must receive substantial
> accessions of territory in the North and West. They feel
> that the opinion of the new Polish Provisional Government of
> National Unity should be sought in due course on the
> extent of these accessions and that the final delimitation of
> the Western frontier of Poland should thereafter await the
> Peace Conference.

This refusal to make a binding decision on Poland's western frontier was a rather pathetic step taken by the Western Allies with a view to retaining their bargaining position *vis-à-vis* the Soviet Union. Churchill and Roosevelt were not disposed to make territorial concessions to a Soviet-dominated Polish government and hoped to bind the recognition of Poland's western frontier to the issue of establishing a truly democratic and representative government. These were part and parcel of British and American proposals at Yalta, and they would have to be fulfilled conjointly. The Soviets never had any intention of fulfilling either.

Still optimistic about the prospects of future co-operation with the Soviet Union, President Roosevelt reported to the American people upon his return from Yalta:[48]

> Throughout history, Poland has been the corridor through
> which attacks on Russia have been made. Twice in this
> generation, Germany has struck at Russia through this
> corridor. To insure European security and world peace, a
> strong and independent Poland is necessary to prevent that
> from happening again.
>   The decisions with respect to the boundaries of Poland
> were frankly a compromise . . . under which the Poles will
> receive compensation in territory in the North and West
> in exchange for what they lose by the Curzon Line in the

East. The limits of the Western border will be permanently fixed in the final Peace Conference. Roughly, this will include in the new, strong Poland quite a large slice of what is now called Germany. . . .

I am convinced that this agreement on Poland, under the circumstances, is the most hopeful agreement possible for a free, independent, and prosperous Polish State.

In a similar tone, upon his return to Great Britain, Prime Minister Churchill addressed parliament and made a motion in the House of Commons:[49]

That this House approves the declaration of joint policy agreed to by the three great Powers at the Crimea Conference, and, in particular, welcomes their determination to maintain unity of action not only in achieving the final defeat of the common enemy but, thereafter, in peace as in war.

With respect to Poland's frontiers he reported:[50]

The three Powers have now agreed that Poland shall receive substantial accessions of territory both in the North and in the West. In the North she will certainly receive, in the place of a precarious Corridor, the great city of Danzig, the greater part of East Prussia West and South of Königsberg, and a long, wide sea front on the Baltic. In the West she will receive the important industrial province of Upper Silesia and, in addition, such other territories to the East of the Oder as may be decided at the peace settlement to detach from Germany after the views of a broadly based Polish Government have been ascertained.

Although Churchill did not elaborate on the meaning of 'substantial accessions', it was clear that according to the Anglo-American plan Poland would *not* be given any German territory west of the Oder River (with the exception of a very small part of Upper Silesia east of the Glatzer (eastern) Neisse River, but west of the Oder). Nor was it at all certain that the Anglo-Americans would approve all of Poland's demands for German territories east of the Oder. As Churchill explained,

it would be a great mistake to press Poland to take a larger portion of these lands than is considered by her and her friends and Allies to be within her compass to man, to develop, and, with the aid of the Allies and the world organisation, to maintain.[51]

Churchill's speech was received enthusiastically by many members of parliament, but critics of the Prime Minister's announced policy were not lacking either. On 1 March 1945, Mr Rhys-Davis posed the following rhetorical question:[52]

> If it is the policy of the Allied Powers to hand over Danzig and East Prussia and other patches of Germany to Poland, to establish a new State by giving patches of Poland to Russia on the other side, do they imagine for a moment they are likely to establish a durable peace in Europe?

On the same day Mr Strauss (Labour Party) observed:[53]

> According to the Prime Minister some parts of Germany, certainly Upper Silesia, are to go to Poland. I hope the Government will hesitate before it finally gives its approval to a proposal of this sort, which can hold out no advantage to anybody but may be exceedingly harmful to the general prospects of a lasting European peace. On what ground is such a proposal put forward? That it is going to be some compensation to Poland. But the whole justification for the Curzon Line is that it was agreed in 1919 at Versailles. Not only was the Curzon Line, but also Poland's Western boundary was agreed at Versailles. If one is fair to Poland, so, presumably, is the other.

But in the context of political horse-trading 'ancient' history like the Treaty of Versailles simply did not play a very significant role. Perhaps the most illuminating and at the same time distressing commentary was that of Mr Davis, who concluded: 'We started this war with great motives and high ideals. We published the Atlantic Charter and then spat on it, stamped on it and burnt it, as it were, at the stake, and now nothing is left of it.'[54] Five months later, the pronouncement of the Potsdam Protocol confirmed the martyrdom of the Atlantic Charter. It too had become a war casualty. The Soviet-Polish frontier was fixed at the Curzon Line and $1\frac{1}{2}$ million Poles had to abandon their homes and migrate west.[55] The Polish-German frontier was also fixed at the Oder-Neisse Line – albeit 'provisionally' – and over 9 million Germans became homeless. As *Time* reported: 'Europe had emerged from history's most terrible war into history's most terrifying peace.'[56]

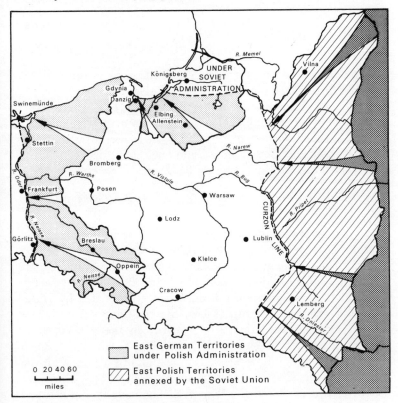

Map 6.   Poland's removal to the West: losses in the East – compensation in the West

CHAPTER FOUR

THE FLIGHT: PRELUDE TO THE EXPULSIONS

The disaster that befell this area with the entry of the Soviet forces has no parallel in modern European experience. There were considerable sections of it where, to judge by all existing evidence, scarcely a man, woman, or child of the indigenous population was left alive after the initial passage of Soviet forces; and one cannot believe that they all succeeded in fleeing to the West.

George F. Kennan, *Memoirs*, 1967, vol. 1, p. 265.

The great westward displacement of the Germans during and after the Second World War went through many phases. The first groups to move west were those Germans of the Baltic States, Volhynia and Bessarabia who opted for German citizenship pursuant to the population transfer treaties negotiated by Hitler Germany with these countries between 1939 and 1941.[1] These ethnic Germans were resettled primarily in the pre-Versailles German Provinces of West Prussia and Posen, which the Reich reannexed in 1939 following the subjugation of Poland. With the collapse of the German military machine in 1944–5 these re-settled Germans shared the fate of all Germans in Eastern and Central Europe.

The second phase of the displacement took the form of military evacuations organized by the retreating German army. These evacuations were often commenced upon short notice, but their harshness was tempered by a modicum of organization.

The third phase was characterized by the disorganized flight of hundreds of thousands of civilians who had not been evacuated in time. Many whose flight was frustrated chose suicide instead as an escape from the avenging Red Army.[2]

The most extensive and possibly the costliest phase was that of the actual expulsions beginning in March and April 1945 and continuing through the year 1948 and even into 1949.

This chapter is mainly devoted to the history and the motivation of the second and third phases of the German displacement: military evacuation and disorderly flight.

THE ARRIVAL OF THE RED ARMY IN EAST PRUSSIA: NEMMERSDORF

Until the summer of 1944 the province of East Prussia had been sheltered from the war. British planes sought their targets mostly in Western and Central Germany. The Ostfront seemed very far away.

Not until the mighty Soviet offensive of the summer of 1944 did the East Prussians commence to lose their sense of security. Although officially it was 'defeatism' to doubt in the *Endsieg*, the rapidly approaching front soon gave even Party officials good reason to become defeatists.

On 16 October 1944 the Red Army launched a massive offensive along a ninety-mile front on the eastern frontier of East Prussia. On 19 October they broke into the Reich and captured the districts of Goldap and Gumbinnen. A vigorous counter-offensive by the German Wehrmacht pushed the Russians out of Germany territory by 5 November 1944. But the short Russian occupation had not failed to leave its mark upon the landscape. Wehrmacht and Volkssturm soldiers who recaptured Goldap and Gumbinnen found very few survivors of the Russian occupation.

The events in the village of Nemmersdorf on 20–21 October deserve special attention, because the word Nemmersdorf was destined to play an important role in the history of the German flight. Not many Americans have ever heard the word 'Nemmersdorf'. It is, however, together with Katyn, one of the best-documented Russian atrocities of the Second World War. To the East Prussian peasant the word came to evoke unspeakable fear. Nemmersdorf, however, was by no means the only East Prussian village where serious excesses were committed by members of the Red Army. Yet, it was Nemmersdorf that became a kind of symbol, and knowledge of what had happened there accelerated the flight of the Germans – not only from East Prussia, but also from Silesia and Pomerania.

But why did the Nemmersdorf massacre happen? Why weren't the German civilians evacuated in time? Experienced military commanders[3] had repeatedly advised the civil authorities in

East Prussia of the dangers associated with the rapidly approaching front. As early as August 1944 General Friedrich Hossbach, Commander-in-Chief of the German Fourth Army, had proposed the precautionary evacuation of civilians from the eastern parts of East Prussia, but the political leadership under the infamous Gauleiter Erich Koch deprecated any proposals of evacuation as confessions of 'defeatism' and proscribed them until the emergency had ripened and the Soviet Army had overrun the eastern districts of East Prussia.[4]

Nemmersdorf was one of the first villages in the Reich to experience the severity of Russian occupation. After more than three years of fighting Germans on Russian soil it appears that Russian soldiers went berserk upon entering the Reich for the first time. The harrowing events are documented below.

On 5 July 1946, before an American tribunal in Neu Ulm, the former Chief of Staff of the German Fourth Army in East Prussia, Major General Erich Dethleffsen stated:[5]

> When in October, 1944, Russian units . . . broke through
> German defences and advanced as far as Nemmersdorf,
> they tortured civilians in many villages south of Gumbinnen,
> nailed some on barn doors and shot many others. A large
> number of women were raped. The Russian soldiers also
> shot some fifty French prisoners of war. The affected
> villages were reoccupied by German forces within forty-
> eight hours.

Another, a first lieutenant of the reserve, Dr Heinrich Amberger, Chief of the Thirteenth Parachute and Armoured Company of the Second Regiment 'Hermann Goering' which had been brought in from the Memel front to counterattack in the zone of Gumbinnen-Insterburg, gave the following sworn affidavit which was later submitted as evidence for the defence in the Nuremberg Trials:[6]

> I saw fully confirmed the rumours regarding the Russian
> massacre of German civilians. On the road through
> Nemmersdorf, near the bridge over the brook Angerapp, I
> saw where a whole trek of refugees had been rolled over by
> Russian tanks; not only the wagons and teams, but also a
> goodly number of civilians, mostly women and children,
> had been squashed flat by the tanks. At the edge of the road

and in the farm yards lay quantities of corpses of civilians
who evidently had not all been killed in the course of
military operations but rather had been murdered
systematically. . . .

On the edge of a street an old woman sat hunched up,
killed by a bullet in the back of the neck. Not far away lay
a baby of only a few months, killed by a shot at close range
through the forehead. . . . A number of men, with no other
marks of fatal wounds, had been killed by blows with shovels
or gun butts; their faces were completely smashed. At least
one man was nailed to a barn door. Yet, not only in
Nemmersdorf itself, but also in the near-by villages between
Angerapp and Rominten similar cases were noted after these
villages were cleared of Russian troops. Neither in
Nemmersdorf nor in the other places did I find a single
living German civilian despite the fact that the Russian
invasion had come as such a surprise that no appreciable
number of civilians could have fled. . . .

Karl Potrek, a civilian from the capital city of Königsberg,
had been recruited into the Volksturm and hurriedly sent as
reinforcement to the area of Gumbinnen and Nemmersdorf. He
later reported:[7]

At the edge of town, on the left side of the road, stands the
large inn 'Weisser Krug'. . . . In the farmyard further down
the road stood a cart, to which four naked women were
nailed through their hands in a cruciform position. Behind
the Weisser Krug towards Gumbinnen is a square with a
monument to the Unknown Soldier. Beyond is another large
inn, 'Roter Krug'. Near it, parallel to the road, stood a barn
and to each of its two doors a naked woman was nailed
through the hands, in a crucified posture. In the dwellings
we found a total of seventy-two women, including children,
and one old man, 74, all dead . . . all murdered in a bestial
manner, except only for a few who had bullet holes in their
necks. Some babies had their heads bashed in. In one room
we found a woman, 84 years old, sitting on a sofa . . . half
of whose head had been sheared off with an axe or a spade. . . .

We carried the corpses to the village cemetery where they
lay to await a foreign medical commission. . . .[8] In the
meantime, a nurse from Insterburg came, a native of

Nemmersdorf, who looked for her parents. Among the corpses were her mother, 72, and her father, 74, the only man among the dead. She also established that all the dead were Nemmersdorfers. On the fourth day the bodies were buried in two graves. Only on the following day did the medical commission arrive, and the tombs had to be re-opened. Barn doors were set on blocks on which to lay the bodies so that the commission could examine them. This foreign commission unanimously established that all the women, as well as the girls from eight to twelve years and even the woman of 84 years had been raped. After the examination by the commission, the bodies were again buried.

Still another witness of the Nemmersdorf massacre was Captain Emil Herminghaus, who reported as follows: [9]

Upon re-entering Nemmersdorf the German troops were greeted by a frightful scene, which for the first time showed the German people what everyone had to expect who fell into the hands of the soviet Soldateska. The women who had been surprised in the village, including several nuns, had been herded together by the Russians, raped and gravely abused. The women had been bestially stabbed or shot. . . . The army immediately invited the neutral Press. Reporters from Switzerland and Sweden as well as some Spaniards and Frenchmen from the occupied parts of France came to witness the frightful scene.

One of the very few survivors of the massacre was a German Hausfrau of Nemmersdorf who was able to disguise herself as a Polish farmhand. In the morning of 20 October 1944 Frau Margot Grimm started off with her husband, mother, mother-in-law, son Joachim,[10] daughter Sabine and six Polish women and their children. Not far away from Nemmersdorf they were overtaken by Russian soldiers who cut their flight. The first wagon was able to get away. In this wagon were the mother, mother-in-law, and the children. The second wagon, driven by Herr Johannes Grimm, was unable to escape. After halting his wagon Herr Grimm was pulled down and summarily shot. His other passengers, including his wife and the Polish workers, were similarly dragged down and robbed of their watches and rings, but they were not shot. The Polish women, who had been in the employ of Herr Grimm, also feared for their lives, but they pleaded with the Russian soldiers in Polish and made them understand that they were not 'the enemy'. Out of loyalty and pity for Frau Grimm, the Polish women threw their shawls about her and tied an old handkerchief over her head. For twenty-four hours Frau Grimm remained disguised and did not speak; later, with the help of the merciful Polish farmhands, she was able to bury her husband and to continue her flight West.

Such was the entry of the Red Army in East Prussia. The mass flight that followed was a direct result of it.

During the First World War East Prussian peasants had also fled upon the advance of the Tsarist Army, but their flight had not been as thorough nor as precipitate as was the case in the winter of 1944-5. The Soviet invasion of the Second World War manifested a different, genocidal character.

Some of the excesses committed by members of the Red Army upon their first contact with civilians in the Reich may, no doubt, be explained as outbursts of vengeance for the atrocities committed by the SS and Einsatzgruppen in the Soviet Union. On the other hand, Russian excesses in East Prussia were not simply a spontaneous eruption of retributive justice. The Red Army had been systematically incited by the propaganda of Ilya Ehrenburg, the fanatical anti-German author whose articles regularly appeared in *Pravda*, *Isvestja* and in the front-line soldier newspaper *Red Star*. This Soviet Julius Streicher[11] inflamed the lust and rapine of the Red Army with hate propaganda such as:

Kill. Nothing in Germany is guiltless, neither the living nor the yet unborn. Follow the words of Comrade Stalin and crush forever the fascist beast in its den. Break the racial pride of the German woman. Take her as your legitimate booty. Kill, you brave Soldiers of the victorious Soviet Army.[12]

Ehrenburg's hate propaganda had started early in the war and reached its high point in the autumn of 1944. In his oft-quoted book *Война* (The War), published in 1942, Ehrenburg proposed to treat all Germans as sub-human. He wrote, for instance:[13]

The Germans are not human beings. From now on the word German means to us the most terrible oath. From now on

the word German strikes us to the quick. We shall not speak
any more. We shall not get excited. We shall kill. If you
have not killed at least one German a day, you have wasted
that day. . . . If you cannot kill your German with a bullet,
kill him with your bayonet. If there is calm on your part of
the front, or if you are waiting for the fighting, kill a German
in the meantime. If you leave a German alive, the German
will hang a Russian and rape a Russian woman. If you kill
one German, kill another – there is nothing more amusing
for us than a heap of German corpses. Do not count days,
do not count versts. Count only the number of Germans
killed by you. Kill the German – that is your grandmother's
request. Kill the German – that is your child's prayer.
Kill the German – that is your motherland's loud request.
Do not miss. Do not let through. Kill.

In sharp contrast to Ehrenburg's propaganda one reads Stalin's
Order of the Day no. 55 of 23 February 1942 in which Stalin
tried to reassure the world:[14]

Some time we hear silly talk about the Red Army intending
to exterminate the German people and to destroy the
German state. This is, of course, a stupid lie. . . . It would
be ridiculous to identify the Hitler clique with the German
people or the German state. Historical experiences prove
that the Hitlers are coming and going but the German people
and the German state remain.

Such reasonable words appear as a sad arabesque upon the harsh
realities of the war in the eastern parts of Germany.

During the first weeks of the invasion posters went up in
East Prussia and Silesia reading: 'Red Army Soldier: You are
now on German soil; the hour of revenge has struck!'[15] Whole
towns were burned down without any military necessity, just
because they were German. Allenstein, for instance, which had
originally fallen almost intact into Russian hands, was devastated.
After the Poles took over they were furious at all the repairing
and rebuilding that had to be done.[16]

George F. Kennan succinctly described what took place in the
Eastern German territories: 'The Russians . . . swept the native
population clean in a manner that had no parallel since the days
of the Asiatic hordes.'[17]

Among the most perceptive witnesses of the behaviour of the
Red Army were Allied prisoners of war who had not been evacuated from East Prussia, Pomerania and Silesia at the time of the
great Soviet offensive. Many recorded their experiences in
veteran newspapers, conveying a thousand stories of flight with
the German civilians or liberation through the Red Army. Those
who remained behind report on the widespread raping and
looting; but this 'sweeping clean' of the population was frequently so indiscriminate that the prisoners of war became
victims themselves. Several hundred French and Belgian prisoners
of war[18] never returned, many being killed by airplanes or
artillery bombardment and many being liquidated outright
because they were 'suspicious' or because they did not have a
watch or a ring to give to a looting soldier. In some cases prisoners
of war were allegedly taken for 'werewolves'[19] and summarily
shot. Russian soldiers simply did not take the time to find out – to
them every moving object in the Reich was 'the enemy' and had
to be destroyed. Belgian prisoners of war were particularly afraid
of identifying themselves as 'belge' for fear of being taken for
survivors of the fascist Degrelle Division. They learned to say
they were 'frankosen' or just 'de Gaulle'. Yet, this did not prevent
many Russian soldiers from mistreating the prisoners of war,
whose best hope was to find a responsible Russian officer who
might honour their protected status.[20] But by the time they were
recognized as prisoners of war they had usually lost their boots,
watches and marriage rings.

Former English prisoners of war were similarly 'liberated' of
their valuables. Upon repatriation into the English zone they
reported on the appalling lack of discipline within the Red
Army:[21]

> In the district around our internment camp – the territory
> comprising the towns of Schlawe, Lauenburg, and Buckow
> [all in Eastern Pomerania] and hundreds of larger villages –
> Red soldiers during the first weeks of their occupation raped
> every woman and girl between the ages of 12 and 60. That
> sounds exaggerated but it is the simple truth.
>
> The only exceptions were girls who managed to remain in
> hiding in the woods or who had the presence of mind to

feign illness – typhoid, diphtheria, or some other infectious
disease. Flushed with victory – and often with wine found in
the cellars of rich Pomeranian land owners – the Reds
searched every house for women cowing them with pistols
or tommy guns, and carried them into their tanks or tracks.

TESTIMONY OF RUSSIAN SOLDIERS

For obvious reasons, few war recollections by Russian authors
contain any reference to the faults of their frequently heroic and –
in any case – victorious soldiers. There are some exceptions.
Alexander Solzhenitsyn, then a young captain in the Red Army,
described the entry of his regiment into East Prussia in January
1945 as follows: 'For three weeks the war had been going on
inside Germany, and all of us knew very well that if the girls were
German they could be raped and then shot. This was almost a
combat distinction.'[22] Party Member and Red Army Intelligence
Officer Lev Kopelev[23] was so appalled by the abuses inflicted on
the German population that he had to intervene on their behalf.
In his war recollections[24] he describes his often fruitless inter-
ventions. Not long after the occupation of Neidenburg in East
Prussia he tried to protect an old lady who was erring through the
streets, half-mad, babbling about her daughter and her food
stamps. He did his best to calm her down and tried to take her
home. On the way an officer named Beljajew grabbed the old
lady's purse in order to inspect her papers, accused her of being a
spy and shot her dead before Kopelev could stop him.[25] In
Allenstein, which had been taken almost without a fight, the
sacking and raping lasted for weeks. For all practical purposes
plunder was legal. Indeed, shortly before the winter offensive
started official permission had been granted to Soviet soldiers to
send packages home. Soldiers could send two packages per
month, each weighing eight kilograms. Officers could send twice
as much.[26] But what was there to send home? Food rations?
Plunder of all kinds and sizes – from silver to grandfather clocks.
But far worse were the rapings. Kopelev remembers a woman
who came imploring to him. The soldiers should not rape her
or her thirteen-year-old daughter any more. The soldiers should
not hit her eleven-year-old son. The daughter told Commissar
Kopelev not to worry – her brother was already dead.[27] Even
Polish and Ukrainian labourers who had stayed in Allenstein to

Убей

Вот отрывки из трех писем, найденных на убитых немцах.

Управляющий Рейнгардт пишет лейтенанту Отто фон Шираху:

«Французов от нас забрали на завод. Я выбрал шесть русских из Минского округа. Они гораздо выносливей французов. Только один из них умер, остальные продолжают работать в поле и на ферме. Содержание их ничего не стоит, и мы не должны страдать от того, что эти звери, дети которых, может быть, убивают наших солдат, едят немецкий хлеб. Вчера я подверг легкой экзекуции двух русских бестий, которые тайком пожрали снятое молоко, предназначавшееся для свиных маток...»

Мы знаем все. Мы помним все. Мы поняли: немцы не люди. Отныне—слово «немец» для нас самое страшное проклятье. Отныне слово «немец» разряжает ружье. Не будем говорить. Не будем возмущаться. Будем убивать. Если ты не убил за день хотя бы одного немца, твой день пропал. Если ты думаешь, что за тебя немца убьет твой сосед, ты не понял угрозы. Если ты не убьешь немца, немец убьет тебя. Он возьмет твоих близких и будет мучить их в своей окаянной Германии. Если ты не можешь убить немца пулей, убей немца штыком. Если на твоем участке затишье, если ты ждешь боя, убей немца до боя. Если ты оставишь немца жить, немец повесит русского человека и опозорит русскую женщину. Если ты убил одного немца, убей другого — нет для нас ничего веселее немецких трупов. Не считай дней. Не считай верст. Считай одно: убитых тобою немцев. Убей немца! — это просит старуха-мать. Убей немца! — это молит тебя дитя. Убей немца! — это кричит родная земля. Не промахнись. Не пропусти. Убей!

24 июля 1942 г.

1 Excerpt from Ilya Ehrenburg's Война (The War), vol. 2, pp. 21–3, 1943 (Harvard University Library HB 477.45.5)

2 *Above* The village of Nemmersdorf in East Prussia was overrun
on 20 October 1944 (Bundesarchiv)

3 *Right* German civilians who were
not evacuated in time
(Bundesarchiv)

4 *Below* Over seventy civilians were
massacred in Nemmersdorf
(Bundesarchiv)

5 *Above* A team of non-German doctors and several foreign journalists were invited to see the victims at Nemmersdorf, Goldap and Gumbinnen (Bundesarchiv)

6 *Left* Nemmersdorf children (Bundesarchiv)

7 *Left* Nemmersdorf farmer (Bundesarchiv)

8 *Right* Winter 1944–5: trek in Silesia (Podzun)

9 *Left* and 10 *Below* Trek in East Prussia (Bundesarchiv)

11 *Above* Machine-gunned trek in East Prussia (Henrich)

12 and 13 *Left* Plundered trek (Bundesarchiv)

14 *Above* Flight over the ice of the Frisches Haff (Podzun)

15 *Below* Low-flying planes did not spare the treks (Bundespresseamt)

16 *Above* The *Wilhelm-Gustloff* sank on 30 January 1945 (Hapag-Lloyd)

17 *Left* The *General von Steuben* sank on 10 February 1945 (Hapag-Lloyd)

18 *Left* The *Goya* sank on 16 April 1945 (Hapag-Lloyd)

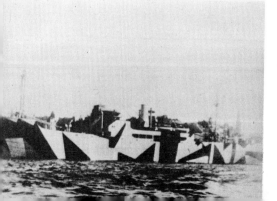

19 and 20 At the time of the fire-bombing of Dresden on 13 February 1945, the city was teeming with hundreds of thousands of Silesian refugees. An estimated 135,000 persons perished (Andres and Irving)

await the arrival of the Red Army were not always spared. Drunken soldiers mistook them for Germans and so raped them or shot them.[28]

Similar excesses were reported by Russian-born author Alexander Werth, who spent most of the war on the Russian front as correspondent for the British *Sunday Times*. He remembers a conversation with a Russian major, who unabashedly told him:[29]

> Any of our chaps simply had to say: 'Frau komm', and she knew what was expected of her. . . . Let's face it. For nearly four years, the Red Army had been sex-starved. . . . In Poland a few regrettable things happened from time to time, but, on the whole, a fairly strict discipline was maintained as regards 'rape'. The most common offence in Poland was 'dai chasy' – 'give me your wrist-watch.' There was an awful lot of petty thieving and robbery. Our fellows were just crazy about wrist-watches – there's no getting away from it. But the looting and raping in a big way did not start until our soldiers got to Germany. Our fellows were so sex-starved that they often raped old women of sixty, or seventy or even eighty – much to these grandmothers' surprise, if not downright delight. But I admit it was a nasty business, and the record of the Kazakhs and other Asiatic troops was particularly bad.

The American General Frank A. Keating, who served in Germany together with Soviet soldiers later wrote that he had observed in them a very deep hatred for the Germans stemming from the knowledge of Nazi atrocities in their homeland and from the thought that revenge was a privilege. He compared some of their 'savagery . . . to that of . . . barbaric hordes'.[30]

THE FEAR OF DEPORTATION TO FORCED LABOUR IN THE SOVIET UNION

In cases where the dangers of remaining in the combat zone did not suffice to convince German civilians of the necessity of fleeing west, the fear of being deported to forced labour in Siberia did induce many a stubborn peasant to abandon everything and trek to safety. As it happened, not many Germans were sent as far as Siberia, but more than two hundred thousand[31] able-bodied men and women from East Prussia, Pomerania and Silesia were deported to remote areas of the Soviet Union for forced labour of indeterminate duration and under conditions[32] that were considerably more barbarous than the conditions under which Hitler-Germany had recruited forced labourers from the occupied countries during the war, a crime for which Fritz Saukel, Reich Plenipotentiary for the Allocation of Labour, was convicted and hanged at Nuremberg.[33]

Since at the Yalta Conference the Western Allies had failed effectively to oppose the Soviet demand for 'reparations in kind'[34] in the form of German labour, the Soviet Army drew up quotas of needed labourers and started implementing them as soon as they conquered German-populated areas. Only with respect to the large-scale deportation of Volksdeutsche of Romania did the Western Allies lodge vigorous protests.[35] Post-war investigations on the mortality in the deportation camps, during the transport and up to the return of the survivors lead to a conservative estimate of 100 to 125,000 deaths among the *Reichsdeutsche* deportees alone.[36]

AN UNNECESSARY FLIGHT?

At this point the above question may appear sufficiently answered. Yet, in spite of incontrovertible evidence of grave excesses by the Red Army, some post-war authors have propagated the theory that the German flight from the Red Army was unnecessary, since the soldiers of the Soviet Socialist Republic did not come as conquerors but rather as liberators. These authors accordingly maintain that there was no reason to panic and that German civilians only fled because of a 'psychotic fear of the Soviet Army'[37] instilled by Goebbels's mendacious propaganda.

Any such theories fall apart when one considers alone the fact that thousands of Germans fled *after* the arrival of the first wave of Red Army soldiers, knowing full well from experience – not from propaganda – what it would mean to be around when the second wave rolled over them. Many who could not escape, especially women, chose suicide as a preferable fate to continued physical abuse and degradation.

The vast number of suicides among the German civilian population has also been written off as motivated by the shock of defeat.[38] No doubt, the arrival of the victorious Red Army was a shock to some fanatic Germans who religiously believed in the German *Endsieg* through miracle weapons. Disappointment and despair drove some of these Germans to suicide, but the majority of the suicides were motivated primarily by fear of rape or by fear of being deported to the Soviet Union.

A FLIGHT OF 'BAD CONSCIENCE'?

Another argument which is frequently heard is that the Germans fled out of feelings of guilt, anticipating Red Army vengeance for the crimes committed by the Nazis in the Soviet Union.[39] Of course, a number of Nazi functionaries knew about the crimes of the political SS and the Einsatzgruppen inside Russia and decided that it would be healthier for them to disappear before the arrival of the Red Army. The number of these Nazi functionaries, however, was limited. To generalize from these few and impute guilt upon millions of German civilians who fled for entirely different reasons would be tantamount to falsifying history. Quite the contrary, the occupying Powers were frequently perplexed by the almost total lack of a sense of guilt among the German people. In his report to President Truman dated 9 November 1945, Byron Price complained that[40]

> Notwithstanding the punishments Germans now suffer and those still before them, there is no apparent realization of collective guilt for the unspeakable crimes committed by the German nation. . . . Intelligence reports indicate clearly that all of our propaganda efforts to instill a sense of collective guilt have fallen flat.

Thus, the principal motivation for the great flight of the Germans should not be sought in the bad conscience of the Germans nor in an unfounded and 'psychotic' fear of the Red Army. Other reasons were determinative of this movement.

Field Marshal Montgomery, who did much to help the German refugees, and who, unlike General Eisenhower, permitted all refugees to find safety within his lines,[41] observed in his *Memoirs*,[42]

> From their behaviour it soon became clear that the Russians, though a fine fighting race, were in fact barbarous Asiatics who had never enjoyed a civilisation comparable to that of

the rest of Europe. Their approach to every problem was utterly different from ours and their behaviour, especially in their treatment of women, was abhorrent to us. In certain sectors of the Russian zone there were practically no Germans left; they had all fled before the onward march of the barbarians, with the result that in the Western zones the crowd of refugees was so great that the problems of food and housing seemed almost insoluble.

THE TREKS

In spite of bad roads and inclement weather, German civilians started moving west late in the autumn of 1944, principally after the events of the Russian occupation in Nemmersdorf became known. Evacuations were carried out in groups of vehicles, mostly horse-drawn, which took their name 'treks' from the South African Boers. These treks could have just as well been called 'wagon trains' as in the legendary American West, but in 1944-5 the interminable columns of covered wagons were not pioneers, but refugees trying to save their lives from a rapidly advancing enemy.

At first the roads were not too congested, but as the weeks passed more and more civilians decided to pack and go, even against Gauleiter Koch's express orders to remain and defend the homeland to the last man. Later evacuations would be hurriedly ordered and not always carried out in an organized manner, even though officials usually accompanied the refugee columns to prevent collisions and other calamities. Not infrequently the leaders of the refugee columns were prisoners of war who preferred to help in the evacuation than wait for the arrival of the Red Army.[43]

The way through icy roads and blinding blizzards was not easy. Horses were constantly slipping and the wagons frequently broke down. Food for the evacuees and milk for the babies were insufficient. Whereas the earlier evacuations had still afforded the refugees the possibility of spending the nights in villages along the road to the West, later evacuations exhibited more and more a 'sauve qui se peut' character.

Attacks of low-flying planes on the refugee columns became an ever-present danger, even though most of the time there were no military objectives surrounding the refugees and any pilot could have distinguished the columns of westward fleeing civilians from enemy military formations.

THE FRISCHES HAFF

Since the way overland was so arduous and the Red Army had succeeded in cutting numerous escape routes to the West, many refugees trekked to the Baltic coast in the hope of being evacuated by sea.

One of the worst chapters of the flight was the perilous crossing of the ice-covered bay separating the inner coastline from the narrow Pillau peninsula on the Baltic.[44] The refugees arrived in greater and greater numbers, mostly from Königsberg and Gumbinnen in the east and from Heiligenbeil and Allenstein further south. It had been bitter cold all the way up to the coast. Suddenly, the refugees wished it were colder still. The ice was thick but it was not thick enough to support the heavy wagons that travelled over it. Some fifteen miles separated that inner coast of Kalholy and Balga from the narrow tongue on the Baltic, and since the Haff was frozen over, rescue ships could not enter in order to evacuate the refugees from the inner coast. It became necessary to continue trekking, partly over ice, partly through freezing water, out to the peninsula and the outer sea.

Sometimes six or eight hours were necessary to cross the ice,[45] sometimes even longer. Exhaustion and exposure took its toll of lives, especially among the very young and the very old.[46] Babies froze and were left by their mothers on the ice, old women fell from their wagons – dead. But the touch of the macabre would still be added by low-flying Russian planes, which mercilessly machine-gunned the refugees and bombed the ice so that many a wagon sank through the broken ice and disappeared in the waters of the Haff.[47] Horses drowned, people drowned. It was an unimaginable trial against despair. Later, in February 1945, the ice became thinner due to warmer temperatures, and the gaps in the ice caused by the air raids did not ice over thickly enough to withstand the weights moving over them. It had become even more dangerous to cross the Haff, but the pocket behind the refugees closed and the arrival of the Red Army was imminent. Therefore, in spite of increased hardships and hazards, thousands of refugees continued crossing the Haff. In all, an estimated half a million East Prussians successfully crossed over to Pillau and to the other ports along the Nehrung where evacuations were taking place.

Arrival on the Nehrung, however, was by no means equivalent with reaching safety, since the air raids continued to inflict heavy casualties among the refugees.[48] There were, of course, military objectives in the port of Pillau, as there are in every port. On the other hand, it is difficult to see sufficient military necessity that could have justified the constant air bombardment of a port where tens of thousands of refugees were being evacuated. The principle of proportionality would seem to indicate that the loss of human life was too high in comparison with the military advantage to be gained. Technically, of course, the air raids on Pillau did not constitute war crimes, but one cannot help observing that here grave inhumanities were committed which could have been easily avoided without altering the conclusion of the war.

SEA RESCUE

In charge of sea rescue operations was Admiral Konrad Engelhardt, who under orders of Grand Admiral Dönitz, engaged every vessel available for the evacuation in the Eastern Baltic. A total of 790 vessels, both of the German Navy as well as of the Merchant Marine and even smaller private boats, were involved in the huge undertaking, some vessels making as many as twelve voyages, each time bringing German civilians, wounded and soldiers.[49]

Dwarfing the memorable evacuation of Dunkerque by the British Navy in May 1940, the Baltic operation was to prove the safest way for large numbers of refugees to reach the West. Yet, the few catastrophes of the sea rescue were so vast that they tend to be over-emphasized, thus conveying the erroneous impression that hundreds of thousands perished.

Although it is impossible accurately to determine the actual number of evacuees, the number of ships lost is known and a plausible estimate of the number of victims has been made. Between 2 and 3 million civilians and soldiers (principally the wounded) were evacuated through May 1945. Between 20,000 and 25,000 persons, approximately 1 per cent of the evacuees, perished when their ships were torpedoed by Soviet submarines or sunk from the air.

The best-documented tragedy was the sinking of the *Wilhelm Gustloff*[50] on 30 January 1945 by the Soviet submarine *S13* under

Captain A. I. Marinesko. The first and largest ship in a convoy, the *Gustloff*, sailed from Pillau with a cargo of some seven thousand human beings and travelled along the Pomeranian Coast toward Mecklenburg. After several hours of sailing it was shaken by three successive explosions and soon started listing to port. It shot distress signals. The Baltic was choppy and the deck was covered with ice. Rescue boats were frozen. Water temperature was two degrees. Only the presence of other ships in the convoy and the fact that the *Gustloff* sank slowly prevented a complete disaster. According to German sources only 838 persons were saved.

Probably the largest sea disaster in history was the sinking of the *Goya* on 16 April 1945 by the Soviet submarine *L-3* under Captain V. K. Konovalov.[51] It has been estimated that between 6,000 and 7,000 refugees had been packed into this freighter. Only 183 persons survived.

The sinking of the *Lusitania* in 1915 had claimed the lives of 1,198 of its nearly two thousand passengers, including 128 Americans.[52] This tragedy became famous because of its not unimportant role in the building of tensions that led to the American declaration of war upon Germany in 1917. Perhaps an even more famous sinking was the iceberg disaster of the *Titanic* on its maiden voyage in 1912 in which 1,517 persons perished. But the *Lusitania* and *Titanic* disasters only became legendary because of their uniqueness at the time of occurrence. By comparison, the sinking of the *Goya* occurred at a time when each day produced major catastrophes. In May 1941 the battleship *Bismarck* had gone down with nearly 3,000 men, several hundred U-Boats had been sunk, the *Gustloff* and the *Steuben* had already gone down. . . .The special tragedy of the *Goya*, on the other hand, was that it happened so close to the end of the war, at a time when the German surrender was within grasp.

But many senseless things are known to happen in wartime. Where was the sense of sinking so many refugee ships in the Baltic when the Russians and Poles had already decided to expel all the Germans from the provinces of East Prussia, West Prussia, Pomerania, etc.? It was precisely from these areas that the refugees were fleeing. Moreover, at the time of the sinking of the *Goya* the Russians had already begun with the actual expulsion of the Germans from the entire Baltic region. Why then send so many thousands of refugees to the bottom of the sea?

Captain Marinesko's submarine also scored the third biggest strike in the Baltic when it sank the *Steuben*, a large transporter of wounded soldiers, on 10 February 1945.[53] Three thousand five hundred evacuees drowned, and, as in the case of the *Gustloff*, no rescue of the shipwrecked was attempted by the Soviets.[54]

Unlike the *Gustloff*, the *Steuben* was a 'Verwundetentransporter' used strictly for transporting wounded soldiers to hospitals in the West. These 'Verwundetentransporter' were similarly equipped as the 'Lazarettschiffe' (hospital ships), but did not enjoy the special protection of the Hague and Geneva Conventions because Germany did not officially register them by notifying the Protecting Power (Switzerland) which would have in turn conveyed to Germany's adversaries the names and particulars of the protected ships. Nor was there time to repaint these vessels as prescribed in the Conventions, since every vessel was required for immediate evacuations in the Baltic. In any event, it would have made no difference whether the 'Verwundetentransporter' qualified as protected ships or not, since the government of the Soviet Union had expressly refused to recognize German hospital ships[55] and attacked them throughout the war as if these were legitimate military objectives.[56] In the course of the evacuations in the Baltic 13 hospital ships and 21 wounded transporters were deployed in repeated voyages; of this number 4 Lazarettschiffe and 8 Verwundetentransporter were sunk.[57]

In spite of these spectacular sinkings, the German Navy and Merchant Fleet continued the rescue undertaking until the very last days of the war. The peninsula of Hela in West Prussia was still teeming with civilians wishing to be evacuated. On 6 May 1945, for instance, 43,000 persons could still be evacuated from Hela.[58] On 8 May the last day before the German unconditional surrender went into effect, 25,000 soldiers from Hela arrived in Schleswig Holstein. Many other boats were still under way midnight of 8 May when hostilities officially ended, and although by the terms of the surrender agreement all ships were to sail immediately into the next available port, refugees who had been already fleeing over hundreds of miles in order to escape the Red Army refused to comply with the agreement when it meant sailing into a port occupied by Soviet forces.

The *Julius Rütgers*, a tanker with some 300 persons on board, thus strained its motors to reach the West before the deadline. At dawn of 9 May the old tanker had not reached its destination.

Suddenly Soviet torpedo planes appeared, dropped their missiles and sprayed the boat with bullets.[59] Only one person was wounded. The torpedoes missed target. Another tanker full of refugees was not so fortunate. On 9 May the *Liselotte Friedrich* was hit by a torpedo and sank near Bornholm, Denmark. Even two weeks after the capitulation ships laden with refugees arrived in Schleswig Holstein. The last ship that reached port completed its long voyage with a broken compass.

On the Hela peninsula thousands of civilians and soldiers remained who could not be evacuated in time. All of the soldiers and many of the civilians were sent to forced labour in the Soviet Union and many never returned.[60]

Simultaneously with the treks and the sea rescue, a lesser number of East Germans were actually evacuated by train, which although frequently unheated and always crowded, were usually a faster means of reaching the West. The fastest evacuation was, of course, by airplane, but only an insignificant and privileged few were able to avail themselves of this escape route, while some very lucky families who still had both an automobile and gasoline were able to make the sad voyage by car.

As long as the war lasted, the story of the refugees did not, of course, end with their arrival in Saxony or Mecklenburg, where they were still to share the grim fate of the West German city-dweller. Many who had survived the rigours of the flight perished under the carpet bombing of thousand-bomber swarms. Berlin and Hamburg experienced these attacks regularly and were at least equipped with air raid shelters. Other cities, however, were not at all prepared for air attacks. By far the largest holocaust of the war, claiming more victims than the bombings of Hiroshima and Nagasaki combined, was the fire bombing of Dresden, the capital of Saxony, on the night of the 13–14 February 1945. This famous baroque city on the River Elbe was overcrowded with some 600,000 refugees from Silesia, many of whom had arrived in trains, while others had come in treks and camped where they could, hoping to stay in Dresden until they could return to Silesia. During more than five years of war Dresden had been exempted from air attacks, not for humanitarian reasons, but because it had no important military objectives that could have justified the attack. It had, of course, a train station and rail lines spreading in many directions. The destruction of the train station could have justified a strategic attack, but not carpet bombing, especially when Dresden was known to be teeming with refugees. Three consecutive air attacks involving more than 1,500 planes were to turn this 'Florence on the Elbe' into an inferno which consumed 90 per cent of the old town and killed well over 100,000 persons, many of them miserable refugees from Silesia.[61]

EPILOGUE TO THE FLIGHT

In observing the phenomenon of mass flight one ought to keep in mind what triggers it. People do not take lightly a decision to abandon everything, to leave their homes and go into the vast unknown.

In 1971 the Bengalese war triggered the flight of some ten million East Pakistanis across the border into India. These East Pakistanis were mostly peasants and innocent of any crime. Their flight was not motivated by bad conscience nor by 'psychotic' fear of the enemy, but rather by the recognition of an imminent danger of being exterminated through genocidal war practices.[62]

Another aspect of every flight is the present hope of the refugees to return to their homes as soon as conditions permit. The Palestinian refugees, for instance, have proved to the world time and again that they want to return to their homeland. Their terroristic methods are criminal and reprehensible, but these are an answer to the insufficient attention which the world had given to their problem. Not only do the Palestinians have *animus revertendi*; they have made it unequivocal that they possess *voluntas revertendi*.

Regarding the German refugees of 1944 and 1945, the overwhelming number of them left their homes with the firm intention of returning. These refugees had no hint of Allied plans to amputate their provinces and forcefully to remove all remaining Germans and resettle them in the truncated Reich. Ignorant of these radical plans, waves of refugees whose escape had been cut off by the Red Army started returning to their villages in the East. After the German unconditional surrender many refugees also decided to attempt a return and face the hardships of occupation in their own villages in the East. Hungry and tired they turned around and commenced trekking back. On many occasions their intentions were frustrated by Soviet or Polish military authorities, who immediately interned them in camps, deported the men to forced labour in the East, or simply blocked the roads and the crossings of the Rivers Oder and Lusatian Neisse.[63] Meanwhile, the refugees who succeeded in reaching their homes often found them destroyed or already occupied by Russians or Poles. Some were lucky enough to be able to enjoy a few months of peace in their villages, only to be rounded up again in the year 1946 and sent off packed in cattle cars to the West, of course, and without any compensation whatever for their property.

CHAPTER FIVE

ANGLO–AMERICAN PLAN OF LIMITED TRANSFERS

> We recognized that certain transfers were unavoidable, but we did not intend at Potsdam to encourage or commit ourselves to transfers in cases where other means of adjustment were practicable.
>
> Secretary of State James F. Byrnes, 19 October 1945.
> *Foreign Relations of the United States*, 1945, vol. 2, p. 1294.

In the early spring months of 1945, as the war approached its conclusion, millions of German civilians from Pomerania, Silesia and East Prussia filled the roads to the West in their desperate flight from the fury of the conquering Soviet Army. Millions, however, had remained behind, and it was at this time that the actual expulsions got under way, beginning as soon as Polish authorities moved into the occupied German provinces. Who authorized these expulsions? Did the Allied decisions at Yalta provide legal justification for the physical removal of Germans from territories subject to belligerent occupation? The fact is that these early expulsions were carried out with the encouragement of the Soviet Government but without the knowledge or authorization of the Western Allies. Of course, as has been shown in earlier chapters, the leaders of Great Britain and the United States had already endorsed the principle of population transfers as applied to the Germans and in this sense they do not escape a share of the responsibility for the excesses that accompanied the actual implementation of the principle. Yet, their endorsement had been a limited one, which the governments of Poland and later Czechoslovakia chose to interpret as green light for indiscriminate expulsions.

In order to determine the degree of Western responsibility it is indispensable to ascertain what manner of transfer they had envisaged. Did the Western Allies envisage a displacement of 16 million persons? Did they authorize transfers into their occupation zones upon the end of hostilities? Contemporary British and American documents reveal a common policy of limiting the transfers to a minimum and executing a gradual and orderly resettlement, which was to commence in the spring of 1946. These documents further disclose the unsuccessful efforts of the Western Allies to induce the expelling countries to desist from further expulsions in 1945 and to wait for directions from the Allied Control Council with respect to the timing and number of subsequent transfers.

NUMBER OF PERSONS TO BE TRANSFERRED

Probably the most important element of the expulsion decision was the number of persons originally intended to be affected by this extraordinary measure. The forcible removal of tens of thousands of persons would have in any event caused grave problems from the technical and humanitarian point of view. The uprooting of millions necessarily spelled chaos, misery and death.

During the early years of the war the Allies formulated no plans for any transfer of Germans. The problem was palpably not acute in 1941–2 when the Germans were still winning victories. Even in 1943–4 no concrete decisions or plans were made. It was, however, at this time that Churchill and Roosevelt started to play with the idea of population transfers as a possible solution of minority problems in Central and Eastern Europe, basing their projections on a rather optimistic assessment of the Greek–Turkish experiment of 1923–6. Only toward the end of the war did Churchill and Roosevelt concern themselves more concretely with numbers, since the British and American occupation zones would be absorbing many of the transferred Germans, who would also 'bring their mouths with them',[1] as Churchill aptly observed.

In May 1944 the Committee on Post-War Programs in the US State Department prepared a memorandum containing policy recommendations with respect to the treatment of Germany in the light of long-term United States interests. On the matter of post-war population transfers it was clear that the Committee only contemplated the transfer of certain groups of Germans, and by no means their immediate transfer upon the end of hostilities. It recommended:[2]

This Government should oppose the mass transfer to the Reich of Germanic people from neighboring countries immediately after the cessation of hostilities but should approve the removal of individuals and groups who constitute an especially difficult problem; the transfer should be made, so far as may be feasible, under humane conditions and without undue strain on Germany's absorptive capacity. (Tentatively recommended: Inter-Divisional Committee on Germany to study further the question of (a) criteria for selecting populations for transfer; (b) an inter-allied occupation of East Prussia, and (c) establishment of an inter-allied commission to supervise transfers of population.)

In November 1944 the Committee similarly recommended:[3]

The United States Government should not favor any general transfer of minorities. . . . The objections to a general transfer of minorities do not necessarily apply to transfers of specially selected groups. However, the United States Government should admit such transfers only where it is convinced that they will improve relations between the countries concerned and contribute to greater stability in Europe. To achieve these ends, transfers should be carried out in orderly manner, over a period of time, with provisions for resettlement, and under international auspices.

This general policy reappeared in a 'Briefing Book Paper' prepared in the State Department dated 12 January, 1945. This paper confirmed that the United States 'should, wherever possible, favor a selective transfer',[4] and concluded, 'the Department favors a policy whereby these transfers would be held to a minimum.'[5]

It is well known, of course, that Prime Minister Churchill did not always express himself quite as carefully. In an impassioned address before the House of Commons on 15 December 1944, he said:[6]

The transference of several millions of people would have to be effected from the East to the West or North, as well as the expulsion of the Germans – because that is what is proposed: the total expulsion of the Germans – from the area to be acquired by Poland in the West and the North.

This rough statement of policy, however, ought to be placed in its proper context and understood as what it was – a rhetorical outburst in the course of a rousing wartime speech. Churchill was not sitting at a conference table in front of maps and making real decisions. Churchill was addressing the House of Commons at a moment of crisis. British efforts to capture Arnhem had failed miserably. The Germans were holding out. Winter had arrived and the mood was low because the British had not achieved what they had set out to achieve. It is not at all surprising that under these circumstances Churchill should have been carried away with 'fire and brimstone' rhetoric before Parliament. Yet, he never used this rhetoric in negotiations with Stalin at Yalta, nor was he to express himself in this way at Potsdam. Whereas in the House of Commons Churchill proved himself an orator with eloquence to move not only members of parliament but also the people and the armed forces, at the conference table he was a cool statesman, prepared to make only considered decisions and aware of the consequences.

Churchill's statement of 15 December 1944 has been quoted by every Soviet-bloc author in support of their 'total expulsion' thesis and in order to shift responsibility to the Western Allies.[7] They interpret Churchill's words as wholesale consent, broad enough to authorize everything that happened. Yet, in the light of Churchill's stance at Yalta and Potsdam, such an interpretation of his 15 December speech is untenable. It need only be mentioned that while on the one hand Churchill agreed to the expulsion of the Germans 'from the area to be acquired by Poland', on the other he intended to limit Poland's acquisition to about half of what Poland eventually took with the help of the Soviet Union and against vigorous protests from both the United States and Great Britain.

MALTA On 1 February 1945, three days before the opening of the Yalta Conference, the Foreign Ministers of the United States and Great Britain conferred on Board *HMS Sirius* in Grand Harbour, Malta. At this meeting British Foreign Minister Eden expressed anxiety over the Lublin government's latest demands for German territory, which, if approved, would have as a consequence the transfer of many more Germans than the British and Americans were willing to take into their occupation zones. The Americans shared this anxiety too and stressed their view that whatever the number of Germans to be affected, 'the transfer of population should be gradual and not precipitate.'[8]

On the same day Eden reported to Prime Minister Churchill on his conversations with Secretary of State Stettinius, summarizing that 'the cessions upon which we and the Americans are agreed would involve the transfer of some $2\frac{1}{2}$ million Germans.'[9] He estimated further that a frontier on the Oder without Breslau and Stettin would affect an additional $2\frac{1}{4}$ millions and a frontier on the western Neisse with Breslau and Stettin some $3\frac{1}{4}$ millions more. In the face of these numbers both the American and British Delegations agreed to oppose the western (Lusatian) Neisse, and concluded that 'even the Oder line frontier would severely tax the Polish capacity for absorption and would increase the formidable difficulties involved in the transfer of millions of Germans.'[10] Churchill and Roosevelt thus went to Yalta well briefed on the magnitude of the population transfers that would result from the planned territorial amputations of Germany.

YALTA In order to reach a considered decision on the transfer of the Germans from the Provinces East of the Oder–Neisse the Western Allies required an estimate of the number of German civilians who had been evacuated by the retreating Wehrmacht or who had fled since the arrival of the Red Army. How many Germans remained east of the demarcation line proposed by the Western Allies, cutting through Pomerania and Upper Silesia? How many remained east of the Oder? How many remained east of the Oder and Lusatian Neisse?

Technical and humanitarian considerations led the Western Allies to favour the removal of only that number of Germans whose transfer to the west would make an adequate amount of land free for the Poles coming from east of the Curzon Line. The removal of more Germans than absolutely necessary to satisfy this aim would create too many other problems.

An entirely different goal was pursued by the Soviet Union and the Soviet-dominated Polish provisional government, both intent on removing the largest possible number of Germans from the east so as to be able to occupy and annex a greater piece of Germany than the Western Allies would have been disposed to approve. One of the methods employed by the Soviets to bamboozle the Western Allies into approval of the Oder–Neisse Line was the deliberate underestimation of the number of Germans remaining in the territories east of the Oder and Lusatian Neisse Rivers, the rationale for this misrepresentation being that if the

Western Allies could be persuaded that all the Germans had voluntarily abandoned their lands and fled west, then they might not object to the Polish government's landgrab. There would be no problem of population transfers from East to West. On the contrary, if the Germans had already fled and were then to be permitted to return after the war, there would be the problem of transferring them from West to East, which would be nonsensical!

On 7 February 1945, during the fourth plenary session at Yalta, Marshal Stalin pressed hard for the Oder and the Lusatian Neisse Rivers as the future frontiers of Poland. Prime Minister Churchill at once objected because 'a considerable body of British public opinion . . . would be shocked if it were proposed to move large numbers of Germans.'[11] Marshal Stalin coolly replied that most Germans in the proposed areas, including the Germans between the two Neisse Rivers, had run away from the Red Army. There were no Germans left in these areas, Stalin maintained. But, in reality, at least 5 million Germans still resided east of the Oder–Neisse in February 1945, and the great cities of Königsberg, Breslau, Danzig and Stettin were still in German hands.

In any case, Churchill said that he was not afraid of a transfer, provided that it should be proportioned to Germany's capability to receive the deportees. He felt that if it were confined to a transfer of the East Prussians and the Upper Silesians this number could be managed.[12] After all, 6 to 7 million Germans had already died in the war and their absence could make room for the same number of deportees.[13] Churchill noted, however, that the problem of transferring the Germans was a complex matter and that it necessitated study not only in principle, but also as a practical matter. Under no circumstances, however, would he approve the western Neisse frontier. On the following day Churchill informed Stalin that he had received a telegram from the War Cabinet deprecating any frontier as far as the western Neisse because 'the population problem is too large to handle.'[14]

The Yalta Conference closed without agreement on a western frontier for Poland and no decisions were made with respect to the number of Germans to be transferred or the timing when these transfers were to begin.

POTSDAM

Five months later, at the Potsdam Conference, the question of the number of Germans still residing in the territories east of the Oder-Neisse was again raised in connection with the drafting of Article XIII. During the fifth session on 21 July 1945 President Truman made reference to the German character of the Oder-Neisse territories and to the 9 million Germans who lived there. Stalin replied that many had been killed during the war and that the rest had fled. He emphasized that no single German remained in the territory to be given to Poland. At that Admiral Leahy whispered to the President, 'Of course not, the Bolshies have killed all of them.'[15]

The Polish delegation, which was invited to express its views with respect to the Oder-Neisse frontier, made an estimate that there were only $1\frac{1}{2}$ million Germans in the disputed territories, and that these would leave voluntarily after the harvest was over.[16]

Contrary to these estimates, there lived at least 4 million[17] Germans in these territories at the time of the Potsdam Conference, while an additional million was attempting to return.[18] The Soviets and the Poles knew this. Neither Churchill/Attlee nor Truman were privies to this information, which was indispensable to their making a binding decision on the fates of millions of persons. An iron curtain separated them from a determination of the facts.[19] In so far as the Soviet Union and Poland were in exclusive possession of the material facts, they had the legal obligation to convey the correct information to the Western Allies at Potsdam. Instead, they deliberately misled Churchill and Truman on this crucial point.

Thus, the theoretical question arises whether Truman and Churchill/Attlee, if correctly informed, would have given their approval to the transfer of an additional 5 million persons from Poland and the Polish-administered territories, at a time when the British and American zones of occupation were already bursting. Only a negative answer can be given to this question. Therefore, to the extent that Western authorization to the transfer of the Germans was obtained through subterfuge and fraudulent manoeuvres by the Soviet and Polish Delegations, this authorization was legally invalid[20] and the expulsions based on this defective authorization accordingly illegal, since Poland did not have any right to deport persons into a country (or occupation zone) which was not willing or prepared to accept the new arrivals.

The Western view on the transfer of the Germans was declaredly limited in scope – not out of pity for the Germans but out of practical considerations with respect to concrete problems of post-war reorganization. Indeed, by assuming authority over Germany and the Germans, the Allies also assumed weighty responsibilities with respect to the feeding and housing of the German population. The Western Allies therefore did not only have the right but also the obligation to regulate migration into their zones in order to prevent chaos and starvation.

During the fifth session of the Potsdam Conference, Churchill registered his unequivocal opposition to the Soviet-Polish plan and argued that any population transfers would have to be held within bounds. Moreover, he proposed that some of the German refugees who had fled to the West should be allowed to return to their homes east of the Oder and Neisse Rivers:[21]

> If there were three or four million Poles east of the Curzon Line then room should be made in the west. So considerable a movement of population would shock the people of Great Britain, but a move of eight and a quarter millions [Germans] would be more than I could defend. Compensation should bear some relation to loss. It would do Poland no good to acquire so much extra territory. If the Germans had run away from it they should be allowed to go back. The Poles had no right to risk a catastrophe in feeding Germany. We did not want to be left with a vast German population who were cut off from their sources of food. The Ruhr was in our zone, and if enough food could not be found for the inhabitants we should have conditions like the German concentration camps.

In the sixth session on Sunday, 22 July, Churchill again emphasized the reasons why His Majesty's Government could not accept the Polish demands:[22]

> The British had grave moral scruples about vast movements of population. We could accept a transfer of Germans from Eastern Germany equal in number to the Poles from Eastern Poland transferred from east of the Curzon Line – say two to three millions; but a transfer of eight or nine million Germans, which was what the Polish request involved, was too many and would be entirely wrong.

Yet, in spite of these weighty objections, the Western Allies did finally approve the transfer of the Germans. Article XIII of the Potsdam Protocol provides in part:[23]

> The Three Governments having considered the question
> in all its aspects, recognize that the transfer to Germany of
> German populations, or elements thereof, remaining in
> Poland, Czechoslovakia and Hungary, will have to be
> undertaken. They agree that any transfers that take place
> should be effected in an orderly and humane manner.

The consent of the Western Allies manifested above, however, cannot be separated from the deliberate misinformation given them by Stalin and Bierut on the number of Germans in the East, nor from the fact that the principal motivation of the Western Allies in adopting Article XIII was the urgency of bringing order into a population movement they could not stop except by military action against the Soviet Union and Poland, a decision which they understandably refused to take after long years of fighting a common enemy in total war.[24]

Moreover, the authorization given in Article XIII was future-oriented, preserving the right of the Allies to regulate the timing and the number of transports to be sent into the occupied Reich. Article XIII did not aim to encourage the transfer of all Germans, but it meant that any transfers that did take place would have to take place in an orderly and humane manner.

In the case of Czechoslovakia the numbers game was played with considerably more skill. Initially a persuasive argument had been made for transferring the Nazis and certain 'disloyal' elements, in any event a relatively small and manageable group. As the war progressed, however, the Czechoslovak government-in-exile tended more and more to a 'final solution' of the Sudeten question. On the eve of the Yalta Conference the United States State Department already estimated that some 1·5 million Sudeten Germans would have to be transferred.[25] By the time of the Potsdam Conference the number had been increased to 2 to 2·5 million.[26] German anti-Nazis, numbering at least 800,000,[27] were supposed to be exempt from expulsion. In the end even the anti-Nazis were expelled from Czechoslovakia, only because they were German.[28]

Can Article XIII of the Potsdam Protocol be cited as proof of Western approval of the expulsion of all 3·5 million Sudeten Germans? Probably the most revealing interpretation of the meaning of Article XIII was given by the American Secretary of State Byrnes two months after the Potsdam Conference in a telegram to the American Ambassador in Czechoslovakia, Lawrence A. Steinhardt:[29]

> We should also point out that Potsdam Agreement only recognized that the transfer of German populations or elements thereof would have to be undertaken. So far as we were concerned we wished to slow down indiscriminate and disorderly expulsions and avoid unnecessary hardships on the transferees and unnecessary burdens on the zones to which the transfers were to be made. We recognized that certain transfers were unavoidable, but we did not intend at Potsdam to encourage or commit ourselves to transfers in cases where other means of adjustment were practicable.

As it turned out, the hope of the Western Allies to regulate the transfer and limit the number of transferees was largely frustrated. British and American dismay at the abuse of the principle of population transfers by the expelling countries would be later voiced by many prominent leaders. Winston Churchill, the early champion of the principle of population transfers, regretted in his widely known address at Westminster College in Fulton, Missouri on 5 March 1946: 'The Russian-dominated Polish Government has been encouraged to make enormous and wrongful inroads upon Germany, and mass expulsions of millions of Germans *on a scale grievous and undreamed-of* are now taking place' [emphasis added].[30] Indeed, the expulsions exceeded by far anything which either Churchill or Truman had been disposed to authorize. Thus, the contemplated westward displacement of 3 to 6 million Germans stampeded into an expulsion of 16 million.

In the light of this history, it would be difficult to credit with good faith any person who would make elaborate assertions of American and British consent to the expulsion of 10 million Germans from Poland and the Polish-administered territories and $3\frac{1}{2}$ million from Czechoslovakia.[31] It is undisputable that the Western Powers bear some responsibility for the mass uprooting of the Germans, but the greater share necessarily falls upon the Soviet Union, Poland and Czechoslovakia. Yet, it was the unwitting consent of the Western Powers that lent a certain mantle of legality and respectability to the expulsion – a mantle torn to shreds by many British and American authors appalled at what they called 'the most inhuman decision ever made by governments dedicated to the defence of human rights.'[32]

TIMING OF TRANSFERS

From the standpoint of minimizing the loss of life connected with a compulsory transfer of population, the timing of the transfer is certainly as important as the method.

Early advocates of the idea of transferring the Germans were aware of the fact that adequate transport would not be available upon the conclusion of hostilities. In the long debate of 8 March 1944 in the House of Lords the Earl of Mansfield expressed the generally accepted view that mass transportation could not be achieved quickly. He continued: 'If the transference of the Greeks and Turks took approximately six years, it may well be that the other transferences [of Germans] ... may take up to twenty years or even more. It is certainly a matter which must not be hurried.'[33] One year later many leaders in the West recoiled at the thought of commencing the transfer of the Germans at a time when the Reich was thoroughly devastated and where starvation and disease were rife. Transfers would doubtlessly add catastrophe to catastrophe. But in those apocalyptic days of the end of the Second World War there were very few cool heads among the victorious leaders of Eastern Europe, who were determined to annex large tracts of the old Reich and to make these areas as free of Germans as possible. They intended to waste no time in the implementation of this programme.

The great Teutonic displacement thus began as soon as the Soviet Army conquered areas where Germans had been living. Millions fled on their own or were evacuated by the retreating German Army. Millions, however, had remained behind and their expulsion began in the spring months of 1945.

By the time of the Potsdam Conference the expulsions were in full swing, and only Soviet, Polish or Czechoslovak authorities could have stopped them. Instead, they deliberately accelerated the expulsions, thereby placing the Western Allies in a situation where these could only hope to delay the inevitable and perhaps arrange for a more orderly transfer by negotiating with the expelling countries.

If the Soviet Union and the provisional governments of Poland and Czechoslovakia had not insisted on it, the Western Allies would not have authorized any transfers of German populations until the spring of 1946.[34] By that time, it had been hoped, the chaos accompanying the German collapse would have been partly overcome and the economy might have been functioning sufficiently so as to permit the absorption of the expellees.

Long before the end of the war the Western Allies communicated their views on the method and timing of transfers to the provisional governments of Poland and Czechoslovakia. These governments accordingly adopted the language of orderly and humane transfers and agreed to observe the timetable to be decided by the Allies.[35]

In November 1944 the Czechoslovak Minister of State Dr Ripka submitted to the Allied governments a memorandum[36] concerning the desire of the Czechoslovak government to transfer the Germans out of Czechoslovakia including the Germans of the Sudetenland, which at the end of the war was to be reannexed by Czechoslovakia.

The American Secretary of State Stettinius responded in a note dated 16 January 1945:[37]

> The American Government therefore feels that transfers
> of the kind contemplated in your Excellency's note should
> only be carried out pursuant to appropriate international
> arrangement, as suggested in your Excellency's address of
> October 8, 1944, and under international auspices. . . .
> *Pending such international arrangements, the American*
> *Government feels that no unilateral action should be taken to*
> *transfer large groups,* and understands from the statements
> cited above that the Czechoslovak Government does not
> envisage any unilateral action to do so [emphasis added].

The British government also avoided a commitment as to when the transfers could begin and limited itself to thanking the Czechoslovak government for its communication and assuring to study it with care and sympathy.[38] The British view was that any final decision on the fate of the German minorities in Eastern Europe should await agreement on the entire German settlement among the major Allies.[39]

With respect to the removal of *Volksdeutsche* from Poland and *Reichsdeutsche* from the territories to be awarded to Poland there were far fewer communications, since neither the Polish government-in-exile in London, nor the Communist Polish government in Poland were co-operative enough to present their plans for the transfer of the Germans to the Western Allies. Nevertheless, the position of the Allies had been unequivocal.

At the Yalta Conference it was understood that the transfers would have to await Allied agreement so as to permit arrangements to be made for reception of the deportees in the various occupation zones. Churchill had repeatedly stated that although he approved the transfer of the Germans in principle, this was a matter that required careful planning on the practical level – that is, no transfers were to be undertaken until the Allies had given their final approval. For reasons already discussed the Western Allies opposed premature expulsions. The Soviet Union, on the other hand, had a political interest in promoting these movements. Thus, expulsions out of East Prussia, Pomerania and Silesia commenced without the consent or knowledge of the Western Allies long before the end of hostilities. In Czechoslovakia and in the Sudetenland, however, no expulsions – disregarding isolated incidents – got under way until after the German capitulation, because the Army of Field Marshal Schörner still occupied most of the German-populated areas there. Immediately after the disarmament of the German Army, however, the 'wild expulsions' began.

On 18 June 1945 the Director of the Office of Strategic Services in the State Department, William Donovan, presented a memorandum to President Truman on the question of the return of the Sudetenland to Czechoslovakia. Among the problems discussed were the transfer of sovereignty to Czechoslovakia and the proposed removal of the Sudeten Germans. Quite unaware that the expulsions had already begun (among others the expulsion of 30,000 Germans from Brno on 30 May 1945 to Austria. See Chapter 6) Donovan surveyed the post-war situation in the light of United States interests:[40]

> One of the most difficult problems will be that arising out of the Czech Government's expressed intention of expelling large numbers of the Sudeten Germans. In this matter the interests of Czechoslovakia and the occupying powers may collide. The Czechs have an interest in expediting this expulsion as much as possible; it would reflect popular feeling against the Germans and would present the occupying powers with a *fait accompli*. It might be to the interest of the occupying powers, on the other hand, to avoid or postpone such large-scale transfers of population in order not to be burdened with this additional responsibility.

Thus, in Donovan's view, the transfer of the Germans from Czechoslovakia was very much an open question with respect to the timing and indeed the size of any eventual transfer. The Western Allies intended to regulate and supervise any population movements into their zones because they would be responsible for the sustenance of the deportees and because the unscheduled arrival of deportees would further aggravate the chaos already existing in their zones.

A telegram of the British Embassy to the Department of State, dated 22 June 1945, reveals the common policy of the Western Allies:[41]

[I]t will be for the Allied Control Commission in Germany, when the main questions of principle have been decided between the Governments, to decide when and by what stages German minorities outside the frontiers of Germany can be admitted into that country.

The Department of State replied in a Memorandum dated 11 July 1945 that the determination of the method and timing of the transfers would be left to the Allied Control Council in Germany.[42]

Meanwhile, Czech militia and the Svoboda Army were engaged in forcing large numbers of Sudeten Germans across the border into the Soviet zone.[43] The Czechoslovak government was also intensifying its efforts to obtain an early legalization of the transfers from the Western Allies.

Without mentioning that expulsions were going on, the Czechoslovak Under Secretary of State for Foreign Affairs, Vladislav Clementis, delivered on 3 July 1945 a long written statement to the American chargé in Czechoslovakia, Klieforth, specifically recognizing the right of the Allies to determine the size and timing of the transfers but expressing the hope that settlement should not be delayed because it would 'considerably disquiet all Czech and Slovak population'.[44]

Klieforth telegraphed this statement to Washington and received a reply on 13 July, reaffirming United States policy that 'transfers as proposed in Zecho notes Nov. 23, 1944 and July 3, 1945 should be carried out only on organized lines and in accordance with international agreement.'[45]

As shown above, international agreement followed at the Potsdam Conference,[46] but, contrary to the wishes of Czechoslovakia and Poland, the Allies decided to call a moratorium on all further expulsions. While the first paragraph of Article XIII of the Potsdam Protocol gave formal approval to the eventual transfer of the Germans from Poland, Czechoslovakia and Hungary, the second paragraph articulated Allied scruples over the disrupting effect of continued expulsions into Germany and the third paragraph expressly called a halt on further expulsions pending a through examination of the problem by the Occupying Powers. The official text of the second and third paragraphs follows:[47]

> Since the influx of a large number of Germans into Germany would increase the burden already resting on the occupying authorities, they consider that the Allied Control Council in Germany should in the first instance examine the problem with special regard to the question of the equitable distribution of these Germans among the several zones of occupation. They are accordingly instructing their respective representatives on the Control Council to report to their governments as soon as possible the extent to which such persons have already entered Germany from Poland, Czechoslovakia and Hungary, and to submit an estimate of the time and rate at which further transfers could be carried out, having regard to the present situation in Germany.
>
> The Czechoslovak Government, the Polish Provisional Government and the Control Council in Hungary are at the same time being informed of the above, and are being requested meanwhile to suspend further expulsions pending the examination by the Governments concerned of the report from their representatives on the Control Council.

These provisions were, of course, adopted at the insistence of the British and Americans, who already had enough problems in their respective zones of occupation without having to cope with the continued arrival of more millions of destitute expellees. Stalin's complete indifference to the fate of the expellees was a matter of more than superficial annoyance to the Western Allies. Stalin would have been contented to expel all the Germans overnight as he had deported the Volga Germans to Kazakhstan in 1941, the Crimean Tatars in 1944,[48] or the Leningrad peasants in 1929–30.[49] When at the Potsdam Conference Churchill argued that it would be necessary to give thought to where the Germans would go, Stalin grimly commented that the Czechs had already evacuated all the Germans of the Sudetenland into the Russian zone of Germany, throwing them out on two hours' notice.[50] Stalin's statement was inaccurate in so far as there were at least 2 million Sudeten Germans and several hundred thousand *Reichsdeutsche* refugees still in Czechoslovakia, but it confirmed the fact that a very large number of Germans had already been expelled by the Czechs into the Soviet occupation zone, and that Stalin viewed this precedent without alarm and considered any delay in further expulsions to be unnecessary. It was only in deference to the protests of the Western Allies that Stalin agreed to the humanitarian language of Article XIII and accepted the Western demand that the three foreign ministers should meet to develop a programme to regulate the flow of the Germans into the various zones of occupation. Stalin, however, merely paid lip service to the necessity of temporarily suspending the expulsions. Soviet authorities in Czechoslovakia and Poland did not take any steps to prevent the continued expulsion of Germans out of these areas into the Soviet occupation zone, so that the moratorium proclaimed in Article XIII of the Potsdam Protocol was not observed by either Czechoslovakia or Poland. Only the Control Council in Hungary refrained from carrying out expulsion measures until January 1946, following direct authorization by the Allied Control Council in Berlin.

Not only did the Soviet Union fail to impress upon the governments of Czechoslovakia and Poland the urgent necessity of suspending further expulsions; wholly in violation of the spirit of Article XIII, Soviet propaganda in both countries effectively agitated against the Western Powers as being pro-German and pro-fascist because these wanted to slow down or stop the expulsions and thereby would thwart the innermost wishes and aspirations of the Czech and Polish peoples.[51] In this fashion the Western Powers as well as local democratic politicians who either sympathized with the West or showed any concern over the fate of the Germans were to be defamed before the people and thus eliminated from the arena. This cunning form of political extortion made it nearly impossible for moderate leaders in Czechoslovakia and Poland openly to oppose the expulsions and even led the Western Allies to give their final consent in the Control Council far earlier than they had originally intended.

For the time immediately after the Potsdam Conference, however, the Western Allies actually believed to have succeeded in gaining a breathing spell during which to attempt to remedy the urgent problems of housing and food before the arrival of the winter of 1945–6, which was feared could bring with it mass starvation and mass dying from exposure and disease.[52] The belief in having gained the necessary breathing spell was supported by the *pro forma* agreement of the Polish[53] and Czechoslovak[54] governments temporarily to suspend the expulsions. The Polish government, however, while agreeing to postpone the expulsions, added a statement with respect to the necessity of getting rid of the Germans from Stettin and Silesia, owing to the desire of the Polish government to reconstruct those areas.[55] Thus, although the Western Allies had been unequivocal that they wanted no more expulsions for the time being, the Poles said 'yes, but' and continued expelling Germans into the Soviet zone. Of course, the deportees often did not stop in the saturated Soviet zone but continued moving west into the British and American zones.

In view of this situation the British government communicated an urgent proposal to the Soviet and American governments that joint representations be made to the Polish provisional government to suspend expulsions at once. On 9 September 1945 the British embassy communicated this proposal to the State Department, observing that,[56]

> despite the requests made to them by the three Governments as a result of the Potsdam Conference, the Polish authorities are continuing, at any rate by indirect means, to expel the remaining German inhabitants from the German territories handed over to Polish administration. The difficulties created for the Control Commission, already formidable as a result of previous expulsions, are thus daily becoming greater.

The American General Eric Wood, Deputy Director of the Prisoners of War and Displaced Persons Division of the Control Council for Germany, reported after a trip to Poland that the Poles had agreed to suspend expulsions 'except from Oppeln and Stettin'.[57] In view of this the American Political Adviser for Germany, Robert Murphy, wired Warsaw to explore the possibility of postponing all expulsions during the fall and winter. On 12 September 1945 Murphy telegraphed Secretary of State

Byrnes requesting State Department instructions with respect to proposing in the Directorate that Poland, Czechoslovakia and the Allied Control Council for Hungary be requested formally to suspend further expulsions until the spring of 1946.[58]

Parallel to the Polish expulsions, the Czechoslovak government similarly bypassed British and American opposition by channelling the greater number of expellees into the Soviet zone of occupation. At a meeting of the Co-ordinating Committee of the Allied Control Council on 3 October 1945, General Vasily Danilovich Sokolovsky stated that most of the refugees entering the Soviet zone at that time were from Czechoslovakia.[59] Several months later, in negotiations with representatives of the United States Military Government on preparations for organized transfers into the US zone, the representatives of the Czechoslovak government stated that since the Potsdam Agreement – that is, in contravention of it – 70,000 to 75,000 Germans had been transferred into the Soviet zone 'in organised transports'.[60] No figure was given for those expelled in other than 'organised transports' or for those simply pushed across the border. Such was the case of many Sudeten Germans who entered the United States zone during this period. Robert Murphy reported the refugee influx in a telegram to Secretary of State Byrnes, dated 25 September 1945, and added:[61]

> Reputedly these entries are result of treatment of German elements in Czechoslovakia that prevents orderly and humane transfer. Commanding General is directed to submit for transmission to State Department a factual report on Czech treatment of Germans and its probable effect upon latter's migration to U.S. and other zones in Germany.

Subsequent reports submitted by United States personnel in Czechoslovakia gave witness to frequent abuses committed on German civilians and resulting in disorganized movements of Germans across the border into the American occupation zone. Indeed, serious outbursts of violence against German civilians had already occurred in various Sudeten German towns, the worst being perhaps the massacre at Aussig on 31 July 1945, where Czech militia went berserk after an explosion in a munitions depot in the near-by village of Schönpriesen. The exact number of victims will probably never be known, estimates varying between 1,000 and 2,700.[62] It is macabre to note that this pogrom against the German population was used by the Czechoslovak government as an argument to induce the Western Allies to accelerate the pace of the 'transfer'. Even though no proof whatever was proffered, a propaganda campaign was mounted around the convenient scare of alleged Werewolf activities in Czechoslovakia. In a speech broadcasted from Prague on 20 August 1945, Minister Ripka stated:[63]

> Our people are worried . . . by the postponement of the transfer. We are fully conscious of the technical and food difficulties which the Allies have to overcome in connection with the deportation of the Germans from Czechoslovakia and Poland to Germany but one should understand the feelings of our people who are being consistently attacked by Werewolf organizations, and whose property is still being destroyed. We witness large-scale sabotage as was recently the case at Usti nad Labem (Aussig on the Elbe). Many of our people still do not feel safe until they know that the Germans will go away.

Yet, it is difficult to imagine how that could be the case after the Sudeten Germans had been disarmed and hundreds of thousands interned in camps awaiting expulsion. Those who remained in their villages could hardly have presented any danger to the Czechoslovak population. The only conceivable motivation for accelerating expulsions was not the security of the Czechs, but the overriding pan-Slavic policy of completing the reannexation of the Sudetenland by the permanent de-Germanization of this area, which for 700 years had been peopled by Germans.[64] This motivation proved stronger than Allied will. Thus, American and British refusal to authorize immediate expulsions did not prevent the refugee situation in their occupation zones from worsening. Although relatively few Sudeten Germans were coming into the American zone directly from Czechoslovakia, many Sudeten Germans and, of course, Germans from the territories east of the Oder-Neisse kept entering the British and American zones after finding no place in the enormously overcrowded Soviet zone.

On 15 September 1945 the London *Economist* commented:[65]

> In spite of the Potsdam declarations calling a halt to the disorderly and inhuman mass expulsions of Germans, the

forced exodus from the provinces of East Prussia, Pomerania, Silesia and parts of Brandenburg – which had a population of some 9 million in 1939 – goes on. So does the expulsion of the $3\frac{1}{2}$ million Sudeten Germans from Czechoslovakia. . . .

The Council of Foreign Ministers must put a stop to this appalling tragedy. The wandering millions in this district are practically without food or shelter. The inhabitable parts of the large urban centres were overcrowded before their arrival, and the countryside has only limited means of housing them. The inevitable result will be that millions of them will die from hunger and exhaustion. The Germans, no doubt, have deserved punishment – but not by torture of this kind. If the Poles and Czechs wish to be rated higher in civilisation than the Nazis, they will stop the expulsions at once.

On the floor of the House of Commons on 10 October 1945, Mr Bower asked Foreign Minister Bevin whether His Majesty's Government had already protested to the government of Poland 'against the atrocities inflicted on German women and children in connection with their expulsion.' Bevin answered in the affirmative:[66]

I have urged the Polish Government to suspend all further expulsion of Germans for the time being, as they were invited to do by His Majesty's Government, the United States Government and the Soviet Government after the Potsdam Conference. The Polish Ambassador in London recently assured the Foreign Office, on instructions from this Government, that strict orders had been given to stop all further expulsions of Germans from Polish-occupied territory.

In spite of this assurance by Secretary Bevin, Captain Marples informed the House of Commons on 22 October 1945 that[67]

according to a recent report by the International Red Cross, protests against unorganised deportations of Germans by the Poles and Czechs have failed to have effect, and refugees are still streaming into Berlin, where thousands die in the streets.

On 25 October 1945 a deputation led by Sir William Beveridge and consisting of seven members of parliament, four bishops, the distinguished publisher Victor Gollancz and several other prominent Englishmen, visited Prime Minister Attlee and urged that in view of the imminent danger of death from starvation and disease of millions of human beings, His Majesty's Government should 'negotiate with the Russian, Polish and Czechoslovak governments with a view to stopping the expulsion of Germans from their homes in Eastern Europe forthwith and throughout the winter, and to develop an agreed inter-Allied policy on this subject before the spring.'[68]

Parliament devoted the next day to a discussion of European conditions. The first speaker in the House of Commons was Sir Arthur Salter (Oxford University), who presented a motion urging His Majesty's Government to take all possible steps to prevent a disaster in Germany, especially[69]

> by using their utmost influence with those Governments who have been expelling vast numbers of Germans from their homes in Eastern Europe, to ensure that this expulsion should be discontinued at least until the winter is over, and if then resumed, should be carried out in an orderly manner as suggested in the Potsdam Declaration, and by agreement with all the four Governments in control of Germany. . . .

In the course of the debate that ensued, Mr Michael Foot condemned the clear and open defiance of the Potsdam Agreement and urged that supreme efforts be made to see that the deportations were stopped during the winter, when it would be absolutely impossible to carry them out according to the terms of the agreement.[70]

In the same spirit *The Economist* commented on 10 November 1945:[71]

> It is an unpleasant, but a hard, fact that the protests of the Western Powers against the immediate expulsions of Germans from the lands on the Oder and the Neisse as well as from the Sudetenland have not been effective. The expulsions go on. . . .

Thus, it was evident that the moratorium called in Article XIII of the Potsdam Protocol had been a total failure.[72] The Governments of Poland and Czechoslovakia, despite assurances to the contrary, refused to grant the Western Powers a breathing spell. The influx of destitute expellees into the devastated British

21 *Above* Cecilienhof Palace, Potsdam. The principal conference room is behind the bay windows in the centre of the photograph (US Army Photograph)

22 *Below* The Conference table at Cecilienhof. President Truman is seated with back to camera, aides on either side; Generalissimo Stalin is seated further on the right, while Prime Minister Winston Churchill and his staff are on the left (US Army Photograph)

23 *Above* The three heads of government and their principal advisers, 1 August 1945. Seated, left to right: Prime Minister Attlee, President Truman, Generalissimo Stalin. Standing, left to right: Fleet Admiral Leahy, Foreign Secretary Bevin, Secretary Byrnes, Foreign Commissar Molotov (US Army Photograph)

24 *Below* Berlin in the summer of 1945 (US Army Photograph)

Rozkaz místního vojenského velitele.

Obyvatelé německé národnosti měst České Lípy, Staré Lípy a Mimoně bez rozdílu věku a pohlaví opustí dne 15. června 1945 v 5 hod. ráno své příbytky a pochodují ulicí Křížovou, jednak Pivovarskou na shromaždiště u pivovaru v České Lípě. V Mimoni se shromáždí v prostoru křižovatky 200 m záp. železničního mostu (silnice směr Zákupy).

Toto nařízení se netýká těchto osob a jejich rodin:

1. Lékaři, zvěrolékaři, lékárníci, ošetřovatelský personál a hasiči.
2. Živnostníci a zaměstnanci potravinářského oboru v provozu.
3. Kováři, zámečníci, správkárny vozidel, krejčí a obuvníci, kteří provozují své zaměstnání.
4. Zaměstnanci továren a podniků v provozu.
5. Zaměstnanci železnic, pošty a dopravních podniků.

Osoby uvedené pod čís. 1—5 se prokáží potvrzením o svém zaměstnání. Vzdálí-li se, budou přivedeny zpět a patřičně potrestány.

II. Vypovědění se nevztahuje na příslušníky komunistické a sociálně-demokratické strany, kteří se prokáží legitimací této strany, a kteří prokáží, že pro své smýšlení a kladný poměr k ČSR byli persekvováni, t. j. zavření nebo zbavení svého místa.

Každý jednotlivec, na něhož se vypovědění vztahuje, může s sebou vzíti:

   a) potraviny na 7 dní;
   b) nejnutnější věci pro osobní potřebu tak, aby si vše mohl sám nésti;
   c) osobní doklady a všechny potravinové lístky s kmenovým listem pro domácnost.

Cenné věci: Zlato, stříbro a z nich zhotovené předměty (prsteny, brože atd.), zlaté a stříbrné mince, vkladní knížky, pojistky a peníze s výjimkou ponechání 100 RM na osobu, fotografické přístroje, musí každý vložiti do sáčku, nebo zabaliti do papíru převázaného motouzem a s podrobným písemným seznamem těchto cenností a s uvedením přesné adresy dosavadního bydliště, bytu a domovního čísla, tyto cenné věci v sáčcích odevzdá na místě shromaždiště.

Upozorňuji, že každý jednotlivec bude podroben přísné osobní prohlídce. Taktéž obsah jeho osobních zavazadel bude podrobně překontrolován.

Proto zatajování vyjmenovaných předmětů, ať u sebe, pod šatstvem, v obuvi a jinde, tak i v příručních zavazadlech, je bezúčelné a bude trestáno.

Domácí zvířectvo ponechte na místě a seznam zvířat s udáním čísla domu a ulice odevzdejte zároveň s klíči na shromaždiště. Nemovitý majetek a zařízení, jako různé stroje, hospodářské stroje a nářadí, musí býti ponechány na místě. Jakékoliv úmyslné poškození tohoto majetku nebo zařízení bude přísně trestáno. Rovněž bude trestáno předávání jmenovaných předmětů a zařízení do úschovy osobám jiným.

Klíče: Při odchodu buďtež všechny vchody do domu, a místností jakož i vchody do budov ve dvorech, po případě do dílen a provozoven uzamčeny a klíče od těchto budov a všech jednotlivých místností buďtež svázány motouzem a opatřeny přesnou adresou dosavadního bydliště nebo bytu na tuhém papíře, který se ke klíčům motouzem připevní. Při opuštění místnosti a budov buďtež všechny jejich vchodové dveře po uzamčení přelepeny páskem papíru přes klíčový otvor tak, aby pásek přesahoval obě dveřní křídla. V domech, v kterých někteří nájemníci zůstanou nadále bydleti, uzamkněte jen všechny vchody do obytných bytů a dveře přelepte páskem papíru.

Po převzetí klíčů budou ihned všechny budovy prohlédnuty vojenskými a četnickými orgány. Osoby, které neoprávněně a úmyslně budovy neopustily, budou přísně potrestány.

Osoby nemocné, avšak transportu vozidly schopné, dopraví příslušníci jejich domácnosti na shromaždiště, odkud budou společně s transportem odvezeny Červeným křížem.

Česká Lípa, dne 14. června 1945.

Místní vojenský velitel:

pplk. VOVES v. r.

Befehl des Militärortskommandanten.

Překlad:

Die Einwohner deutscher Volkszugehörigkeit der Stadtgemeinden Böhmisch-Leipa, Alt-Leipa und Niemes, ohne Unterschied des Alters und des Geschlechtes, verlassen am 15. Juni 1945 um 5 Uhr früh ihre Wohnungen und marschieren durch die Kreuz- und Bräuhausgasse auf den Sammelplatz beim Bräuhaus in Česká Lípe.

In Niemes versammeln sich diese im Raum Kreuzung 200 Meter westlich der Eisenbahnbrücke (Straße in der Richtung Reichstadt).

Die nachstehend betrifft: den nachstehend angeführten Personen und die Familien derselben:

I. 1. Aerzte, Tierärzte, Apotheker, Pflegepersonal und Feuerwehr. 2. Gewerbetreibende und Angestellte der im Gange befindlichen Versorgung-unternehmungen. 3. Schmiede, Schlosser Kraftfahrzeug-Reparaturwerkstäl len, Schneider und Schuhmacher, die ihr Gewerbe betreiben. 4. Angestellte der in Gange befindlichen Fabriken und Unternehmungen. 5. Angestellte der Eisenbahn, der Post sowie der Verkehrsunternehmungen.

Die unter Nr. 1— 5 angeführten Personen haben sich mit einer Bestätigung über ihre Beschäftigung auszuweisen. Falls sie sich entfernen, werden sie zurückgeführt und entsprechend bestraft.

II. Die Ausweisung findet keine Anwendung auf Angehörige der kommunistischen und der sozialdemokratischen Partei, die sich mit einer Legitimation der Partei legitimieren und nachweisen können, daß sie für ihre Gesinnung und den bejahenden Einstellung zur ČSR verfolgt d. h. inhaftiert oder ihres Postens enthoben wurden.

Jeder Einzelperson, auf die sich die Ausweisung bezieht, ist es gestattet, mitzunehmen: a) Lebensmittel auf 7 Tage und b) die allernotwendigsten Sachen für ihren persönlichen Bedarf in einer Menge, die sie selbst tragen kann; c) Personalbelege und alle Lebensmittelkarten samt der Haushalts-Stammkarte.

Wertsachen: Gold, Silber und alle aus diesen Metallen hergestellten Gegenstände (Ringe, Broschen usw.), Gold- und Silbermünzen, Einlagebücher, Versicherungen, Bargeld, mit der Ausnahme von 100 RM, pro Kopf sowie Photoapparate sind in ein Säckchen einzulegen oder in verschnürte Papierpäckchen einzupacken, unter Beischließung eines genauen schriftlichen Verzeichnisses dieser Wertsachen und unter Anführung der genauen Anschrift des bisherigen Wohnortes, der Wohnung und der Hausnummer. Diese Wertsachen in Säckchen werden an der Versammlungsstelle abgegeben.

Ich mache aufmerksam, daß jede Einzelperson einer strengen Leibesvisite unterzogen wird. Auch der Inhalt der Gepäckstücke wird genau überprüft werden. Es ist daher jede Verhehlung der angeführten Gegenstände bei sich, sowohl in der Kleidung, als auch in den Schuhen und anderen Stellen, so z. B. im Handgepäck, zwecklos und wird bestraft werden.

Haustiere bleiben an Ort und Stelle, das Verzeichnis der Tiere ist unter Angabe der Hausnummer und der Straße gleichzeitig mit den Schlüsseln an der Versammlungsstelle abzugeben. Unbewegliches Eigentum und Einrichtung, wie verschiedene Maschinen, landwirtschaftliche Maschinen und Geräte, ist an Ort und Stelle zu belassen. Jede absichtliche Beschädigung dieses Eigentums oder der Einrichtung wird streng bestraft werden. Desgleichen wird die Übergabe der angeführten Gegenstände und Einrichtungen an andere Personen zwecks Aufbewahrung straft werden. Schlüssel: Beim Abgang sind alle Haus- und Wohnzimmereingänge sowie die Eingänge der Hofgebäude bzw. der Werkstätten und Betriebsstätten zu verschließen, die Schlüssel von diesen Gebäuden und aller einzelnen Räumen sind mit Schnur zusammenzubinden, und mit der genauen Anschrift der bisherigen Wohnstelle oder der Wohnung auf starkem Papier zu versehen, die an den Schlüsseln mittels Schnur zu befestigen ist. Vor dem Verlassen der Schlüssel werden alle Eingangstür verschlossen und mit einem strikten Papier sie versehen und an den Schlüsseln mittels Schnur zu befestigen ist. In Häusern, in denen einige Mieter weiter verbleiben, werden bloß alle Eingänge der verlassenen Wohnräume verschlossen und die Türen mit Papierstreifen überklebt. Nach Übernahme der Schlüssel werden die Gebäude sofort von Militär- und Gendarmerieorganen durchsucht werden. Jene Personen, welche unberechtigt und absichtlich die Gebäude nicht verlassen haben, haben eine strenge Bestrafung zu erwarten. Kranke, jedoch des Transports in einem Beförderungsmittel fähige Personen, werden von den Angehörigen ihres Haushalts zur Versammlungsstelle gebracht, von wo sie gemeinsam mit Transport durch das Rote Kreuz weiter befördert werden.

Böhmisch-Leipa, den 14. Juni 1945.

Der Militärortskommandant pplk. Voves e. h.

5 Czechoslovak expulsion order, 14 June 1945
Sudetendeutsches Archiv)

26 *Right* Expulsion from
Czechoslovakia in the
summer of 1945
(Sudetendeutsches Archiv)

27 Expulsion in open cars (Podzun)

28 *Above* Homeless war victims in Berlin (Bundespresseamt)

29 *Below* Pomeranian refugees in Berlin at the time of the Potsdam Conference (US Army Photograph)

30 . . . and the expulsions continued. The majority were transferred by train
(Bundesarchiv)

31 Some were compelled to trek to the border
(Sudetendeutsches Archiv)

32 *Above* Expellee quarters in the American zone (US Army Photograph)

33 *Below* Expellees from Sudetenland (US Army Photograph)

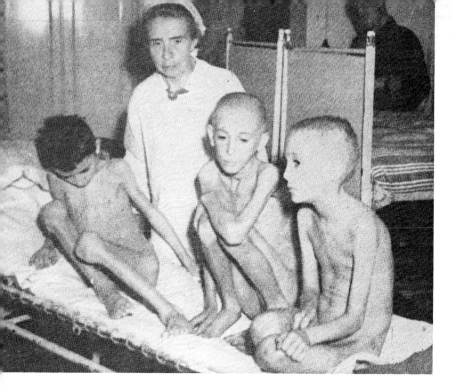

34 *Above* German children expelled from an orphanage in Danzig. This picture was first printed in *Time*, 12 November 1945, p. 27 (Blackstar)

35 *Right* Thousands of expellees died of undernourishment and disease shortly after arriving in the West. View of the cemetery outside the refugee reception centre in Friedland, near Göttingen (Schmidt)

and American zones had continued. Appeals to postpone expulsions until after the winter of 1945 had all been useless.

Under these circumstances, the best way of preventing a further aggravation of conditions in the American and British zones of occupation was to approve a plan for the orderly transfer of Germans. Such a plan would have the advantage of rendering the time and number of arrivals predictable, and this element of predictability would at least allow the possibility of making some minimal but indispensable preparations.

The Allied Control Council produced such a plan on 20 November 1945, providing that of the 3,500,000 Germans estimated to be still within Poland and all the areas administered by Poland, 2 million were to be admitted into the Soviet and the remainder into the British zone; of the 2,500,000 Germans estimated to be in Czechoslovakia and the Sudetenland, 1,750,000 were destined for the American and 750,000 for the Soviet zones; half a million Germans from Hungary were to be admitted into the American zone; and 150 Germans from Austria were to be sent to the French zone, with all transfers to be completed by 1 August 1946.[73]

It was considered possible to proceed with the admittance of population from the above-mentioned countries in accordance with the following schedule:[74]

During December 1945 at the rate of 10 per cent of the total number.

During January and February 1946 at the rate of 5 per cent of the total number.

During March 1946 at the rate of 15 per cent of the total number.

During April 1946 at the rate of 15 per cent of the total number.

During May 1946 at the rate of 20 per cent of the total number.

During June 1946 at the rate of 20 per cent of the total number.

During July 1946 at the rate of 10 per cent of the total number.

This schedule, however, was tentative, and as it turned out, no 'organized transfers' began until the middle of January 1946. The Allied Control Council plan also provided that transports would be cancelled during inclement weather and at other times when the occupying Power on the receiving end could not accommodate the new arrivals.

The forecast of completing the transfer of the Germans by August 1946 could not be kept because of the enormous difficulties that arose. It was no easy task for the Occupation authorities to care for the destitute millions who were arriving in a country where daily rations had already sunk to 1,000 calories,[75] where in some cities available housing was 10 to 20 per cent of the pre-war level,[76] and where fuel scarcity led to numerous cases of frozen families.[77]

In reviewing the catastrophe of the expulsion of the Germans, the International Committee of the Red Cross observed:[78]

> Had it been borne in mind that the repatriation of some 1,500,000 Greeks from Asia Minor, after the first World War, had taken several years and required large-scale relief schemes, it would have been easy to foresee that the hurried transplanting of fourteen million human beings would raise a large number of problems from the humanitarian standpoint, especially in a Europe strewn with ruins and where starvation was rife.

But the world had seen too much suffering and death. The plight of the German expellees therefore fell on blunted sensibilities.[79] Thirty years after the war the magnitude of this human catastrophe boggles the mind.

CHAPTER SIX

'ORDERLY AND HUMANE' TRANSFERS

> If the conscience of men ever again becomes sensitive, these expulsions will be remembered to the undying shame of all who committed or connived at them. . . . The Germans were expelled, not just with an absence of over-nice consideration, but with the very maximum of brutality.
>
> Victor Gollancz, *Our Threatened Values*, 1946, p. 96.

Any large-scale resettlement of population necessarily involves hardship and suffering. It is an extraordinary measure conceivable only in extraordinary times.

Retrospectively one may well be of the opinion that the Western Allies underestimated the difficulties involved in transplanting the Germans; yet, placing this historical event in its proper context, one realizes that in the summer of 1945 the expulsion of the Germans appeared to most politicians as an anti-climax to the war. Parliamentary debates, official memoranda, briefing-book papers and other documents attest to this fact and also reveal the sanguine belief – shared by most Western leaders – that the resettlement of the Germans could be carried out in an 'orderly and humane' manner. In the light of later developments certain features of the Anglo–American plan appear utopian. Adequate compensation, for instance, was to be given to the resettlers for the movable and immovable property left behind.[1] Transfers were to be gradual and internationally supervised.[2] Transports could be called off in winter and when occupation authorities so ordered. . . .

Earlier in this study it was pointed out that over 2 million Germans did not survive their displacement. Probably about 1 million perished in the course of the military evacuations and the flight of the last months of the war. The rest – mostly women, children and old people – perished as a result of the ruthless method of their expulsion. Of course, not all transfers were carried out in a brutal manner. Transports into the Western zones in the summers of 1946 and 1947 were relatively organized and gave rise to considerably fewer casualties. On the other hand, the expulsions of 1945, winter transports in general and most movements into the Soviet zone of occupation were catastrophic in method and consequences.

Three periods or phases ought to be differentiated. The first, the ante-Potsdam period, was characterized by 'wild' expulsions unilaterally undertaken by the governments of Poland and Czechoslovakia without the consent of the Western Allies but with the encouragement of the Soviet Union. During this period Poland and Czechoslovakia accelerated expulsions so as to be able to present a *fait accompli* at Potsdam; however, the task of moving so many millions of persons proved to be greater than anticipated, so that the intended *fait accompli* remained instead a *fait à accomplir* or *mission à liquider*. Thus, the second and third expulsion periods correspond to post-Potsdam expulsions, which according to the express language of Article XIII of the Allied protocol should have been 'orderly and humane' transfers.*

Expulsions that occurred immediately following the Potsdam Conference and through the end of the year 1945 exhibited the same relentless virulence that had characterized the ante-Potsdam period. No organized transports could get under way, because the Allies had declared a moratorium on transfers in order to gain time to make preparations for the arrivals. And even after the Control Council in Berlin issued official directives for the transfer on 20 November 1945, its timetables were seldom observed and disorderly expulsions continued in spite of repeated protests by the Western Powers.[3] Only gradually were greater numbers channelled into the organized transports of 1946 and 1947, which, although indubitably severe upon those transferred, proved to be far less deadly than the earlier expulsions.

THE ANTE-POTSDAM PERIOD: WILD EXPULSIONS

Long before the end of the war Polish authorities were given

---

* Of course, it is not at all easy to imagine how the involuntary uprooting of millions of persons, guilty and innocent alike, could ever be considered 'humane' in any sense of the word; still, there is little doubt that much suffering and death could have been avoided if the transfers had at least been 'orderly'.

permission by the Soviet occupation to move into the German provinces of East Prussia, Pomerania and Silesia. Evictions of the native Germans followed and frequent excesses by members of the Soviet and Polish armed forces drove many of the Germans who had not yet been evicted from their homes to abandon everything and flee west, thus making their later expulsion unnecessary.[4]

Meanwhile in Czechoslovakia expulsions did not begin until after the German capitulation. In the weeks immediately following the German unconditional surrender tens of thousands of Sudeten Germans were forced to trek to the frontier with Austria or Germany.

The relatively few reports that appeared in contemporary British and American newspapers reveal a uniform picture of misery and death among the German expellees. The London *Daily Mail*, for instance, featured an article by Rhona Churchill dealing with conditions in the newly emerged Czechoslovak State and in particular with the expulsion of the Germans from (Brno) Brünn, the capital of Moravia, on 30 May 1945:[5]

Here, for instance, is what happened last month in Brno when young revolutionaries of the Czech National Guard decided to 'purify' the town.

Shortly before 9 p.m. they marched through the streets calling on all German citizens to be standing outside their front doors at 9 o'clock with one piece of hand luggage each, ready to leave the town forever.

Women had ten minutes in which to wake and dress their children, bundle a few possessions into their suit-cases, and come out on to the pavement.

Here they were ordered to hand over all their jewellery, watches, fur and money to the guards, retaining only their wedding rings; then they were marched out of town at gun-point towards the Austrian border.

It was pitch dark when they reached the border. The children were wailing, the women stumbling. The Czech border guards pushed them over the frontier towards the Austrian border guards.

There more trouble started. The Austrians refused to accept them; the Czechs refused to readmit them. They were pushed into a field for the night, and in the morning a few Rumanians were sent to guard them.

They are still in that field, which has been turned into a concentration camp. They have only the food which the guards give them from time to time. They have received no rations. . . .

A typhus epidemic now rages amongst them, and they are said to be dying at the rate of 100 a day.

Twenty-five thousand men, women and children made this forced march from Brno, amongst them one English-woman married to a Nazi, an Austrian woman of 70, and an Italian woman of 86.

Concentration camps for Germans are now opening up all over the territory and the Germans are being thrown indiscriminately into them while waiting visa for Germany. Even German Jews and anti-Nazis recently released from Gestapo concentration camps are not immune. . . .

F. A. Voigt, for many years Berlin correspondent of the *Manchester Guardian* and in 1945 editor of the influential monthly magazine, *Nineteenth Century and After*, observed in an article entitled 'Orderly and Humane':[6]

One of the chief strongholds of the Sudeten labour movement was Bodenbach. When it was occupied by the Russians, there was a reign of terror, of looting, and of outrage to women. The Czechs suffered as well as the Germans. Special measures were then taken against the Germans, but many of these were certified as 'anti-Fascists' and were spared. When the new Czech authorities took over, these certificates were cancelled and Germans were expelled or sent to concentration camps regardless of their past allegiance. They were robbed, and otherwise maltreated – even women and old men were whipped by Czechs on the slightest provocation. The N.S.B., mostly young men who, even in appearance, resembled the S.S., used whips and rifle-butts indiscriminately. They continued the looting begun by the Russians; some people were killed for concealing valuables. The deportees were allowed to take a small amount of luggage, but this was usually stolen *en route* by Czech soldiers who 'controlled' the roads. There are four concentration camps in the neighborhood and the screaming of maltreated people can be heard by those who reside near by.

On July 31st there was an explosion in the cable-works near Usti (Aussig, on the Elbe).* The explosion was attributed to 'Werewolves' but without the slightest evidence. Terrible excesses against the Germans began even before the explosion. A massacre followed. Women and children were thrown from the bridge into the river. Germans were shot down in the streets. It is estimated that 2,000 or 3,000 persons were killed.

The Joint Relief Commission of the International Red Cross, which attempted to help those expellees arriving in Berlin and elsewhere in Germany also recorded the senselessness and the inhumanity of the expulsion:[7]

These uprooted masses wandered along the main roads, famished, sick and weary, often covered with vermin, seeking out some country in which to settle. Wherever they appeared, they were passed on, now in this direction, now in that. Take as an example the case of a man and a woman who were expelled from Silesia. They got as far as Mecklenburg, where they received official instructions to return to Silesia. The man returned to his cart and placed his wife in it since she could no longer walk. They then returned to Silesia. No sooner had they arrived than they were once more ejected. . . .

Take also the case of the children. On 27 July 1945, a boat arrived at the West Port of Berlin which contained a tragic cargo of nearly 300 children, half dead from hunger, who had come from a 'home' at Finkenwalde in Pomerania. Children from two to fourteen years old lay in the bottom of the boat, motionless, their faces drawn with hunger, suffering from the itch and eaten up by vermin. Their bodies, knees and feet were swollen – a well-known symptom of starvation.

---

* 'We [the editors of *Nineteenth Century and After*] have two independent accounts of what followed, both of them by reliable persons, one of them the British officer who made a visit of enquiry to the Sudetenland in September, 1945.' Cited also in *Congressional Record*, 29 March 1946, p. 2805. See also F. A. Voigt, 'Dark Places', *Nineteenth Century and After*, February 1946, pp. 52–5.

THE POST-POTSDAM PERIOD: AUGUST–DECEMBER 1945

Article XIII of the Potsdam Protocol contained the first official authorization for the transfer of the Germans. It was, however, not a blank cheque for expulsions. As discussed in Chapter 5, this article expressly provided for a temporary moratorium on expulsions, because war-torn Germany was not capable of absorbing any more expellees; furthermore it conditioned Allied consent to the transfer on the obligation of the governments of Poland, Czechoslovakia and Hungary to observe the all-important 'orderly and humane' standard.

Winston Churchill, one of the principal architects of the expulsion policy, was among the first to express his concern about the manner in which this policy was being implemented. In his oft-quoted and eloquent speech of 16 August 1945 before the House of Commons, he said:[8]

> I am particularly concerned, at this moment, with the reports reaching us of the conditions under which the expulsion and exodus of Germans from the new Poland are being carried out. . . . Sparse and guarded accounts of what has happened and is happening have filtered through, but it is not impossible that tragedy on a prodigious scale is unfolding itself behind the iron curtain which at the moment divides Europe in twain. . . .

Other voices were also raised in protest.

On 19 October 1945 Bertrand Russell, appalled at the reports on the mass expulsion of the Germans, wrote in *The Times*:[9]

> In eastern Europe now mass deportations are being carried out by our allies on an unprecedented scale, and an apparently deliberate attempt is being made to exterminate many millions of Germans, not by gas, but by depriving them of their homes and of food, leaving them to die by slow and agonizing starvation. This is not done as an act of war, but as part of a deliberate policy of 'peace'. . . . It was decreed by the Potsdam agreement that expulsions of Germans should be carried out 'in a humane and orderly manner.' And it is well known, both through published accounts and through letters received in the numerous British families which have relatives or friends in the armies of occupation, that this proviso has not been observed by

our Russian and Polish allies. It is right that expression
should be given to the immense public indignation that has
resulted, and that our allies should know that British
friendship may well be completely alienated by the
continuation of this policy.

But the relentless expulsions continued in spite of the obvious
consequences. On 8 December 1945 Bertrand Russell, writing
in the *New Leader*, protested again:[10]

It was agreed at Potsdam that these expulsions should take
place 'in a humane and orderly manner,' but this provision
has been flouted. At a moment's notice, women and
children are herded into trains, with only one suitcase each,
and they are usually robbed on the way of its contents. The
journey to Berlin takes many days, during which no food is
provided. Many are dead when they reach Berlin; children
who die on the way are thrown out of the window. A member
of the Friends' Ambulance Unit describes the Berlin station
at which these trains arrive as 'Belsen over again – carts
taking the dead from the platform, etc.' A large proportion of
those ejected from their homes are not put into trains, but
are left to make their way westward on foot. Exact statistics
of the numbers thus expelled are not available, since only
the Russians could provide them. Ernest Bevin's estimate is
9,000,000. According to a British officer now in Berlin,
populations are dying, and Berlin hospitals 'make the sights
of the concentration camps appear normal.'[11]

It has been said that readers do not care for long quotations.
Maybe. Those who would be disinclined to read these reports
because of their length should realize that millions of men,
women and children had to endure these expulsions, not merely
read about them. Typical of the Press reports that motivated the
letters of Betrand Russell are the following:

Under the bomb-wrecked roof of the Stettiner Railway
Station – the Euston or King's Cross of Berlin – I looked
this afternoon inside a cattle truck shunted beside the
buffers of No. 2 platform.
    On one side four forms lay dead under blankets on cane
and raffia stretchers; in another corner four more, all women,
were dying.

One, in a voice we could hardly hear, was crying out for water.

Sitting on a stretcher, so weakened by starvation that he could not move his head or his mouth, his eyes open in a deranged, uncomprehending stare, was the wasted frame of a man. He was dying, too.

As I walked about the station a score of others came up to me, all ravenous and starved, for whom also, like those in the cattletruck mortuary, nothing could be done – until death.

Two women sanitary helpers did what they could in ministering to the small wants of the dying.

The train from Danzig had come in. It had taken seven days on the journey this time; sometimes it takes longer.

Those people in the cattle truck, and hundreds who lay on bundles of belongings on the platform and in the booking hall, were the dead and dying and starving flotsam left by the tide of human misery that daily reaches Berlin, and next day is turned back to take train to another town in a hopeless search of food and succour.

Thousands more – up to 25,000 in a day – trek on foot to the outskirts of Berlin, where they are stopped and forbidden entry to the already overcrowded city.

Each day between fifty and 100 children – a total of 5,000 already over a short period – who have lost both parents, or have been abandoned, are collected from Berlin's stations and taken to orphanages or found foster-mothers in Berlin.

That is all that Berlin charity can do.

For this problem at the moment is the Germans' own; the Allies have made no move to render relief or even give the Social Welfare Organisation, with its staff of thirty-three and 220 helpers all told, any assistance whatever.

Without any central control (no telephone lines or cars are put at the organisation's disposal, and the only means of co-ordinating any plan, even if it existed, is by occasional cycle courier at the mercy of sympathetic military road controls) the Welfare Committees are trying to grapple with a problem that is beyond their powers.

Here in Berlin we are living under this shadow, not just of hunger and want, but of death, and epidemics on a scale that the world has not seen in recorded history.

The expulsion of Germans from Polish-occupied Germany east of the Oder, and the mass transfers of population into the provinces of Pomerania, Mecklenburg, Brandenburg and Saxony, are projecting a tragedy of the greatest magnitude. It is almost already out of hand.

At a conservative estimate – given me by Dr. Karl Biaer, anti-Nazi, now installed as head of Berlin's Social Welfare Committee – there are 8,000,000 homeless nomads milling about the areas of the provinces around Berlin.

If you take in the Sudeten Germans expelled from Czechoslovakia and those on the move from elsewhere the figure of those for whom no food can be provided rises to 13,000,000 at least. . . .

What is aggravating the problem beyond all solution is the continuation by the Poles of the ejection of German nationals from their homes, literally at a moment's notice.

This is in direct defiance of the Potsdam Declaration, which urged that the transfers of population must be carried out 'in an orderly and humane manner.'

A woman I met at the Stettiner Station had left Danzig on August 13th – eleven days after the standstill order was made. . . .

Other things I saw when the Danzig train came in I am bound to record. Apart from the women rocking in tears and anguish, and the famished children asleep in their arms or crying for food, there was a group of young men – all Poles – who sat apart, waiting for the next train to go out.

Then they would board it, and going through the train, would force these unprotected mothers and women to give up any possessions of value, including watches and jewels.

The guards on the train and at stopping places are shot if they attempt to intervene.

> Norman Clark (writing from Berlin),
> *News Chronicle*, August 24th.

One woman [among those seen at the Stettiner station], emaciated, with dark rings under her eyes and sores breaking out all over her face, could only mutter self-condemnation because she was unable to feed her two whimpering babies. I watched her trying desperately to force milk from her

milkless breasts – a pitiful effort that only left her crying at
her failure.

Charles Bray (writing from Berlin),
Daily Herald, August 24th.[12]

No reliable evidence is available of the number of evicted
Germans who are passing through the Russian zone from the
eastern frontier, but they probably run into millions, and in
their desire to move to the west large numbers of them are
coming up against the sealed frontiers of the British and
American zones, which already have trouble enough on their
hands. . . .

The Potsdam Declaration, it will be remembered, called
for the humane treatment of expelled German nationals,
and in view of the distressing reports laid before the
Conference from such cities as Breslau and Stettin, the
countries concerned were urged to postpone further
expulsions.

No evidence exists that these directives have been
observed. In the Robert Koch Hospital here, which I
visited this morning, there are more than sixty German
women and children, many of whom were summarily
evicted from a hospital and an orphanage in Danzig last
month, and, without food and water or even straw
to lie on, were dispatched in cattle trucks to Germany.
When the train arrived in Berlin they said that of
eighty-three persons crammed into two of the trucks
twenty were dead.

A woman recovering from typhoid had, she stated, seen
her husband beaten to death by Poles and she had then been
driven from her farm near Danzig to work in the fields. Now
she has survived the journey to Berlin with two young sons,
and, without money, clothes or relations, cannot see what
the future holds.

Three orphans I saw aged between eight and twelve are still
almost skeletons after ten days' treatment, owing to the
almost complete lack of fats in Berlin; none of them weighed
more than three stone.

Another small boy turned out of Danzig had a scrawled
postcard attached to him stating that his soldier father was

long since missing and that his mother and two sisters had died of hunger.

It is surely not enough to say that the Germans brought these miseries upon themselves; brutalities and cynicism against which the war was fought are still rife in Europe, and we are beginning to witness human suffering that almost equals anything inflicted by the Nazis. There is an urgent need for complete information on these mass expulsions; all the control council could do to-day was to refer the subject to its co-ordinating committee for full study.

Berlin Correspondent of *The Times*, writing on September 10th.[13]

In November 1945 F. A. Voigt reported in the *Nineteenth Century and After*:

Millions of Germans, Danzigers and Sudetenlanders are now on the move. Groups of 1,000 to 5,000 will take the road, trek hundreds of miles, and lose half their numbers by death through disease or exhaustion. The roadsides are dotted with graves. Children have arrived in Berlin looking like the emaciated creatures shown in pictures of Belsen.

One train, which arrived in Berlin on August 31st, started from Danzig on the 24th with 325 patients and orphans from the Marien Hospital and the Orphanage in the Weidlergasse. They were packed into five cattle trucks, with nothing to cover the floors, not even straw. There were no doctors, nurses or medical supplies. The only food provided when the journey began was twenty potatoes and two slices of bread for each orphan. The patients had nothing, but the train stopped from time to time so that those of the passengers who were fit enough could forage. . . .

Between six and ten of the patients in each truck died during the journey. The bodies were simply thrown out of the train. When the train arrived in Berlin, sixty-five of the patients and orphans were removed to the Robert Koch Hospital, where nine of them died. We have no information as to what happened to the rest. . . .[14]

About the same time, a transport of Sudetenlanders – men, women, and children – arrived from Troppau. They had been travelling in open cattle trucks for eighteen days.

They numbered 2,400 when they set out and 1,350 when they arrived, so that 1,050 perished on the way.[15]

Donald Mackenzie, Berlin correspondent for the New York *Daily News* reported on 7 October 1945:[16]

In the windswept courtyard of the Stettiner Bahnhof, a cohort of German refugees . . . sat huddled in groups under a driving rain and told the story of their miserable pilgrimage, during which more than 25 percent died by the roadside and the remainder were so starved they scarcely had strength to walk.

Filthy, emaciated, and carrying their few remaining possessions wrapped in bits of cloth, they shrank away crouching when one approached them in the railway terminal, expecting to be beaten or robbed or worse. That is what they have become accustomed to expect.

A nurse from Stettin, a young, good-looking blond, told how her father had been stabbed to death by Russian soldiers who, after raping her mother and sister, tried to break into her own room. She escaped and hid under a haystack with four other women for 4 days, she said, then remained on in the city working for the Poles who had taken over a portion of the city, until she had bartered everything she owned for food. . . .

On the train to Berlin she was pillaged once by Russian troops and twice by Poles who, she said, were far more savage than the Russians. Women who resisted were shot dead, she said, and on one occasion she saw a Polish guard take an infant by the legs and crush its skull against a post because the child cried while the guard was raping its mother. . . .

An old man said that when his party reached Kustrin a typhoid epidemic broke out in the train and all who were sick were pushed out on the platform, where they lay day and night until they died. . . .

Another woman with whiplash bruises across her face said that as the party with which she marched to the railroad from Upper Silesia was passing through Sagan, Polish civilians lined both sides of the road and the refugees were systematically robbed and beaten as they walked by. . . .

She concluded that she thought she was pregnant. She had been raped 30 times on the journey to Berlin.

Even allowing a generous margin for human exaggeration and journalistic sensationalism, it may be said with certainty that frightful excesses were happening in connection with the expulsion of the Germans from the East. Foreign Minister Ernest Bevin, who witnessed the plight of the expellees in Berlin, reported to the House of Commons:[17]

It was a pathetic sight – the stream of perambulators and small vehicles of one kind or another, and the people were nearly all women and children, with very few men at all. One could not help saying, 'My God, this is the price of stupidity and war.' It was the most awful sight one could see.

American authorities in Berlin were similarly appalled at the catastrophe unfolding before their eyes.

It was with this background of utter chaos and intense human suffering that Robert Murphy, United States Political Adviser for Germany, wrote an urgent Memorandum to the State Department reporting:[18]

In the Lehrter Railroad station in Berlin alone our medical authorities state an average of ten have been dying daily from exhaustion, malnutrition and illness. In viewing the distress and despair of these wretches, in smelling the odor of their filthy condition, the mind reverts instantly to Dachau and Buchenwald. Here is retribution on a large scale, but practiced not on the *Parteibonzen*, but on women and children, the poor, the infirm. . . .

Knowledge that they are the victims of a harsh political decision carried out with the utmost ruthlessness and disregard for the humanities does not cushion the effect. The mind reverts to other mass deportations which horrified the world and brought upon the Nazis the odium which they so deserved. Those mass deportations engineered by the Nazis provided part of the moral basis on which we waged war and which gave strength to our cause.

Now the situation is reversed. We find ourselves in the invidious position of being partners in this German enterprise and as partners inevitably sharing the responsibility. The United States does not control directly the Eastern

Zone of Germany through which these helpless and bereft people march after eviction from their homes. The direct responsibility lies with the Provisional Polish Government and to a lesser extent with the Czech Government. . . . That deportations have not gone further in the Sudetenland has been in part due to the presence of our forces whose Commanders, in friendly but firm fashion, have told the local Czechs that certain acts simply cannot be tolerated in the name of humanity, but even so, ruthless evictions have occurred on a sufficiently large scale to antagonize many of our troops against the liberated Czech people.

At Potsdam the three Governments agreed that the transfer of populations should be conducted in an orderly and humane manner, and that Poland and Czechoslovakia should be requested to suspend temporarily evictions of Germans. Despite official assurances, evidence seems to show that little regard has been paid to either point, especially to Poland. . . .

As helpless as the United States may be to arrest a cruel and inhuman process which is continuing, it would seem that our Government could and should make its attitude as expressed at Potsdam unmistakably clear. It would be most unfortunate were the record to indicate that we are *particeps* to methods we have often condemned in other instances.

Berlin, October 12, 1945

On 26 October 1945, Secretary of State Byrnes sent a Telegram to Murphy reaffirming the United States position that 'any transfers that take place should be effected in an orderly and humane manner', and expressing concern over informations to the contrary which were reaching him from various sources.[19]

Since the situation in Berlin was getting progressively worse and winter was approaching, Murphy sent another telegram to Byrnes on 23 November 1945 in which he deplored the dire situation of the German expellees:[20]

Members of my staff who have seen the refugee trains from the East arrive state that the condition of these people is in most instances pitiable. The stories told by individuals talked to at random indicate that they were evacuated from their former homes with little advance notice and in many cases were harried from the time they left their homes almost until the time they reached Berlin. They tell tales of progressive robbing and the taking of the few possessions they were allowed to remove from their homes and most of the individuals arriving in Berlin had only a small amount of hand luggage. While final conclusions cannot be deduced from these limited observations, other evidence which has come to the attention of the Mission from widely assorted sources indicates that the pattern of ill treatment and robbery is widespread.

In view of these distressing reports Secretary of State Byrnes sent a telegram on 30 November 1945 to the American Ambassador in Poland, Arthur Lane, instructing him to convey the American displeasure to the provisional Polish government:[21]

US Govt has been seriously perturbed by reports of continued mass movements of German refugees who appear to have entered Germany from areas east of the Oder-Neisse line. These persons presumably have been expelled summarily from their homes and dispossessed of all property except that which they can carry. Reports indicate that these refugees – mostly women, children, and old people – have been arriving in shocking state of exhaustion, many of them ill with communicable diseases and in many instances robbed of their last few personal possessions. Such mass distress and maltreatment of weak and helpless are not in accord with Potsdam Agreement . . . nor in consonance with international standards of treatment of refugees.

Instead of immediately conveying the message, Lane telegraphed back suggesting that the Germans were probably exaggerating their ill-treatment 'in keeping with their characteristic of whining after losing war',[22] and warned of the undesirable political consequences of making such a statement at a time when the powerful Communist party in Poland was making considerable gains by branding its enemies, mainly Mikolajczyk, and the Western Allies as pro-German and pro-fascist. In a second telegram Lane indicated that the British Ambassador in Warsaw, Victor Cavendish Bentinck, fully agreed with him on the unwisdom of making representations to the Polish government with regard to the treatment of the Germans, because such protests would only serve to irritate the Poles and would hardly alter conditions.[23]

Aware of the repercussions that the American statement could elicit, Byrnes allowed Lane to confine his representations to an oral statement instead of a written note, and further allowed him to clarify to the Polish government that the United States action was in no way a reflection of lack of appreciation of what the Poles had suffered at the hands of the Germans, but was based entirely on the interest of the United States government in seeing that Article XIII of the Potsdam Agreement was observed and that transfers of Germans be carried out in humane manner in accordance with the spirit in which the Article had been adopted.[24]

In spite of these new and more conciliatory instructions, Lane was still rather reluctant to approach the Poles on the matter of the Germans. The British Ambassador Bentinck was just as indifferent to the fate of the Germans and even more reluctant to do anything about it. Bentinck proposed 'like Nelson at bombardment of Copenhagen to hold his telescope to his blind eye'.[25]

In any event, there appeared to be little to be achieved by approaching the Polish government on this matter. The British *chargé d'affaires*, Robin Hankey, had already spoken with the Polish Minister of Foreign Affairs, Wincenty Rzymowski, who had given his assurance that the Polish government did not propose to aggravate the confusion in Germany by expelling large numbers of Germans, although Poland did plan to get rid of the Germans of Stettin and Silesia as soon as possible in order to start reconstructing those areas. When Lane later spoke to Rzymowski, he received virtually the same answer,[26] and the expulsions continued in the same precipitous and disorderly manner. Tadeusz Zebrowski, Chief of the Anglo-American Department of the Ministry for Foreign Affairs of the Polish provisional government, who was present at the interview of Lane and Rzymowski, observed that the Germans were not being treated worse than the Poles who were being expelled from Eastern Poland by the Soviet Union.[27] In a telegram to Secretary Byrnes, Lane mentioned that he had heard many complaints with respect to the Eastern Poles who were sent westward in open freight cars in spite of the cold weather 'resulting in death of six children last week in trainload'.[28]

With respect to Czechoslovakia the American Ambassador Lawrence Steinhardt was similarly instructed to approach the Czech government to impress upon them the need for suspending the transfer of the Germans and for using the most humanitarian methods in effecting any future deportations. Although the Czech government gave repeated assurances that the expulsions had ceased,[29] they did not; nor did the method of the expulsions significantly improve during the year 1945.

In September 1945 the United States Forces, European Theater, Main Headquarters, advised General Patton, Commanding General, Eastern Military District, that reports were being received indicating that Germans were entering the United States zone in violation of the policy agreed upon at Potsdam. The reason for these entries was believed to be the treatment of the Germans in Czechoslovakia, which drove many to seek safety and refuge across the American lines.[30]

Numerous affidavits in the Ost-Dokumente at the Koblenz archives attest to the flight of several Sudeten German families who during this period fled to the American lines because of actual physical abuse by the Czech militia or out of fear of imminent danger.[31]

In the midst of these reports it is interesting to mention that Ambassador Steinhardt did not believe that the treatment of the Germans was unduly harsh. In a note to Secretary of State Byrnes he commented: 'It is surprising that there has been so little ill-treatment of the Germans in Czechoslovakia and so few irregular expulsions or voluntary departures.'[32]

Maltreatment, of course, is a relative thing. . . . But what makes this comment of Ambassador Steinhardt all the more peculiar is the fact that US military personnel in Czechoslovakia had been eye-witnesses to many instances where Germans had been forcibly evicted from their homes, 'frequently being stripped there or on the road of the few personal possessions they could still carry, and being beaten if resistance was shown'.[33] As Robert Murphy twice reported to Secretary Byrnes,[34] US military authorities were increasingly concerned over the anti-Czech sentiments which had developed among US soldiers as a consequence of these frequent abuses committed upon defenceless civilians. Indeed, American soldiers had to intervene many times to protect German women and children from excesses by the Czech militia.[35]

THE YEARS 1946–7: THE 'ORGANIZED' TRANSFERS

Following the issuance by the Allied Control Council of directives for the transfer of the Germans from Czechoslovakia, Poland and Hungary, the possibility for controlling the movement improved.

However, one of the main problems that was to plague the Western Allies in the years 1946 and 1947 was their failure at Potsdam to provide for appropriate machinery to ensure that the transfers were in fact carried out in an orderly and humane manner. On 30 January 1946 the Lord Chancellor of the British House of Lords, Lord Jowitt, stated in reply to a question posed by the Lord Bishop of Chichester:[36]

> There is no international machinery for carrying out transfers or for supervising their execution. The arrangements are left to be worked out directly between the Government of the expelling country and the authorities of the zone in Germany to which the immigrants are to be expelled.

The Lord Chancellor further expressed the hope that representatives of the British government would be allowed to observe the process of transfer out of Czechoslovakia. On the other hand, he noted that in Poland no British representatives had been thus far permitted to observe the process of the transfers from that end, nor did he consider it likely that any such opportunity would be offered in the future.[37]

Meanwhile, the International Committee of the Red Cross had been trying without success to have its delegates in Czechoslovakia[38] and Poland authorized to supervise the transfers and to assist in reducing the suffering of the expellees.

A false report in the official Radio of Prague to the effect that the expulsion of the Germans out of the Carlsbad area was taking place under the supervision of the ICRC had to be denied by the International Committee in Geneva:[39]

> Le Comité international de la Croix-Rouge, pour sa part, tient à préciser qu'il n'exerce aucun contrôle sur les transferts de populations d'origine allemande hors de Tchécoslovaquie et qu'il n'a d'ailleurs pas été appelé à le faire.
>
> En effet, les décisions relatives à des transferts de populations et à leurs modalités sont du ressort exclusiv des gouvernements intéressés.

Unable to supervise the expulsions at the source, the International Committee of the Red Cross could devote itself merely to the relief of the expellees once they reached their destination.

General Lucius Clay, Deputy Military Governor of the US Zone 1945–6 and Military Governor 1947–9, described the first expulsions of the year 1946 from the receiving end:[40]

> The first trainload from Hungary was a pitiful sight. The expellees had been assembled without a full allowance of food and personal baggage, and arrived hungry and destitute. As a result of representations repeated many times, arrangements were made to permit a small baggage allowance and to provide each expellee with RM 500. Difficulties were likewise experienced with the Czechs, not only in the withholding of personal possessions but also in withholding young, able workers while sending to us the aged, the women, and small children. Only after halting the movement temporarily could we remedy these conditions by negotiations.

The expulsions from Poland into the British zone were also heart-rending, although conditions had improved since the catastrophic year of 1945. According to a despatch from The Manchester Guardian's correspondent at Lübeck, writing on 10 March 1946:[41]

> In spite of the Potsdam agreement that the transfer of the German population from the East should be orderly and humane, the Polish authorities are evicting Germans from the newly acquired Polish territories with as little as ten minutes' notice and are sending them into the British zone without food in overcrowded trains.
>   A man of 73 and a child of 18 months were found dead in the first transport which arrived in Lübeck under the 'Operation Swallow' scheme on March 3. The second transport had three dead. On the average 1,500 people are packed in trains of 26 coaches, which are unheated and for the most part damaged. The fourth transport brought 2,070 people, so that most had scarcely enough room to stand, much less sit.
>   The British and Polish authorities agreed that the Poles should provide rations for a journey of two days, but scarcely any food is provided. On the first train each person received half a loaf of bread for the journey. On the second train a 3lb. loaf was divided among eight people, and a

pound of sugar among 60. On the third train there was no food, only tea and hot water. These rations cover the journey only from Stettin to Lübeck, which lasts about 22 hours. But before the refugees reach the Stettin assembly point they often have to travel seven days, so that most have no real meal for ten days. They arrive at the transit camps exhausted or sick. In the first transport 350 people were ill, and 250 of them had to be taken to hospital in Lübeck. In later transports the figures have been higher. The majority suffer from scabies, but so far there have been no cases of typhus.

Generally their physical condition is worse than that of previous refugees from the Russian zone, and many still bear visible traces of maltreatment. Most of the women, it was established by the examining British medical officers, had been violated, among them a girl of 10 and another of 16.

Most of the refugees are over fifty; many in their eighties. They include sick and cripples, although the British and Poles agreed that the sick should not be sent. There are conspicuously few young people, and it appears that they are kept in Poland to do forced labour. Cases are known where children have been forcibly separated from their parents. The refugees officially are permitted to bring with them bedding and cooking utensils as well as personal belongings, but few have bedding and fewer still their cooking utensils. This is partly due to the short notice given them to leave — it has been established that ten minutes was allowed in some cases; in other no notice was given, but the house simply turned over to a new Polish settler. Also a fair amount of their luggage, especially their personal belongings, has been stolen by Poles, mainly on the journey to Stettin.

Matters have slightly improved since a British medical team arrived in Stettin to supervise the train arrangements. Food is now likely to get better; the danger of epidemics is being lessened by the use of D.D.T. powder sent from the British zone; and the indiscriminate sending of the sick and of unaccompanied children is likely to be stopped. But so far nothing is being done to supervise the treatment of refugees on the first stage of their journey from their homes to Stettin.

Altogether one and a half million refugees are expected to arrive in the course of the next few months, 1,500 a day by train, another 1,000 by boat. The figure is, however, likely to be nearer the two million mark. . . .

Anne O'Hare McCormick, special correspondent to the *New York Times*, reported from Germany in February 1946:[42]

it was also agreed at Potsdam that the forced migration should be carried out 'in a humane and orderly manner.' Actually, as every one knows who has seen the awful sights at the reception centers in Berlin and Munich, the exodus takes place under nightmarish conditions, without any international supervision or any pretense of humane treatment. We share responsibility for horrors only comparable to Nazi cruelties. . . .

In October 1946 Miss McCormick again described the progress of the transfer:[43]

The scale of this resettlement and the conditions in which it takes place are without precedent in history. No one seeing its horrors first-hand can doubt that it is a crime against humanity for which history will exact a terrible retribution. . . .

Although these reports do not necessarily suggest an improvement, conditions did improve during the year 1946 and the death toll was significantly reduced. Later, when the winter 1946–7 arrived, Western military authorities were able to cancel several train movements,[44] and thus prevented a repetition of the disaster of the winter 1945–6 when thousands died of exposure or froze to death during the slow transport in unheated wagons.

Meanwhile the delegation of the International Committee of the Red Cross in Warsaw succeeded in taking up the problem directly with the Polish Ministry of the Interior. Early in 1947 it was able to induce the Ministry to postpone some deportations in view of the fact that convoys of expellees sent to Germany in January of 1947 had been arriving in a deplorable condition.[45] Unfortunately, only some deportations – principally out of the internment camps – were postponed, while others continued unabated.

On the whole, the 'organized transfers' involved some six million persons, and although the expelling countries frequently did not observe the minimum standards set by the Western Allies with respect to proviant and humane treatment of the expellees, the very fact that the Western Allies knew in advance when transports were to arrive and how many persons to expect, saved the lives of many.[46] Indeed, if there had been no 'organized transfers' and if all the Germans had been expelled in the brutal manner that characterized the 1945 expulsions, the loss of life attributable to the flight and expulsion would not have been 2 million but perhaps 3 million or even more.

INTERNMENT CAMPS

What happened to those Germans who were not immediately expelled? Their fates varied from province to province, from district to district, from village to village. Those who were permitted to remain in their homes usually suffered the least, although many were subjected to abuses and in general lived close to the starvation level. By comparison, however, those who were interned in camps to await expulsion fared much worse. As it turned out, the Germans who were promptly expelled were relatively fortunate, because their chances of survival were greater in the West – provided, of course, that they survived the transfer itself.

Conditions in many internment camps approached those of the murderous Nazi period, in which sadism was given free rein and internees were left to starve slowly to death.[47] This was one of the reasons why the International Committee of the Red Cross had so much difficulty in gaining access into the camps. Even the few camps which delegates of the ICRC were permitted to visit were found to be 'unsatisfactory'. In the camp of Svidnik in Czechoslovakia, for instance, German civilian internees were employed on mine-clearing until strong protests by the delegation of the ICRC at Bratislava succeeded in having this stopped.[48] Since the interned Germans enjoyed no international protection, the ICRC advocated that in view of the fact that the only grounds for their internment previous to expulsion was their German origin, they should logically be classed with 'civilian internees'[49] and the ICRC should be authorized by the interning powers to provide all the necessary relief in the camps until the time of actual expulsion. Although the ICRC was not so authorized by any of the interning powers, the government of Czechoslovakia was less restrictive than the other Eastern European governments and permitted the ICRC to provide relief in many of its camps.

On 14 March 1946 the ICRC sent a general memorandum to the Prague Government. Whilst having to refrain from taking a stand against the expulsion decision itself,[50]

> the ICRC recalled that it held it to be its duty to contribute, to the best of its ability, to rendering the carrying out of these transfers as humane as possible. Generally speaking, the ICRC was of opinion that, in view of the unsatisfactory conditions in these camps, it was important to put an end to the provisional internment as soon as possible.

One of the worst camps in post-war Czechoslovakia was the old Nazi concentration camp of Theresienstadt. Conditions under the new Czech administration are described by H. G. Adler, a former Jewish inmate as follows:[51]

> Many amongst them [the new inmates] had undoubtedly become guilty during the years of occupation, but in the majority they were children and juveniles, who had only been locked up because they were Germans. Only because they were Germans . . . ? This sentence sounds frighteningly familiar; only the word 'Jews' had been changed to 'Germans'. The rags the Germans had been clothed with were smeared with swastikas. The people were abominably fed and maltreated, and they were no better off than one was used to from German concentration camps. . . .

In Poland the situation was not better. In many internment camps no relief from outside was permitted. In some camps relatives would bring packages and deliver them to the Polish guards, who regularly plundered the contents and delivered only the rest, if that much. Frequently these relatives were so ill-treated that they never returned. Internees who came to claim their packages were also mistreated by the guards, who insisted the internees should speak Polish, even if they were Germans born in German-speaking Silesia or Pomerania. The under-dog had become top-dog, and pan-Slavism had supplanted pan-Germanism.[52]

Frightful excesses occurred in Camp Lamsdorf in Upper Silesia, where a camp population of 8,064 Germans was literally decimated through starvation, disease, hard labour and physical maltreatment.[53] One of the surviving German doctors recorded the death of 6,488 inmates of Lamsdorf, including 628 children.

It was not until June 1946 that the ICRC was able to post a delegate in Poland. During his first months in Warsaw this delegate experienced considerable difficulty in getting recognition of his right to investigate the problem of the German minority.[54] In spite of repeated demands, the ICRC delegate was not permitted to visit any internment camp until 27 June 1947, his first visit being to the Kalawsk Camp.[55] By the summer of 1947, however, a majority of the Germans had already been expelled, and many of the camps had been dissolved, including the infamous Lamsdorf camp. Still there remained a number of camps into which the ICRC was not invited.[56]

With respect to the civilian internee camps in Yugoslavia the ICRC received private appeals and reports to the effect that 'conditions of internment were not satisfactory as regards food, hygiene and treatment'.[57] The ICRC was hardly able to take any action on behalf of the civilian internees, since permission to increase the strength of the ICRC Delegation in Yugoslavia was denied and the Delegation thus had to be confined to its customary work for the German prisoners of war.[58]

Requests by the ICRC to visit civilian internee camps in Romania were consistently denied since March 1945.[59] In Hungary some visits were authorized in November 1945 and January 1946. Following these visits the ICRC delegation submitted requests to the Hungarian Government with the object of improving conditions.[60]

The civilian internees who survived to be expelled recorded the horrors of months and years of slow starvation and maltreatment in many thousands of affidavits. Allied authorities in the American and British zones were able to investigate several cases, including the notorious concentration camp at Budweis in Southern Bohemia. The deputy commander of this camp in the years 1945–6, Vaclav Hrnecek, later fled Czechoslovakia and came to Bavaria where he was recognized by former German inmates of the camp. Hrnecek was brought to trial before an American Court of the Allied High Commission for Germany presided by Judge Leo M. Goodman. The Court based an eight-year sentence against Hrnecek upon findings that the Budweis camp was run in a criminal and cruel way, that although there were no gas chambers and no systematic, organized extermination, the camp was a centre of sadism, where human life and human dignity had no meaning. The Court went on to affirm the impartiality of democratic justice, where a man like Hrnecek, even though his victims had all been Germans, had to be punished, and where the necessity of deterring sadism required heavy punishment.[61]

EVALUATION

More than two decades have elapsed since the Hrnecek Trial and since the end of the agony of the expulsions. The Western world outside Germany, however, remembers surprisingly little about these events. With the passing of time the idea of an orderly 'repatriation' of the Eastern Germans has even gained some ground, particularly in the United States and France. Recent West German statements with respect to the grave inhumanities committed in the course of the expulsions have been rejected by the entire Soviet-bloc Press as 'provocations' and 'falsifications of history'.[62] West German scholars engaged in research into these matters have been labelled chauvinists, revanchists, irredents and even neo-Nazis.[63] It is as if an Orwellesque Ministry of Truth were rewriting the history of this sad period.

In approaching this very complex subject Polish and Czechoslovak authors have consistently directed all attention to Allied authorization and overall responsibility for the transfers. They have thereby neglected to mention that a great many of these 'transfers' actually took place without the authorization or even in contravention of the directives of the Great Powers.

As the late Professor Boleslaw Wiewiora wrote in his widely read treatise on the Polish-German Frontier:[64]

> The transfer of the German population from Polish post-war territories was part and parcel of a general settlement on the question of national minorities agreed upon by the Allies towards the close of the Second World War.

This is partly true. To be complete this statement would require elaboration on the wide discrepancy that existed between Polish wishes and Allied consent, especially with respect to the number and timing of the transfers. It would also be necessary to come to grips with the question of the manner of execution of the transfer. Indeed, if the terminology dictated by the requirements of political expediency is rejected, then the transfers are exposed as criminal expulsions.

Professor Ludwik Gelberg of the Polish Academy of Sciences has similarly justified the expulsion of the Germans by referring to the Allied decision in Article XIII of the Potsdam Protocol.[65] Like Wiewiora he has failed to mention that the Western Allies had envisaged the transfer of several million persons *fewer* than the number ultimately expelled.[66] Nor has he given any explanation why the government of Poland violated the moratorium on transfers imposed by the Allies in Article XIII.

In discussing the millions of casualties suffered during the expulsion, the late Freiherr von Braun, Director of the Göttingen Research Committee in West Germany, pointed to the fact that 'these were primarily children, women, and aged persons.'[67] In answering Herr von Braun, Professor Gelberg did not address himself to the issue of the responsibility for these innocent deaths and chose to evade the problem by referring to the Nazi extermination of the Jews.[68] The monstrous crimes of the Nazi regime are, of course, more than well known. But was revenge upon innocent women and children ever legitimate?[69] The draconian *lex talionis* was abandoned long ago by civilized peoples.

At the same time a concerted effort has been made to attribute all expulsion losses to the war itself. This is the thesis of a widely distributed book entitled *Truth or Conjecture? German Civilian War Losses in the East,* published in 1966 by the Polish Western Press Agency in Warsaw. This book attempts to do as some Nazi apologists have tried to do in reverse – to cloud the issues, throw doubt upon statistical methodology and the integrity of the statisticians, avoid discussion of the methods of expulsion (or extermination), and play with the number of victims so as to convey an impression that 'it wasn't all that bad'. The Polish Government, of course, did not establish the elaborate system of concentration camps which characterized the Nazi extermination policy. It is none the less true that tens of thousands of German civilians perished in Polish internment camps while awaiting their 'transfer' to Germany. Predictably, *Truth or Conjecture* does not mention anything about Lamsdorf, nor for that matter about any of the other internment camps.

With respect to the expulsions from the Sudetenland and Czechoslovakia, the *Memoirs* of Dr Eduard Benes also present a very incomplete picture. While paying lip service to the principle of an orderly transfer, 'the transfer could be closely controlled and co-ordinated and could be carried out under decent and humane conditions',[70] Benes did not admit the fact that such idealized transfers were clearly the exception – not the rule. Dr Benes briefly regretted that 'our subordinate authorities committed some, very few, excesses which were unworthy of the country of Masaryk.'[71] These 'very few excesses', however, claimed 240,000 victims.[72]

In his book *The Transfer of the Sudeten Germans*, the Czech jurist, Dr Radomir Luza, did concede that 'molestations, beatings and killings occurred between May and July 1945'[73] but he gave a very low estimate of the number. Unlike Dr Benes, he mentioned the abuses that occurred in Brno (Brünn)[74] and in Usti nad Labem (Aussig),[75] adding that 'the evacuations were often carried out under excessively harsh conditions, the Germans being transported in trains or forced to march to the border. Frequently the Germans were notified only several hours prior to their departure.'[76] He also noted that 'a wave of German suicides accompanied this initial phase of the transfer.'[77] Yet, he concluded that 'on the whole, however, the organized transfer was carried out decently, in a humane way.'[78] This is unfortunately an inaccurate description.

The Report of the Walter Commission, United States House of Representatives, with respect to the expulsion of the Germans described the fate of the Sudeten Germans as follows:[79]

> About one-quarter of a million Sudeten Germans were inhumanely evicted into Germany from the border provinces by the independent action of the 'partisans.' The balance, amounting to a total of approximately 2·5 million, were sent to Germany in late 1945 and 1946 in the organized expulsion arranged by the Czechoslovak Government. *Conditions were such that neither movement can be termed humane and orderly.* Sudeten Germans who had remained loyal to Czechoslovakia in 1938 and therefore suffered under the Nazi regime were included, for the most part, in the mass expulsions [emphasis added].

This was the 'tragedy on a prodigious scale' that unfolded in Eastern and Central Europe after the war, an outrage for which there can be no justification.

It remains, of course, theoretically possible that a transfer of population, if internationally supervised and carried out gradually, in an 'orderly and humane' manner, might be compatible with international law standards. But a transfer of population accompanied by the atrocities and inhumanities that characterized the expulsion of the Germans from Poland and Czechoslovakia would in any case constitute a serious violation of positive international law in the dimension of a 'crime against humanity'.[80] One may debate the relative merits of population transfers as a means of achieving legitimate ends – such as a more permanent peace settlement – but when these transfers claim the lives of over 2 million innocent civilians, then the illegality of the means ineluctably condemns the end.[81]

CHAPTER SEVEN

FROM MORGENTHAU PLAN TO MARSHALL PLAN

Under the Potsdam agreement, the United States Government has unwittingly become a partner to mass starvation, particularly in Germany, contrary to the established and humanitarian concepts of international law, which have always placed upon the victor the responsibility of protecting to the best of its ability the innocent victims of the population conquered.

Hon. Charles W. Vursell, Appendix to the *Congressional Record*, Friday, 1 February 1946, p. A-397.

THE MORGENTHAU PLAN AND JCS/1067

It has been said that the Morgenthau Plan was the blunder of the American Civil War Reconstruction applied to Germany. The analogy is not altogether without validity. In the latter President Lincoln's 'malice-toward-none-charity-for-all' plan was supplanted by the old *vae victis* idea of Northern radicals whose plan for dealing with the beaten South was to crush it thoroughly so that it would never rise again. Similarly, after the Second World War, the humanitarian ideal of the Atlantic Charter was sacrificed to an ill-conceived plan which envisaged the elimination of the industrial potential of Germany by making it a strictly pastoral land.[1] The plan was worked out on the basis of a memorandum prepared by Secretary of the Treasury Henry Morgenthau, Jr. for the Quebec Conference of 11–16 September 1944, which was attended by President Roosevelt, British Prime Minister Churchill and by the Canadian Prime Minister MacKenzie King.[2]

Although the Morgenthau Plan was not officially adopted by the Western Allies, much of it reappeared in JCS/1067[3] and in this form played an important role in shaping American and British occupation policy in the first months and years following the German surrender, during which a thoroughgoing de-industrialization of Germany was carried out.[4]

131

JCS/1067 was a directive from the Joint Chiefs of Staff to the Commander-in-Chief of the United States Forces of Occupation, General Dwight D. Eisenhower, issued in April 1945. It instructed General Eisenhower in part:[5]

> You will take no action that would tend to support basic living standards in Germany on a higher level than that existing in any other of the neighboring United Nations and you will take appropriate measures to ensure that basic living standards of the German people are not higher than those existing in any one of the neighboring United Nations when such measures will contribute to raising the standards of any such nation.

For numerous reasons this directive was disproportionately harsh. For one, Germany had traditionally enjoyed a higher standard of living than most of her neighbours, being the most highly industrialized country in Europe. Thus, the attempt to lower her standard of living to the level of Poland or Yugoslavia was as revolutionary and abnormal as might have been a proposal to depress the standard of living in the United States below that prevalent in Mexico or Guatemala. In this sense Directive JCS/1067 was clearly a punitive measure aimed at enforcing retrogression in Germany and preventing the restoration of the *status quo ante*.[6] Furthermore, while this directive warned American authorities to watch out that the German standard of living did not rise above that of her neighbours, it failed however to set up machinery that could adequately measure and compare the standard of living of the various countries to be considered. As a result of this, Allied commanders in occupied Germany usually assumed that the standards of living in the other European countries were still lower than that in Germany, and thus blocked private relief initiatives which could have saved many Germans, mainly the destitute expellees, from starvation and disease.[7]

This ill-considered directive together with other aberrations of the Morgenthau 'Plan' reappeared in Western argumentation at the Potsdam Conference, which was in part devoted to shaping the future of the German economy. Point 12 of Article III of the Potsdam Protocol provided: 'At the earliest practicable date, the German economy shall be decentralized for the purpose of eliminating the present excessive concentration of economic power as exemplified by cartels, syndicates, trusts and other

36 Henry Morgenthau, Jr (US Army Photograph)

37 *Below* Dismantling German power plant for shipment to Russia (US Army Photograph)

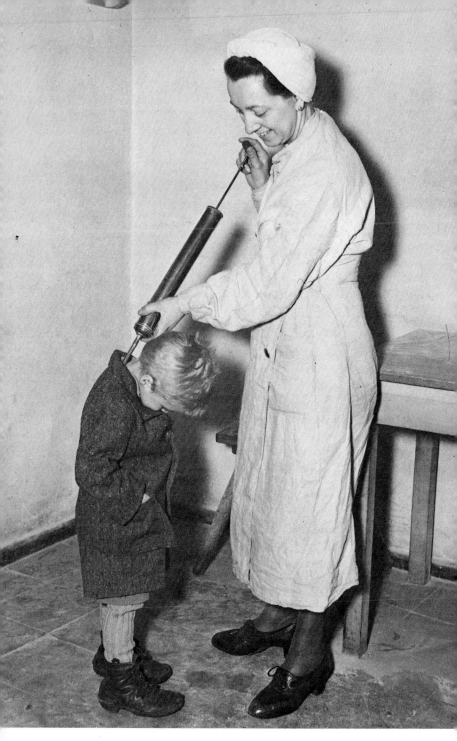

38 Reception centres provided for disinfection of the expellees, who often arrived covered with vermin (US Army Photograph)

39 *Above* Hungry expellee children 'scrape the pot', Berlin, 1947 (US Army Photograph)

40 *Below* Refugee girls at camp in Berlin in November 1947 (US Army Photograph)

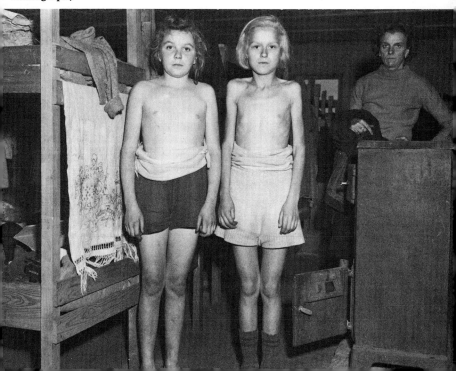

41 *Left* Boy in Hamburg searching for food (Gollancz)

42 *Below* Outside the American barracks in Berlin, April 1946 (US Army Photograph)

3 *Right* Victor Gollancz during his 1946 visit to the British zone of Germany (Gollancz)

4 *Below* Hungry expellee boy in the American zone (US Army photograph)

45 *Above* Secretary of State Byrnes delivering his controversial Stuttgart speech of 6 September 1946 (US Army Photograph)

46 *Below* Winston Churchill at Fulton, Missouri, where he delivered his famous 'iron curtain' speech on 5 March 1946 (UPI)

47 *Right* George F. Kennan (Keystone Press Agency)

48 *Below* Secretary of State Marshall speaking to the American people after the fiasco of the London Conference (UPI)

49 *Above* General Lucius Clay with his political adviser Robert D. Murphy (US Army Photograph)

50 *Below* CARE packages saved many Germans from starvation (US Army Photograph)

monopolistic arrangements.'[8] Point 13 formulated the idea of pastoralizing Germany as follows: 'In organizing the German economy, primary emphasis shall be given to the development of agriculture and peaceful domestic industries.'[9] Point 15 repeated the overall policy of depressing Germany's standard of living by imposing Allied controls 'to assure the production and maintenance of goods and services . . . essential to maintain in Germany average living standards not exceeding the average of the standards of living of European countries.'[10]

It was in pursuance of Point 15 that the occupation authorities in all four zones repeatedly rejected the entreaties of the International Committee of the Red Cross on behalf of the starving German population and prevented the delivery of shipments of food and medicine for many months. The first zone to allow Red Cross shipments was the British zone in October 1945,[11] followed by the French in December 1945. The American and Soviet zones, however, refused to permit deliveries during the very severe winter of 1945–6. US military authorities advised the ICRC delegate in Berlin to send all available relief shipments to other needy areas of Europe, even though large Irish and Swiss donations had been specifically earmarked for Germany.[12] This decision was particularly hard on the expellees, 'whose situation was far more precarious than that of the populations permanently domiciled in that zone'.[13] Relief was finally allowed to enter the American zone in March 1946 and the Soviet zone in April 1946.[14] By that time, however, tens of thousands of Germans had died of starvation or disease and many others were still to die before the available stocks of Red Cross relief could reach them.

In a letter to President Truman dated 14 December 1945 Senator Hawkes had urgently advocated the immediate restoration of postal services in Germany and official permission for private relief efforts. President Truman's reply of 21 December 1945 seemed to echo the voice of the Morgenthau Plan:[15]

> While we have no desire to be unduly cruel to Germany, I cannot feel any great sympathy for those who caused the death of so many human beings. . . . Until the misfortunes of those whom Germany oppressed and tortured are oblivated, it does not seem right to divert our efforts to Germany itself. I admit that there are, of course, many innocent people in Germany who had little to do with Nazi terror. However,

the administrative burden of trying to locate those people and treat them differently from the rest is one which is almost insuperable.

Thus, according to President Truman, American policy toward Germany, while not designed to be 'unduly cruel', was apparently intended to be at least somewhat cruel. This was Morgenthauism, although it would be erroneous to suggest that President Truman felt himself in any way bound to follow the plan of the outspoken Secretary of the Treasury.[16] Truman, in fact, had never approved of Secretary Morgenthau's incursions into foreign policy during the Roosevelt administration, and after Roosevelt's death he made it abundantly clear that Morgenthau's dilettantish incursions would not be welcome in his administration. It was precisely over this matter that Morgenthau took his leave, for when he learned that President Truman did not want him along at the Potsdam Conference he tendered his resignation. Truman accepted it on the spot.[17]

Secretary Morgenthau's resignation did not, however, bury the Morgenthau Plan.[18] As mentioned above, many of the policies adopted at the Potsdam Conference were closely related to Morgenthau's proposals, in particular the de-industrialization programme. For this reason many government critics kept the label 'Morgenthau Plan' to refer to the quasi-Carthaginian peace which was initially imposed upon Germany. Thus, nearly one year after the official shelving of the Morgenthau Plan, Senator Henrick Shipstead delivered on the floor of the Senate a scathing attack on United States occupation policy, condemning what he called 'America's eternal monument of shame, the Morgenthau Plan for the destruction of the German-speaking people'.[19]

While some of the worst aspects of the Morgenthau Plan were indeed jettisoned, in some respects the Potsdam Agreement had proved to be even more severe than the Morgenthau Plan. German boundaries as envisioned by Secretary Morgenthau, for instance, provided that 'Poland should get that part of East Prussia which doesn't go to the U.S.S.R. and the southern portion of Silesia.'[20] There was no suggestion of giving Poland, even for purposes of 'provisional administration', any portion of the provinces of Pomerania and Brandenburg nor the northern half of Silesia. There was no mention of the Oder and Neisse Rivers as western frontiers for Poland.[21]

Still, in spite of several important differences, the Morgenthau Plan and the Potsdam Programme shared a crucial conceptual flaw: central to both schemes was the paradoxical policy of transforming Germany into an agricultural economy while at the same time depriving it of its most valuable agricultural regions and displacing the native population of these regions into the overcrowded rump, which next to Holland[22] and Belgium[23] possessed the highest population density in Europe.[24] Even pre-First World War Germany,[25] which was almost 60 per cent larger than the truncated torso of 1945, had been only 80 per cent self-sufficient[26] in agricultural products. In 1922, after the loss of 12,355,700 agricultural acres (Posen, Corridor, North Schleswig, Alsace-Lorraine, Eupen, Malmedy and part of Upper Silesia) as a result of the Treaty of Versailles, Germany was only 75 per cent self-sufficient.[27] Following the loss of an additional 17,643,960 acres of food-producing lands at the end of the Second World War, Germany was reduced to a mere 61 per cent self-sufficiency.[28] How could Germany ever become a pastoral country as envisaged in the Morgenthau Plan and in point 13 of Article III of the Potsdam Protocol? To any amateur economist it would be evident that rump Germany could not feed itself, let alone export any food. But, it would have to export something in order to be able to buy a minimum diet for its own people. What did Germany have to export? Not unlike Great Britain, Germany's only significant mineral resource was and is coal, the mining of which has been long required to meet Germany's own domestic needs. Even though a surplus of coal could have been exported, it would have never sufficed to pay for food imports. The economic realities of Central Europe determined that Germany could only survive as an industrial producer, or it would starve to death. The Allies themselves, by taking away a quarter of Germany's arable land, unwittingly created a situation in which Germany's existence would necessarily be even more dependent on industrialization than before the war.[29]

Yet, in spite of the various manifestations of the Morgenthau syndrome, which may be attributable to transitory malevolence and rancour remaining after the war, American and British public opinion did not countenance mass starvation in Germany as a permanent situation. A 'modest proposal' in the sense of Jonathan Swift was not contemplated.[30]

Decisive for the gradual abandonment of the Morgenthau Plan, however, was the apprehension that if Germany remained Europe's slum, social unrest would force it into the Communist camp and that the rest of Europe could well follow. Developments in Central and Eastern Europe had already taken an ominous turn. The anti-Communists in Poland had been forced out of government and only a few had been able to escape to safety. The same undemocratic developments were subverting Romania, Hungary and Czechoslovakia. The Communist parties in France and Italy intensified their activities and caused several general strikes. Europe was ripe for a Communist takeover. Perhaps more than any humanitarian consideration, the spectre of a Communist Europe finally led the Western Powers to a thoroughgoing revision of their occupation policy in Germany. This opened the way for the implementation of the promises of the Atlantic Charter, point 4 of which had articulated a sensible policy that could be applied in re-establishing a democratic and friendly German nation. As the British and Americans had pledged in 1941,[31]

> they will endeavor, with due respect for the existing obligations, to further the enjoyment by all States, great and small, victor and vanquished, of access, on equal terms, to the trade and to the raw materials of the world which are needed for their economic prosperity.

THE BIRTH OF THE MARSHALL PLAN

Und neues Leben blüht aus den Ruinen.
(And new life blossoms out of the ruins.)

Friedrich von Schiller
Wilhelm Tell, Act 4, scene 2, line 2427

THE ECONOMIC SITUATION IN EUROPE   The fiasco of the Moscow meeting of the Council of Foreign Ministers in March 1947 convinced the Western Powers of the urgent necessity of striking out a new course independent of the Soviet Union. Total economic disintegration in Europe was imminent. Moreover, as George F. Kennan observed, 'it was plain that the Soviet leaders had a political interest in seeing the economies of the Western European peoples fail under anything other than communist leadership.'[32] At this critical moment in European history, the United States was the only country in the world capable to shore up the ailing European economies. The new American Secretary of State proposed to do just that.

General George C. Marshall had been a capable military strategist during the Second World War. He proved himself an even better statesman. As Secretary of State under President Truman (1947–9) Marshall worked closely with George F. Kennan in the implementation of 'containment' politics and the Truman Doctrine. A key element of this policy was the European Recovery Program, better known as the Marshall Plan, which was developed in response to Secretary Marshall's famous Harvard Address of 7 June 1947. The plan was not only in the best American tradition of humanitarian help to the needy – it was also intelligent politics.

It is interesting to note that the recovery plan originally envisaged by Marshall was designed to promote the economic recovery of Europe on both sides of the iron curtain. The countries in the Soviet sphere of influence were thus to benefit as much from American aid as were the Western democracies. Of course, such aid would have necessarily placed the beneficiary States in a position of relative dependence on the benefactor. Understandably, the Soviet Union was not enthusiastic about promoting ties of its satellites with any other Great Power. It therefore took steps to prevent any of the Eastern European countries from participating in a programme which it termed an imperialistic ploy of the West. Only Czechoslovakia had affirmatively answered the invitation of Foreign Ministers Bevin and Bidault to the 1947 conference in Paris in which a joint recovery plan for Europe was to be discussed. After a visit to Moscow by Premier Klement Gottwald and Foreign Secretary Jan Masaryk, Czechoslovakia withdrew its acceptance to attend the conference.[33]

The Soviet Union further boycotted the Marshall Plan by organizing a rival recovery programme for Eastern European nations, to be known as the 'Molotov Plan'. The Cominform, with headquarters in Belgrade, co-ordinated trade agreements within the Soviet sphere and diverted to the East a large volume of trade that had previously flowed to Western Europe. In October 1947 the Cominform urged Communists everywhere to help defeat the Marshall Plan as an instrument for 'world domination by American imperialism'.[34] The Marshall Plan withstood the challenge. On 12 July 1947 representatives of Austria, Belgium, Denmark, France, Greece, Iceland, Ireland, Italy, Luxemburg, the Netherlands, Norway, Portugal, Sweden, Switzerland, Turkey and the United Kingdom met in Paris to discuss common economic problems. Occupied Germany, which was in a far more desperate situation than any of the other nations, was not a participant in this initial conference. However, all three Western occupants were themselves from the beginning the principal parties in the programme.

Although from 1945 to 1947 the Allies had implemented a harsh peace upon Germany, economists soon recognized that Western Europe could only recover when the principal industrial nations, including Germany, returned to a healthy economy.[35] As General Lucius Clay aptly stated, 'it was apparent that Western Europe could not recover if there was an economic vacuum left in Germany.'[36]

THE ECONOMIC SITUATION IN GERMANY   In 1947 the economic situation in occupied Germany could hardly have been bleaker. Industrial output was only 27 per cent of pre-war volume.[37] This alarming decline was attributable partly to the extensive dismantling of German industries pursuant to the Potsdam policy of taking 'reparations in kind', partly to wartime devastation, partly to the economic disruptions caused by the zonal division of Germany, and partly to inadequate manpower, since millions were still prisoners of war and those who were in Germany could hardly work efficiently because they were too weakened by undernourishment and disease.[38]

The removal of plant and equipment from Germany beyond what could be effectively used elsewhere was one of the first Morgenthauist policies to run into extensive criticism from influential persons in the United States and Great Britain. Dismantled German plants were rusting away in warehouses throughout the Soviet Union, Poland and even France. This represented a net loss to European as well as to German output and was retarding the recovery of the continent as a whole.[39]

Since most of the industrial dismantling went to the Soviet Union, the problem was solved in the Western occupation zones when in the spring of 1946 shipments were stopped. General Clay explained his decision to the irate Russians by quoting to them Points 14 and 15 of Article III of the Potsdam Protocol which required that during Four-Power occupation Germany should be treated as a single economic unit and that essential commodities be equitably distributed between the several zones, so as to produce a balanced economy throughout Germany and reduce the need for imports.[40] Since the Soviet Union was not pooling resources with the other occupation Powers but extracting maximum reparations out of its zone without giving an accounting to the other Powers, the dismantling of plants in the West for the benefit of the Soviet Union was cancelled.

The economic disruptions occasioned by Germany's zonal partition also continued to plague the recovery of the area. The Soviet zone oriented itself more and more toward the East and the French zone stagnated, partly because of France's unwillingness to co-operate in any all-German programme until the question of the Saar[41] was solved in France's favour and partly because of her fear of a revival of Germany's strength.

But the recovery of Western Europe could not be made to wait for the unification of all of Germany. Even before Secretary Marshall's Harvard address the American and British zones had merged in common economic endeavour.[42] The extension of this bi-zonal occupation to include the French zone, however, was not achieved until 8 April 1949,[43] the same date of the entry into force of the Occupation Statute.[44] The establishment of the Federal Republic of Germany followed on 24 May 1949.[45]

Millions of dollars of Marshall Plan funds were poured into the young Federal Republic, and the rapid recovery of its economy exceeded by far the hopes of the United States government, which in fact had devoted only a relatively small percentage of Marshall Plan funds to the German recovery programme.

For the period from 3 April 1948 to 30 June 1952, the Marshall Plan allocated 3,176 million dollars to the United Kingdom, 2,706 million to France, 1,474 million to Italy and only 1,389 million to Western Germany.[46] Yet, the biggest results were to be seen in Germany:[47]

> the effects had been prodigious, equaled in no other
> European country, although Germany got only a relatively
> small proportion of Marshall Plan aid. Europe received in
> all $20,000,000,000 from the United States; in 1954 the
> figures per capita had amounted to $39 for Germany as
> against $72 for France, $77 for England, $33 for Italy and
> $104 for Austria. But in Germany the help came at precisely
> the right time, when the accumulated pressures for both

physical and psychological reconstruction had reached a bursting point.

This phenomenal success of the Marshall Plan in Germany was to contribute materially to the success of the plan in the rest of Europe, and indubitably led to the early assumption of full sovereignty by the Federal Republic of Germany on 5 May 1955.

Pursuant to the 'Agreement between the Federal Republic of Germany and the United States of America regarding the settlement of the claim of the United States of America for post-war economic assistance to Germany'[48] dated 27 February 1953 the Federal Republic agreed to repay one billion dollars of Marshall Plan Aid to the United States over a period of thirty years. Grateful to have had a helping hand at a time when survival was at stake, the Federal Republic of Germany has already repaid the entire amount.

THE ROLE OF THE EXPELLEES IN THE GERMAN 'WIRTSCHAFTSWUNDER'

From 1945 to 1948 the prospects of recovery in an acutely over-populated and undernourished Germany had seemed slim indeed. Grave food, fuel and housing problems had been enormously compounded by the constant arrival of expellees from the East. What could be done with these destitute millions? Germany's de-industrialized post-war economy could not even provide employment for the native population of the Western Provinces, let alone for the newcomers. For this reason many American[49] and French[50] politicians asserted that the only solution for Germany was large-scale emigration to other countries including the United States and Australia. As late as 1950 a United States Congressional Committee under the chairmanship of Representative Francis E. Walter recommended:[51]

Granted that maximum efforts as envisaged above are made to integrate the bulk of the refugees into the German economy, slightly in excess of 1,000,000 German expellees and refugees should be offered emigration opportunities.

This proposed emigration, however, did not take place, because through Marshall Plan funds Germany was able to turn its expellee liability into a prime asset. The phenomenal *Wirtschaftswunder* made possible by the influx of dollars rested no less on the availability of skilled workers who had previously been unemployed. At once two important ends were achieved – rapid economic recovery and the integration of millions of expellees.[52]

Although the areas from which most of the expellees came were primarily agricultural, it should not be overlooked that these areas also possessed significant industries, and that many expellees accordingly brought with them valuable industrial expertise and ideas.[53]

East Prussia and Pomerania, for instance, had well-developed wood and paper industries, thanks to abundant forests. Both provinces also boasted important ship-building concerns that had flourished on the Baltic towns of Elbing, Danzig, Stettin, etc. The textile industry and in particular the manufacture of ready-made clothes was also quite considerable in the city of Stettin.

Much more industrialized than either East Prussia or Pomerania was the province of Upper Silesia, which possessed much mineral wealth, including Germany's second largest coal deposits. Heavy machines produced in Silesia had been sold throughout Germany and exported to foreign countries. Thirty-seven per cent of Upper and Lower Silesia's working force were industrial workers.

The Sudetenland also possessed coal deposits, principally in the northern part of Bohemia and in the old province of Austrian Silesia which was contiguous to Prussian Silesia. Among the diverse industries of the Sudetenland were the manufacture of musical instruments, fine crystal, jewellery and furniture, as well as the brewing of Pilsener beer, one of the prides of Czechoslovakia.[54]

Thus, the integration of millions of expellees was achieved peacefully through the combination of hard work and benevolent help from abroad.

Unlike the Palestinian expellees who became terrorists in spite of millions of dollars of United Nations help, the German expellees transformed Marshall Plan Aid into work which not only enabled them to survive but also gradually to rebuild their lives in a liberal, democratic – and peaceful – society.

CHAPTER EIGHT

PEACE WITHOUT A PEACE TREATY

From the beginning our aims for Germany and the Soviet aspirations were at odds. Within a year of the installation of the machinery for quadripartite administration of Germany, it was obvious that the Western powers wanted a self-supporting Germany, while the Soviet Union was interested in exploiting German industry, agriculture, and labour for the benefit of the U.S.S.R.

Robert Murphy, 25 June 1955. Department of State, *Bulletin*, vol. 33, p. 46.

PEACE WITH GERMANY'S AXIS PARTNERS

Throughout the history of Europe wars have been terminated by treaties of peace or by subjugation.[1] The case of Germany after the Second World War is *sui generis* in so far as the victorious Allies did not offer Germany a peace treaty nor complete the act of subjugation by annexing the conquered Reich.[2] Thirty years after the Nazi surrender Germany remains divided and no peace treaty has been signed.

By contrast, the Allies completed treaties of peace with all of Germany's former Axis partners and associated countries. In the State of the Union Message delivered by President Truman to the Congress on 6 January 1947, he announced that 'peace treaties for Italy, Bulgaria, Rumania, and Hungary have finally been prepared.'[3] The treaty of peace with Italy was signed in Paris on 10 February 1947[4] and was ratified by Italy and most of the Allies in the summer of 1947. At approximately the same time treaties of peace went into force with Bulgaria, Romania and Hungary.[5]

Japan, the other major Axis partner, had to wait longer for a treaty, because the Soviet Union, which had entered the war against Japan barely one week before the Japanese surrender, voiced all sorts of objections to the American treaty proposals.[6]

Finally, the treaty of peace with Japan was signed at San Francisco on 8 September 1951, and entered into force on 28 April 1952,[7] without ratification by the Soviet government.

A peace treaty with Germany could have similarly been ratified by a majority of the Allies without the Soviet Union, if Germany had not been divided into zones at the Yalta Conference.[8] What had happened was that from the first moment of actual occupation, the Soviet Union commenced to communize its zone. The proverbial iron curtain[9] soon descended to isolate the Soviet zone from the rest of Germany, even though it had been agreed by the Allies that Germany would not be dismembered and would, instead, be treated as a unit.[10]

At the time of the Potsdam Conference the Allies, including the Soviet Union, also committed themselves to the idea of terminating the war with Germany by way of a peace treaty. Article II of the Potsdam Protocol established a Council of Foreign Ministers, which was given the task to prepare 'a peace settlement for Germany to be accepted by the government of Germany when a government adequate for the purpose is established.'[11]

The Council of Foreign Ministers, however, moved slowly. Over a year after the end of hostilities Foreign Minister Bevin reported to the House of Commons: 'Our ultimate goal is the preparation of a peace treaty, but there is a large amount of preliminary work to be done before that can be accomplished.'[12] Progress was not easy and friction was building up over many issues of the occupation.

As shown in Chapters 5 and 6 the Soviet Union misused for its own political ends the issue of the German minorities in Poland and Czechoslovakia by accusing the Western Allies of being pro-German and of opposing legitimate Polish and Czechoslovak aspirations. The precipitate expulsions which caused so many difficulties in the British and American zones were carried out with the support or connivance of Soviet authorities, even though the Soviet government had consented to Article XIII of the Potsdam Protocol which called a temporary halt on the expulsions. The enormous influx of Eastern Germans into the Western zones aggravated the already critical food situation there, and while the Soviet Union was receiving dismantled German plants from the Western zones, it was not making any grain from East Germany available by way of exchange to the more industrial British and American zones. As Bevin observed in parliament:[13]

We and the Americans have had to buy food and other goods to send into Western Germany, while the Russians are taking similar goods from Eastern Germany into Russia. This is a situation which cannot go on. We must either have Potsdam observed as a whole, and in the order of its decision, or we must have a new agreement.

Friction was also building up in Berlin, where early in 1946 three municipal judges who had rendered judgments contrary to the views of the German Communist leaders disappeared, arrested by agents of the Soviet Military Administration. General Lucius Clay protested vigorously – and to no avail.[14] Another incident reflecting the hidden tensions occurred in April 1946 when Soviet troops attempted to remove railroad track from the American sector of Berlin. Only the prompt arrival of American tanks prevented the continuation of this daring infringement.[15]

Far more serious was the friction that developed from the radically different conceptions of the new Germany. It soon became evident that the Soviet Union had an interest in either bringing Germany into the Soviet sphere or in thoroughly de-industrializing it so that in future Germany could never again become a threat to Soviet power in Europe. The Western Allies, on the other hand, knew that Germany's economic prosperity was vital to European recovery and therefore started advocating a gradual rebuilding of Germany's peaceful industrial potential.

The first indications of this development came in the speeches of Secretary of State Byrnes. The stern tone of Byrnes's Statement on the Meaning of the Potsdam Declaration on 12 December 1945[16] was softened noticeably in his memorable Stuttgart Speech of 6 September 1946.[17] On the constructive side Byrnes announced at Stuttgart, 'We favour the economic unification of Germany. If complete unification cannot be secured, we shall do everything in our power to secure the maximum possible unification.' And as a warning to the Soviet Union, whose Communist propaganda was causing uncertainty in the West, he said 'As long as an occupation force is required in Germany, the Army of the United States will be a part of that occupation force.' This last statement proved to be one of the most welcome parts of the speech, not just in Germany, but throughout Western Europe. In the House of Commons on 22 October 1946, Foreign Minister Bevin echoed British approval of the Stuttgart speech.[18]

The year 1947 witnessed the gradual disintegration of effective four-Power control over occupied Germany. The Allied Control Council in Berlin could claim no important accomplishments and matters awaiting consideration were constantly on the increase. Meanwhile, the Council of Foreign Ministers made even less progress towards the drafting of a peace treaty. From 10 March to 24 April the Foreign Ministers met in Moscow, principally in order to discuss the German peace settlement. Although in the months before the Conference the Western Powers had made very extensive preparations, they failed to co-ordinate their presentation of objectives and means of implementation, so that the Russians were able to take advantage of minor differences of opinion and constantly came up with objections and amendments which effectively frustrated all Western proposals. As Stalin candidly told the new American Secretary of State General Marshall, 'These are only the first skirmishes of reconnaissance forces on the German question.'[19]

Because of the very unco-operative attitude of the Russians, the Moscow Conference proved to be a complete failure. It is true that the Western Powers had not really expected to reach full agreement on a German peace treaty, but it had been hoped that the Moscow conference would have laid a solid foundation and that a peace treaty would have been agreed upon within reasonable time. Instead, Soviet-American relations deteriorated progressively after the abortive conference. The cold war was developing with bewildering speed. Robert Murphy, who as Political Adviser of the American Military Government for Germany participated in the conference, observed, 'it was the Moscow Conference of 1947, I believe, which really rang down the Iron Curtain.'[20]

THE LONDON CONFERENCE AND THE BERLIN BLOCKADE

The second and last concerted effort to reach agreement on the preliminaries for a peace treaty was made in the London session of the Council of Foreign Ministers held in November and December 1947. In spite of widening differences with the Soviet Union, the ministers were still talking in terms of concluding a treaty of peace with Germany and establishing an all-German government under Allied control, which would then sign the treaty and gradually take over responsibility for the conduct of German life.[21] It was the failure of this meeting that led to a decision by the Western Powers to establish a separate government in Western Germany and to assure its economic success by pouring Marshall Plan dollars into it. This decision, of course, aroused keen alarm among the Soviet leaders. In an ill-conceived effort to bring the Western Powers back to the negotiating table, the Russians blockaded the Western sectors of Berlin, the first steps in this direction being taken in March 1948. Following the publication of the so-called London Programme on the modalities of the procedure for establishing a separate West German government, the Russians made the blockade complete in June 1948.[22] During the winter months of 1948-9 the operational levels of the United States government were fully occupied with the Berlin airlift as a means of frustrating the Soviet blockade, and with the implementation of the London Programme. West German political leaders were meanwhile drawing up a democratic constitution for the new West German State and the British, French and American occupation authorities were drafting a new occupation statute that would come into effect simultaneously with the establishment of the new West German government.

As the date of the new Council of Foreign Ministers meeting drew closer, the London Programme was taking final shape. On 8 May 1949 the constitution for the West German government was adopted and on 12 May the new Occupation Statute was transmitted to the West German representatives.[23] General Lucius Clay, who particularly prized the London Programme, regarded its final adoption as a personal achievement and did not want to see it sacrificed to any new and uncertain agreement with the Russians.

On 23 May 1949 the Council of Foreign Ministers assembled in Paris to discuss the German question. In spite of the very slim chance of success, the Western Powers used this occasion to invite the various Länder (provinces) in the Soviet zone to enter the West German Federation on the liberal terms of the London Programme. Predictably, Soviet authorities blocked the proposed union, just as two years earlier they had proscribed Czechoslovakian and Polish participation in the benefits of the Marshall Plan. As already mentioned, Soviet policy since the beginning of the occupation had been to prevent a German recovery, or at least to assure that any recovery operated to Soviet benefit and not to the benefit of European recovery generally. Thus, when the Soviet government was faced with the *fait accompli* of the London Programme, a programme conceived without them, they categorically rejected it.

This breakdown of attempts to reach agreement with the Russians on the future of Germany and especially the establishment of a separate West German State confirmed the division of Germany and of Europe. It is, however, doubtful whether any course of action on the Western side short of surrender to the Russian position would have resulted in a reunification of Germany. The Russians would have co-operated only in the establishment of a Socialist Germany à la Czechoslovakia, a Germany that would have ripened and fallen into the Soviet sphere in the same way that Czechoslovakia did in 1948.[24]

It is interesting to note at this point how realistically George F. Kennan had assessed the situation in a draft written in the summer of 1945, long before the development of the Cold War:[25]

The idea of a Germany run jointly with the Russians is a chimera. The idea of both the Russians and ourselves withdrawing politely at a given date and a healthy, peaceful, stable, and friendly Germany arising out of the resulting vacuum is also a chimera. We have no choice but to lead our section of Germany – the section of which we and the British have accepted responsibility – to a form of independence so prosperous, so secure, so superior, that the East cannot threaten it.

And indeed, out of Germany's smouldering ruins two new Germanies were to arise. Buried sources of spiritual strength were tapped. In the Western zones of occupation a rebirth from inside would again release that creative power which for centuries had been one of the pillars of the Western world. Every step was watched – indeed, guided – by the occupation authorities which acted as a sort of board of trustees. Of course, these trustees committed many blunders, but as the new Federal Republic of Germany matured, the trustees gradually let the young republic assume the powers as well as the appearance of sovereignty. By contrast, the Eastern zone became a Soviet colony[26] in which not only the economy, but also the labour unions, the Press and the universities were subservient to Moscow. Gradually, a modicum of autonomy was granted to the so-called German Democratic Republic. The phoenix would be allowed to fly, but only within its cage.

TERMINATION OF WAR BY PROCLAMATION

In view of the fact that no peace treaty with a united Germany was achieved, the Western Powers, principally for domestic reasons, moved to end the state of war by unilateral proclamation.[27]

The process of moving from total war to the state of peace was a long one. Actual fighting ceased, of course, on 9 May 1945 as a result of the German unconditional surrender. Minor skirmishes continued for several days or weeks when individual soldiers or splinters either did not know or did not accept the fact of capitulation. These were, however, infrequent exceptions. The great mass of the German armed forces became prisoners of war – or what was termed 'surrendered enemy personnel'. Yet, even though Germany had surrendered, the legal state of war against Germany continued for six more years.

On 31 December 1946 President Truman issued a Proclamation Terminating the Hostilities of the Second World War.[28] It read in part, 'Although a state of war still exists, it is at this time possible to declare, and I find it to be in the public interest to declare, that hostilities have terminated.' As a result of this proclamation a number of war and emergency statutes went out of force, and government powers were reduced to a quasi-peacetime basis. The American occupation policy in Germany, however, was not affected by this proclamation.

In April 1949 the Western Powers handed over the administration of their occupation zones to the government of the Federal Republic of Germany, but at the same time a new Occupation Statute went into effect that substantially restricted the sovereignty of the new republic. Also at about this time the Soviet Union set up a rival East German government. In either case, no substantial change occurred in the legal nature of the authority exercised by the Allied Powers.[29]

In spite of this factual division of Germany into two republics, President Truman proclaimed the Termination of the State of War *with all of Germany* on 24 October 1951.[30] This proclamation reaffirmed the American position with respect to a German peace treaty:

It has been and continues to be the policy of the United
States to bring about the conclusion of a treaty of peace with
the government of a united and free Germany, but efforts to
this end have been frustrated and made impossible for the
time being by the policy of the Soviet Government. . . .

Truman further explained the reason for the temporary substitution of a proclamation for a treaty:

it has nevertheless been considered desirable to bring the
existing state of war with Germany to a close and to remove
Germany from its present enemy status, thus eliminating
certain disabilities affecting German nationals. . . .

This Presidential Proclamation of 1951, however, did not restore
sovereignty to the Federal Republic of Germany. This was
achieved with the coming into force on 5 May 1955 of the Treaty
of Termination of the Occupation Regime in the Federal Republic
of Germany, signed at Paris on 23 October 1954.[31]

CONVENTION ON RELATIONS BETWEEN THE THREE POWERS AND THE FEDERAL REPUBLIC OF GERMANY

Of special significance to the future of Germany was the Convention on Relations Between the Three Powers and the Federal
Republic of Germany,[32] in which the Three Powers reaffirmed
their commitment to the reunification of Germany and to the
signing of a peace treaty with all of Germany. Article 7 of the
Convention provides in part:[33]

1. The Signatory States are agreed that an essential aim of
their common policy is a peace settlement for the whole
of Germany, freely negotiated between Germany and her
former enemies, which should lay the foundation for a
lasting peace. They further agree that the final
determination of the boundaries of Germany must await
such settlement.
2. Pending the peace settlement, the Signatory States will
cooperate to achieve, by peaceful means, their common aim
of a reunited Germany enjoying a liberal-democratic
constitution, like that of the Federal Republic, and
integrated within the European community. . . .
4. The Three Powers will consult with the Federal Republic

on all matters involving the exercise of their rights relating to Germany as a whole.

The Paris Agreements also included a resolution by NATO accepting the Western European Union as part of the NATO defence system. An important declaration by the Federal Republic was annexed to the NATO Resolution, whereby the Federal Republic undertook 'never to have recourse to force to achieve the reunification of Germany or the modification of the present boundaries of the German Federal Republic', and to resolve all disputes between Germany and other states by peaceful means.[34] In spite of this provision, however, membership by the Federal Republic of Germany in NATO was a source of great apprehension in the Soviet bloc nations and served to perpetuate the division of the two Germanies. Predictably, East Germany joined the Warsaw Pact[35] and thereby became militarily as well as economically a vassal of the Soviet Union.

The question of German reunification was thus entirely out of German hands and depended exclusively on the political horse-trading of the Great Powers.

In the course of the cold war years Washington and Moscow persevered in their divergent views as to the first stage in German reunification. Washington supported the thesis that Bonn alone was entitled to speak for all Germans and envisaged German reunification through some form of electoral arrangement which could hardly fail, on the basis of numbers alone, to bring about the absorption of the Democratic into the Federal Republic. On the other side Moscow, which had established diplomatic relations with Bonn in 1955, continued to seek wider recognition of the government of the 'Democratic Republic', and at the same time emphasized that reunification of the two Germanies could only come about through some form of confederation. The Moscow plan envisaged each State retaining certain salient economic and political characteristics. Although this plan sounds superficially reasonable, it involved compulsion and denied the free exercise of the right of self-determination. Moreover, it was feared that according to the Moscow Plan the opportunity for subverting the free-enterprise system in the West would increase enormously.

The East-West conflict also manifested itself in the divergent approaches to the question of timing. Washington and Bonn urged progress towards German reunification first, and the signing of a peace treaty only when this had been achieved. Moscow and East Berlin proposed an early start on a peace treaty, which presumably both German States would have to sign, and only then would they consider discussing reunification plans. There was no progress on either count.[36] Still, in 1957 there seemed to be a special urgency in the search for a solution of the German problem. In the third talk of the famous Reith Lectures[37] given by George F. Kennan during the height of the Cold War, the problem of German reunification was discussed in very blunt terms. It was conjectured in the West that if the problem of the division of Germany could be removed, then the reunification of Europe East and West might follow. On the other side, the Russians seemed to be especially interested in preventing the nuclear armament of Western Germany by NATO. Was this finally the moment for political horse-trading? Would the Russians consent to a reunification of Germany if it were neutralized as Austria had been neutralized in 1955?[38] Perhaps. But this idea went counter to what Chancellor Adenauer had specifically stated at the NATO Council meeting in Bonn in May 1957, that reunification could not be obtained by the neutralization of Germany and that neutralization would not reduce tensions. Germany was much too important to gamble on its neutrality. It was considered improbable that the Soviet Union would merely watch the development of a truly neutral Germany without seeking to subvert it and for this reason the Western Powers refused to risk a communist takeover of the entire country. Under the circumstances it was considered more prudent to consolidate the free Federal Republic of Germany even at the expense of permanently losing East Germany.

One of the most impressive critics of the idea of German reunification was Raymond Aron, who maintained that the partition of Europe could not be changed because it was, in fact, less dangerous than any other solution. Elaborating further Mr Aron explained American foreign policy in very candid terms:[39]

The present situation of Europe is abnormal, or absurd. But it is a clear-cut one and everybody knows where the demarcation line is and nobody is very much afraid of what could happen. If something happens on the other side of the Iron Curtain – and we have the experience of a year ago

> [Hungary] – nothing happens on this side. So a clear
> partition of Europe is considered, rightly or wrongly, to be
> less dangerous than any other arrangement.

Admittedly an abnormal situation, but better than an *equivocal*
situation, in which the danger of nuclear confrontation would be
much greater. For this reason it seems that in the late 1950s no
one in authority in Europe or America really wanted to see the
division of Europe removed.[40] The nineteen years that have
elapsed since the Reith Lectures have proved that Western
statesmen are more than ever committed to the *status quo* and do
not seriously consider the reunification of Europe or the reunification of Germany, even though from time to time someone
still pays lip-service to it. It seems that the decision to leave
Europe divided for an indefinite time was taken long ago, even
if it was never announced. This division was again illustrated
during the Czechoslovak crisis of 1968, which showed unequivocally that the Soviet Union has no intention of relaxing its
hold over its satellites and that the Western Powers are unwilling to risk a war with the Soviet Union by actively interfering
on behalf of liberty and human rights in Central or Eastern
Europe.

CHAPTER NINE

RECOGNITION OR REVISION OF THE ODER-NEISSE FRONTIER

With regard to the Polish-German frontier, the starting point for our consideration must be the Potsdam protocol which provided that 'The final delimitation of the western frontier of Poland should await the peace settlement.' Mr. Molotov presented the view that the decision regarding the western frontier has been taken. This is clearly not the case as the quotation just referred to indicates. A just settlement of this frontier, as I stated at our meeting in Moscow on April 9, 1947, requires that we give careful consideration to the needs of the populations which will be directly affected and keep equally in mind the importance of this frontier for the economic and political stability of Europe.

Secretary of State George C. Marshall on 27 November 1947 during the London meeting of the Council of Foreign Ministers. Department of State, *Bulletin*, vol. 17, p. 1078.

OSTPOLITIK AND THE TREATY OF WARSAW OF 1970

After two and a half decades of Western denunciation of the Oder-Neisse frontier, the government of the Federal Republic of Germany decided to strike a new course in foreign policy and concluded a Treaty with Poland affirming the inviolability of this frontier. Article I of the treaty, signed in Warsaw on 7 December 1970, provides in part:[1]

The Federal Republic of Germany and the People's Republic of Poland state in mutual agreement that the existing boundary line the course of which is laid down in Chapter IX of the Decisions of the Potsdam Conference of 2 August 1945 as running from the Baltic Sea immediately west of Swinemunde, and thence along the Oder River to the confluence of the western Neisse River and along the western Neisse to the Czechoslovak frontier, shall

constitute the western State frontier of the People's
Republic of Poland.

The political significance of this treaty, at least for the present
time, is indisputable. The legal significance, however, is rather
unsettled. The treaty is paradoxical for a number of reasons.
For one, the Federal Republic of Germany and Poland do not
have any common frontiers, although from the moment of its
establishment the Federal Republic has consistently claimed to be
the successor of the German Reich in its frontiers of 1937.
Departing from this traditional position, the Federal Republic
consented to the Oder-Neisse frontier in the Treaty of Warsaw
not in its capacity as representative of all Germany, but merely
as Federal Republic.[2] Thus, this ambiguous agreement appears
to have left the door ajar for future claims which a reunited
Germany – should a union ever materialize – might make for the
return of its pre-war provinces east of the Oder-Neisse. These
are, of course, legal conjectures which would only become
relevant if unforeseeable political developments should render a
political union of East and West Germany and subsequent frontier
adjustments with Poland open to negotiation. No such changes in
the political landscape of Europe were realistically thinkable
before the Treaty of Warsaw, because the Soviet Union and
Poland opposed German reunification and categorically maintained the finality of the frontier at the Oder-Neisse. Thus, by the
Treaty of Warsaw the Federal Republic merely recognized the
fact that for the time being no frontier revisions were possible.

Regardless of what might happen in the future, the country
now sharing the Oder-Neisse frontier with Poland is the Communist regime of East Germany, which as early as 1950 concluded an agreement of its own with Poland recognizing the
Oder-Neisse as the final 'peace boundary' between Germany and
Poland.[3] Much more so than the Treaty of Warsaw of 1970, the
Görlitz Agreement of 6 June 1950 had more political than legal
significance, for at that time the so-called 'German Democratic
Republic' was not de facto or de jure a sovereign State nor was it
recognized as such by the overwhelming majority of the members
of the United Nations. In any case, the Görlitz Agreement could
hardly have been taken seriously in international law, in view of
the fact that the German Democratic Republic was not em-
powered to conclude agreements on behalf of all of Germany,

against which a formal state of war still existed in 1950, and over which various peace treaty proposals were still being discussed.

Far more important than any agreement concluded by the Federal Republic or by the German Democratic Republic is the actual recognition or non-recognition of the Oder-Neisse frontier by those States which at the conclusion of the Second World War were legitimately entitled to decide the fate of Germany. These were the United States, Great Britain, the Soviet Union and France.[4]

The Warsaw Treaty of 1970 does not impair the rights of the Big Four. In fact, Article IV expressly states: 'The present Treaty shall not affect any bilateral or multilateral international arrangements previously concluded by either Contracting Party or concerning them.' Moreover, in the notes sent by the Federal Republic to the Four Powers, and in the reply notes of the Western Powers it is reaffirmed that the treaty 'does not and cannot affect the rights and responsibilities of the Four Powers as reflected in the known treaties and agreements.' Thus, no final determination of the Polish-German frontier can be legally effective until the Four Powers give their official approval.

The Soviet Union, as principal architect of the Oder-Neisse frontier, has, of course, recognized it as final.[5] Contrary to popular assumption, none of the Western Powers has made an act of formal recognition, neither individually nor collectively, although with the passing of time their public opposition to the Oder-Neisse frontier has considerably reduced in intensity.[6]

Officially, the United States, Great Britain and France maintain the legal position that according to the Potsdam Agreement the Oder-Neisse frontier is a provisional frontier subject to approval or revision in a final peace treaty with Germany.[7] Yet, since the Soviet Union has made a treaty of peace with Germany impossible by preventing reunification except under communist auspices,[8] the Oder-Neisse frontier will probably remain legally defective until the Western Powers officially relinquish their right to insist on the fulfilment of the Potsdam Agreement.

Is there any justification for non-recognition on the part of the Western Powers after the Federal Republic itself has relinquished its claim to the former German provinces east of the Oder and Neisse Rivers? The answer to this question is a political, not a legal one. The United States, for instance, has nothing to gain by recognizing the Oder-Neisse frontier. Nor does it have much to lose by doing so. Yet, any affirmative act on the part of the United States should logically have a motivation, which at the present time would be difficult to formulate in favour of recognition. Moreover, the United States, has no honourable way of accepting the legality of a frontier which was established by illegal means and in direct violation of international agreements to which the United States was a party.

Reviewing the history of the Oder-Neisse, the record shows that the United States and Great Britain vigorously opposed the methods by which the Soviet Union and Poland sought to establish the post-war German-Polish frontier. As shown in Chapter 3, both Roosevelt and Churchill rejected Stalin's proposals at Yalta. Four months later, when the Big Four assumed sovereignty over Germany by the Berlin Declaration of 5 June 1945, they formally and expressly assumed sovereignty over Germany in its frontiers 'as they were on 31st December, 1937'[9] and agreed that the final determination of Germany's frontiers would be made in the peace treaty.

THE POTSDAM CONFERENCE REVISITED

Western approval of the annexation of German territory by Poland was a matter that depended directly on the theory of compensation. The amount of compensation to be given Poland was the subject of frequent discussions at Potsdam, yet, because of disagreement among the Allies, no commitment was reached that would be binding at the peace conference. In spite of the formal postponement of the frontier question, however, the government of Poland, with the encouragement of the Soviet Union, prematurely annexed or claimed to have annexed all of Germany east of the Oder and Neisse Rivers,[10] far more territory than the Western Powers were disposed to concede in the peace treaty. These annexations effectively denied the Western Powers a source of possible reparations and, more importantly, a source of food for the German population in the Western zones of occupation. Anglo–American protests were emphatic, but wholly ineffective. As Admiral Leahy, a participant in the Potsdam Conference put it, 'we would have had to be prepared to take military action to overturn the Soviet *fait accompli*'.[11]

In spite of these abuses, however, the Western Allies approved the controversial Article IX of the Potsdam Protocol, granting

Poland provisional administration over the Oder-Neisse territories. What legal and historical significance does this Article have? There is a widespread prejudice among persons unfamiliar with the nature of the Potsdam Conference which confuses the Potsdam decisions with those of a peace treaty. The Potsdam Conference was not a second Versailles; it was understood by all participants to be one of several preliminary conferences before the actual peace conference, and was devoted primarily to concrete problems arising out of Germany's unconditional surrender. One of the most inveterate errors associated with this basic misconception of Potsdam is the assertion that Article IX of the Protocol finally settled Poland's post-war western frontier at the Oder-Neisse. Actually, the language itself of the article precludes any such interpretation, IXb providing in relevant part, 'The three heads of government reaffirm their opinion that the final delimitation of the western frontier of Poland should await the peace settlement.' It is of especial significance that here the Allies used the word 'delimitation' and not 'demarcation', thus indicating that the tentative frontier could be revised in any direction. The line still had to be 'delimited', i.e. defined.[12] Consequently, there was no cession of territory pursuant to this article and de jure Poland was not entitled to exercise sovereignty.

As indicated above, the reason for this awkward postponement of the final frontier settlement was quite simply that a deadlock developed. The Western Allies, especially Truman, did not want to be bogged down at the Conference over this relatively unimportant point in a long agenda of more important matters. At Potsdam – like five months before at Yalta – the Western Allies would have consented to the cession to Poland of the southern half of East Prussia, the Free City of Danzig, the eastern tip of Pomerania and the province of Upper Silesia. This territory, although smaller than the Polish territory annexed by the Soviet Union east of the Curzon Line, was far more valuable due to rich mineral resources, developed industries and fertile agricultural lands. If Poland and the Soviet Union had been satisfied with this settlement, the Western Allies would have given their approval and a firm commitment would have followed. But Poland insisted on more spoils. As Churchill observed at Potsdam, 'Poland deserved compensation for the land east of the Curzon Line which she was going to lose to Russia, but she was now claiming more than she had given up.'[13] In spite of this reluctance, it is even possible that the Western Allies might have gone as far as consenting to a frontier on the Oder – just in order to get the issue out of the way. The Poles and the Soviets, however, demanded additional German lands west of the Oder as far as the western Neisse River. This was out of the question. Churchill was even prepared to risk a break with the Soviets over the western Neisse,[14] for he feared that once provisional administration was given to Poland over these territories it would prove too difficult to regain any agricultural lands for post-war Germany, which had twice the population density of Poland and simply could not be allowed to develop into a permanent slum. Obviously, an overcrowded and starving Germany could easily become a danger to the peace of Europe. Churchill therefore advised Truman to take a strong stand, which was in fact taken through the ninth plenary session at Potsdam on 25 July 1945. After this session Churchill returned to Great Britain to await the results of the British elections, which quite unexpectedly voted the Labour Party in and Churchill out. Had Churchill returned to Potsdam after the British elections it is probable that the western Neisse would have been rejected altogether, even as a provisional line. The new team of Attlee and Bevin, however, lacked the experience and stamina to stand up to Stalin, while Truman, weary of the troublesome frontier question, decided to consent to provisional Polish administration over the area, which in any event was already in their hands. In the eleventh plenary session on 31 July 1945, the question was so settled. Yet, although the Western Allies bent, they did not break. Truman expressly stated that the cession of territory was a matter for the peace treaty.[15] Secretary of State Byrnes summed up that the three Powers would agree to the administration *in the interim* by Poland in order that there would be no further dispute between them in regard to the administration of the area by the Polish provisional government, but that all understood that no cession of territory was thereby effected.[16] The record does not reveal that either Stalin or Molotov challenged this statement. Thus, clearly, no commitment on the Polish western frontier was made – a deliberate avoidance which was further obviated by the express promise given by the Western Allies (Article VI) that they would support the Soviet claim to Königsberg in the peace conference.

'In the light of this history', Secretary of State James Byrnes wrote, 'it is difficult to credit with good faith any person who asserts that Poland's western frontier was fixed by the conferees, or that there was a promise that it would be established at some particular place.'[17]

Upon returning to the United States on 9 August 1945, Truman delivered a broadcasted speech to the nation in which he reported on the more important aspects of the Potsdam Conference. With respect to Germany's frontiers he said that the Polish provisional government of national unity had agreed, as well as the Big Three,[18]

> that the final determination of the borders could not be accomplished at Berlin, but must await the peace settlement. However, a considerable portion of what was the Russian zone of occupation in Germany was turned over to Poland at the Berlin Conference for *administrative purposes until the final determination of the peace settlement* [emphasis added].

President Truman also said:[19]

> The territory the Poles are to administer will enable Poland better to support its population. It will provide a short and more easily defensible frontier between Poland and Germany. Settled by Poles, it will provide a more homogeneous nation.

The latter statement has been frequently quoted out of context[20] to imply that Truman considered the Oder-Neisse frontier to be final, in spite of the fact that in the very same speech he had just finished saying that he did not. Obviously, Truman's statement does not mean that all of the territory the Poles were to administer would in the end become theirs, although according to Western recommendations probably half of it would. In any event, it is not reasonable to think that in a summary to the nation President Truman would go into the refinements of a frontier agreement that had not coagulated yet. To suggest, as has been suggested by Polish and Russian scholars, that Truman's statement has the 'character of authoritative interpretation'[21] is ridiculous. Truman's position at Potsdam was much too clear for anyone to seek an 'authoritative interpretation' in a presidential message to the American people who knew little and cared even less about the problems of the German-Polish frontier. In his *Memoirs*, which read almost like minutes and in fact follow very closely the official American protocols of the Potsdam Conference,

Truman recalls, 'We had agreed on a compromise on the frontiers of Poland, which was the best we were able to get, but we had accepted it only subject to a final determination by the peace treaty.'[22]

Compelling proof of the fact that the Soviet Union and Poland well understood that the territorial settlements at Potsdam were only provisional is given in the Soviet-Polish Treaty of 16 August 1945 concerning their tentative frontier across German East Prussia, the final settlement of which was expressly postponed until the peace treaty.[23] Indeed, if Poland's frontiers had been no longer subject to revision after the Potsdam Conference, this provision in the Soviet-Polish Treaty would have been entirely superfluous.

THE WESTERN ALLIES AND POST-POTSDAM DEVELOPMENTS

Winston Churchill, the loser in the British elections, made his first full-length speech as Opposition leader in the House of Commons on 16 August 1945. On the question of Poland's western frontier he reaffirmed the position of the British government and continued:[24]

> I must put on record my own opinion that the *provisional* Western frontier agreed upon for Poland . . . comprising as it does one quarter of the arable land of all Germans, is not a good augury for the future . . . [emphasis added].

Many sceptical authors, particularly Polish authors, have attempted to disqualify Churchill's statements as opposition leader as mere politicking.[25] This charge does not stand rigorous historical analysis, for the record shows that Churchill's agreement to compensate Poland at the expense of Germany was always tempered by his demand that such compensation be proportioned to the Polish loss and to the capability of the Germans to receive any transferences from the areas in question.[26] Hardly three weeks before his controversial speech of 16 August 1945, Churchill had said basically the same thing to the Polish delegation at Potsdam. In the afternoon of 24 July the representatives of the Polish provisional government, headed by Prime Minister Bierut, a Stalin protégé, had paid a visit on Churchill, primarily in order to support the Polish claim to the Oder-Neisse territories. Churchill began by reminding them that Great Britain had entered the war on account of Poland and always had shown sympathy for Poland's welfare. On the other hand, Churchill advised Bierut that Poland's territorial demands were excessive in the eyes of the Western Allies and that these demands would deprive Germany of her best agricultural lands and of substantial mineral resources. The result would be that Poland would have the food and the fuel of the Germans while the American and British Occupation Authorities would have the additional burden of filling the mouths and the hearths of 9 million Germans from the areas taken over by Poland.[27] Bierut replied that only $1\frac{1}{2}$ million Germans would have to be shifted, since the rest had either fled or been killed.[28] Furthermore,[29]

> most of the inhabitants of the areas the Poles claimed, especially Silesia, were really Poles, though attempts had been made to Germanise them. These territories were historically Polish, and East Prussia still had a large Polish population in the Masurians.

In the face of such contorted arguments Churchill did not pursue the question of the frontier and moved on to the equally thorny question of free elections in Poland.

In the morning of 25 July Churchill had a second talk with Bierut, in which he emphasized that the frontier question was entangled with the problems of reparations and supply. He unambiguously told Bierut that Poland was asking too much and that Great Britain and the Americans would oppose these demands. Churchill observed in his memoirs: 'My appeal came to nothing. The world has yet to measure the "serious consequences" which I forecast.'[30] Nor was Churchill's position on the Oder-Neisse frontier unique to him or to the British Conservative Party. Indeed, the Labour Party, which came to power after the ninth session of the Potsdam Conference, had no greater sympathy for the Soviet-Polish *fait accompli*. On 10 October 1945 Foreign Minister Ernest Bevin laid bare the policy of his party with respect to the Oder-Neisse Line:[31]

> His Majesty's Government are in no way committed to support the existing provisional arrangements at the Peace Conference . . . the policies followed by the Polish authorities in the territories now placed under their temporary administration will certainly influence the attitude which

His Majesty's Government will adopt in any eventual
discussion of a final territorial settlement in these
regions.

This was not party-politicking. It was a clear statement of the fact
that Great Britain, regardless which party, would finalize Poland's
western frontier only under certain conditions.

Yet, the chances for democracy in Poland were steadily decreasing as the Communist Poles with the help of the Soviet occupants
denied freedom of the Press to the opposition parties, falsified
the results of the referendum of 30 June 1946 and later arrested or
murdered many members of the democratic opposition.[32]

Other events in Poland shocked British public opinion, such
as the pogrom that took place in Kielce in south-eastern Poland
on 4 July 1946. This violent anti-Jewish disturbance claimed the
lives of forty Jews who were thought by the Polish crowd to have
engaged in ritual murder of Polish children.[33] Britain's relations
with the Polish government cooled accordingly.

On 22 October 1946 Foreign Minister Bevin repeated the well-
known British position that the Oder-Neisse frontier was not
final and that recognition depended on many factors that had not
been fulfilled. In his address before the House of Commons he
stated:[34]

As regards the Polish frontier, I will not try to conceal the
fact that it was with the greatest reluctance that we agreed
at Potsdam to the vast changes upon which our Russian
Allies insisted. . . . Our own assent to the provisional
arrangements at Potsdam was given in return for various
assurances made by the provisional Polish Government, to
the effect that they would hold free and unfettered elections
as soon as possible . . . We see no reason why we should
finally ratify the cession of this vast territory to Poland,
without being satisfied that those assurances have been fully
carried out. We should also wish to be assured that the
Poles were able to develop this territory so that the economic
resources were properly used, and that it did not become a
wilderness from which the Germans had been excluded, but
which the Poles were unable to populate.

Similarly, the American Secretary of State James J. Byrnes found
it necessary to reaffirm the American position on Poland, rejecting

the Soviet claim that Poland's western frontiers had been settled at the Potsdam Conference. In his controversial Stuttgart speech of 6 September 1946, he said:[35]

> As a result of the agreement at Yalta, Poland ceded to the Soviet Union territory East of the Curzon Line. Because of this, Poland asked for revision of her northern and western frontiers. The United States will support a revision of these frontiers in Poland's favour. However, the extent of the area to be ceded to Poland must be determined when the final settlement is agreed upon.

With respect to this 'final settlement' Sumner Welles, United States Under Secretary of State, wrote in the same year:[36]

> The general line of the Oder has been tentatively agreed upon by the four major powers as Germany's new eastern frontier . . . If the peace makes this tentative decision a final one, they will perpetrate an injustice and a social and economic blunder which will inevitably make for lasting friction and for European insecurity. . . . Much of the territory lying between the Oder and the western boundary of the former Polish Corridor is rich farm land. A portion of it at least should be available for German food supplies as well as for German homes. The new German frontier with Poland, if drawn with just regard for the economic needs of the German people, would run considerably to the east of the Oder Line.

This was the situation in November–December 1946 when the Council of Foreign Ministers met in New York to discuss the German peace settlement. In order to determine what the new frontiers of Germany should be, the Council decided to ask the views of the member governments of the United Nations that had participated with their armed forces in the common struggle against the Axis.[37] Predictably, the countries of Eastern Europe, which had already fallen into the Soviet sphere, all recommended settlement upon the Oder-Neisse Line as desired by the Soviet Union and the Soviet-dominated Polish government.[38]

The Belgian and Dutch representatives stated their view that no peace would endure unless it included partial restoration of the

German territories placed under Polish administration or in the alternative 'some arrangement whereby this area and its output would be available for Germany's over-population and food requirements.'[39]

The South African government explicitly called for revision of the *de facto* Polish-German frontier, opposing 'any attempt to block off large, specifically German, homelands'.[40] On the other hand, it conceded that 'a moderate readjustment of boundaries in favour of Poland should be feasible.'[41]

The government of Canada, while recommending that large numbers of Germans should not be allowed to remain outside Germany's future frontiers, observed that 'extensive movements of population which are made on political grounds without reference to economic and social conditions have grave disadvantages and may create serious dangers.'[42]

The government of Australia proposed that the fixing of Germany's frontiers 'should be based on the Atlantic Charter and on the Charter of the United Nations, taking into account, however, that certain claims made on grounds of security may be of paramount importance.'[43]

Since the Atlantic Charter provided for 'no territorial changes that do not accord with the freely expressed wishes of the peoples concerned' and the United Nations Charter specifically adhered to the principle of the self-determination of peoples (Articles 1 and 55), it would appear that at least in the view of the Australian government, the millions of Germans already expelled from the territories east of the Oder-Neisse and the millions still to be expelled in 1947 and 1948 should have been consulted. On the other hand, Article 107 of the United Nations Charter had been expressly adopted to give the victorious Allies a free hand in dealing with the Germans. Neither the Atlantic Charter nor the self-determination provisions of the United Nations Charter were seen by most of the members of the United Nations as obstacles to a hard settlement with Germany.

Thus, none of the governments consulted recommended a *restitutio in integrum* of the territories east of the Oder-Neisse to Germany. All seemed to agree that part of these territories should be permanently detached from Germany and given to Poland. Some governments, however, declined to formulate an opinion on this question, presumably because the issue was irrelevant to them.

51 *Above* Berlin airlift (US Army Photograph)

52 *Below* The 'raisin bombers', 1948, broke the Soviet blockade
(Bundespresseamt)

53 Robert Murphy and the first post-war Chancellor of West Germany, Konrad Adenauer, in Bonn, 1955 (Bundespresseamt)

54 President Kennedy at the Berlin Wall, 1963 (Bundespresseamt)

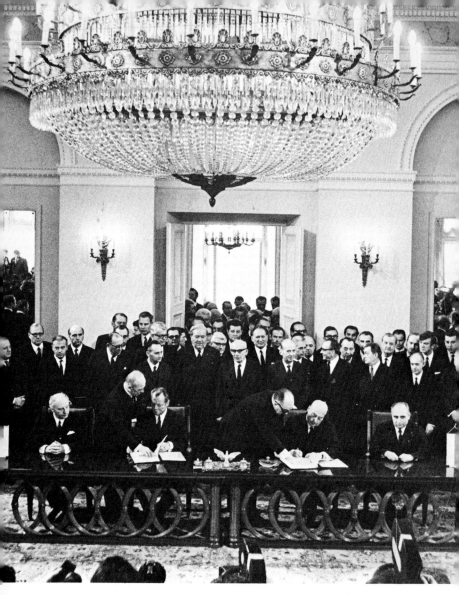

55 *Above Ostpolitik* in action: Chancellor Willy Brandt and Polish Party Leader Gomulka, sign the Treaty of Warsaw on 7 December 1970 (Bundespresseamt)

56 *Above* Dr Herbert Czaja, Member of the West German Parliament and President of the Bund der Vertriebenen, speaks at a meeting of expellees in Bonn, 1972 (Mukker)

57 Annual meeting of the Sudeten Germans in Nuremberg, 1975, attended by an estimated 250,000 Sudetendeutsche and their children (dpa)

58 *Left* German immigrants
from Upper Silesia arriving
at reception centre in
Friedland, near Göttingen, 19
(Schmidt)

59 *Below* The Charter of the
Expellees of August 1950
was reaffirmed in 1975 (Bohn)

60 *Above* President Gerald Ford with Chancellor Helmut Schmidt, 1975 (Bundespresseamt)

61 *Below* Chancellor Schmidt with Polish Party Leader Gierek, 1975 (Bundespresseamt)

62 Chancellor Schmidt at the Helsinki Conference speaking with GDR Party
Leader Honnecker (Bundespresseamt)

THE MOSCOW CONFERENCE OF THE COUNCIL OF FOREIGN MINISTERS

The German peace settlement, of course, was not a matter of irrelevance to Great Britain and the United States. Conscious of the problems of over-population and food scarcity in Germany, Secretary of State Marshall went to the Moscow Conference of the Council of Foreign Ministers in March 1947 prepared to fight for a boundary commission which would draw a more reasonable frontier between Germany and Poland, a frontier which might reduce irredentist sentiment to a minimum and promise to be lasting. Secretary Marshall emphatically rejected Molotov's contention that a decision regarding the western frontier of Poland had been taken at Potsdam, and quoted the language of Article IX of the protocol that had tabled the matter until the peace conference. He reaffirmed that 'Poland is justly entitled to compensation for her war losses and the United States wishes to honor this obligation.' But he also observed 'we must bear in mind that much of the territory now under Polish administration has long been German and contains agricultural resources of vital importance to the German and European economy.'[44]

British Foreign Minister Bevin made more concrete proposals with respect to a revision of the Oder-Neisse Line. Basing his argument on empirical observation of hunger in West Germany, where in the English zone the population was gradually starving upon rations of 1,042 calories per day,[45] Bevin demanded the return of agricultural lands, especially Pomerania and the rich Silesian soil between the Lusatian and Glatzer Neisse Rivers.[46]

Molotov categorically rejected these proposals, making the specious argument that the frontier drawn at Potsdam (Article IX) logically had to be final because the Allies had consented to the expulsion of the Germans from these areas pursuant to Article XIII.[47]

This is, in fact, a rather plausible argument for persons unfamiliar with the history of Article XIII. It has been repeated by numerous Polish[48] scholars and found an echo even in the United States,[49] where unfamiliarity with the Potsdam record is really not excusable. Indeed, if the Great Powers had ordered Poland to expel all the Germans from the territories east of the Oder and Lusatian Neisse, then it would have been rather preposterous for the Western Allies to maintain two years later that the expulsions had only been meant to be 'provisional' and that the frontier should be redrawn permitting the expelled Germans to return. Had it been so, the Soviet-Polish argument would have had some validity. The record, however, reveals an entirely different situation. The Western Powers never 'ordered' Poland to expel the Germans, but had found themselves at Potsdam confronted by a wholly chaotic situation which compelled them to take immediate action with respect to millions of Germans who were already being expelled by the Poles and the Czechs. Short of military intervention there was no practical way of stopping these expulsions, and Great Britain and the United States hesitated to fight their Eastern Allies over the fate of the vanquished Germans. A truce was struck, which was the best that could be obtained in the summer of 1945. The Western Allies thus devised a formula, Article XIII, to bring some order into the chaos that the expulsions were causing in all of Germany, including their occupation zones. First, they stated that transfers should be carried out in an 'orderly and humane manner'. Second, they said that transfers should be suspended for the time being so as to give the Allied Control Council time to prepare for the reception of the expellees.

In this sense it is a very questionable endeavour to read Articles IX and XIII as an 'organic entity'. Article IX drew provisional frontiers. Article XIII was an emergency measure to deal with an avalanche of human misery. The two articles were not conceived together and were not meant to be read together.

ARTICLE XIII IN THE LIGHT OF ARTICLE IX: PROBLEMS OF INTERPRETATION

At this point it would not be unprofitable to note that the edge of Article XIII cuts both ways. If Article XIII were indeed inseparable from Article IX, then the Allies should have drafted Article XIII more carefully, because Article XIII only authorized expulsions from 'Poland' and not from 'Poland including the German territories placed under provisional Polish administration pursuant to Article IX'. In so far as 'Poland' was nowhere defined in the Potsdam Agreement and the settlement of its western frontier was postponed until the peace treaty, then, according to traditional principles of interpretation, 'Poland' as used in Article XIII could only mean Poland *without* the German territories east of the Oder-Neisse, over which Poland was formally exercising only provisional administration and not full sovereignty, which it could only gain by virtue of a peace treaty.

Therefore, Molotov's mixing of Article XIII with Article IX was a very dangerous thing for his own legal argument, because 'Article XIII Poland' could not be greater than 'Article IX Poland', i.e. Poland without sovereignty over the German provinces. In this sense, as German jurists have not failed to point out, any expulsions from East Prussia, Pomerania, East Brandenburg and Silesia were necessarily illegal, since Article XIII of the Potsdam Protocol had not expressly authorized transfers out of these territories. Thus, at best Molotov could have complained that Article XIII was poorly drafted, but in the form in which it was adopted it did not give aid and comfort to his proposition.

The ambiguity of the text of Article XIII did, of course, come to the attention of American jurists and politicians. General Lucius Clay, for instance, who had participated in the Potsdam Conference, did not think that it applied to the Germans of the territories east of the Oder-Neisse.[50] On the other hand, in October of 1945 Secretary of State Byrnes instructed the United States Political Adviser for Germany, Robert Murphy, that Article XIII of the Potsdam Protocol should be interpreted as applying both to Poland and to the Oder-Neisse territories, but emphasized at the same time that Article XIII 'is not intended to prejudice agreement at Potsdam that final delimitation of Poland's western frontier should await peace settlement'.[51]

Arthur Lane, the American Ambassador to Poland 1945–7, was also confused as to the precise meaning and function of Article XIII and, presumably under the influence of Polish diplomats, had commenced to construe Article IX in connection with his version of Article XIII. On 9 May 1947, shortly after Lane's resignation as Ambassador, Secretary of State Marshall elucidated the problem in a conversation with him in Washington:[52]

> The President had been obliged to accept at Potsdam an arrangement that was distasteful to him. The Russians had the territory at the time. The Russians had deliberately twisted the meaning of the agreement arrived at, however, as the minutes and the statements of those attending the Conference clearly showed that we had not agreed to a definite frontier.

Marshall further told Lane that back in 1945 he (Lane) had been instructed to raise the question of humanitarian transfer with the Poles 'because the Poles were actually proceeding to deport the German population, but this did not mean that we had agreed to this.'[53]

THE ARGUMENT OF POLISH 'RECOVERED' TERRITORIES

Soviet reaction to American and British refusal to accept the *fait accompli* of the Oder-Neisse frontier was vehement. While still maintaining the untenable proposition that Poland's western frontier had been settled at Yalta and confirmed at Potsdam, Soviet and Polish Press organs inaugurated a genuinely pan-Slavic line of attack characterized by an inveterate appeal to ancient history. Suddenly it was no longer a question of compensating Poland for the land it lost to the Soviet Union east of the Curzon Line,[54] but a matter of securing 'old Polish lands'.

An *Izvestia* article remonstrated on Secretary of State Marshall's statement of 28 April 1947:[55]

Despite his obviously unsuccessful attempts to confuse the issue and to misrepresent the attitude of the US delegation in Moscow in favour of the revision of the Crimean decisions, Marshall's broadcast does not leave any doubts that what happened in the Council of Ministers was a test of the new US policy, which runs contrary to the interests of Poland in objecting to the transfer of old Polish lands and in favouring the Germanisation of these Polish Provinces. It was an attempt to go back on the Potsdam decisions. It is now being impressed on Poland that the new frontiers would make things difficult for the Poles, and that they would not help Poland at all. Hence, the frank suggestion to deprive Poland of her new western lands, to return them to Germany, and to eliminate in this way all future difficulties. The fact that these suggestions constitute a blatant breach of faith does not worry the originators of this scheme.

Using the same line of argument an *Izvestia* article also castigated the British Foreign Minister on 22 May 1947:[56]

Bevin tried to use the notoriously futile argument, as if the question of Poland's western frontier was an unsettled question, and as if the matter was that of some sort of 'compensation' and not of a return of old Polish lands. Here, too, we are confronted by an obvious attempt to revise the Potsdam agreement and to go back on certain pledges resulting from this agreement. The question of Poland's western frontier has been settled once and for all and is not subject to any revision.

This campaign to convince the world that Pomerania, Silesia and East Prussia were, after all, part of Poland's holy earth, intensified in the year 1947. No opportunity was wasted to propagate the pan-Slavic claim that these territories had never lost their true Polish character, even though Germans had lived there for over 700 years.

Any talk of Breslau or Stettin as old Polish cities, or for that matter of the Oder River as an old Polish boundary, should be placed in historical perspective by recalling that Kiev and Smolensk had also once been Polish. Whereas during the Slavic western migrations the westernmost Slavs occupied the former homes of the Vandals and Goths on the Vistula and Oder Rivers,[57] the subsequent Polish 'Drang nach Osten' also brought them in control of the Ukraine and Byelorussia.

The so-called 'Polish Western Territories' or 'recovered territories' had ceased being Polish for the most part during the twelfth and thirteenth centuries. These sparsely populated areas soon had German majorities living under German princes with German law and German language. By the end of the thirteenth century all of Silesia, Pomerania, the Corridor and Danzig were part of the Holy Roman Empire; East Prussia had been conquered and settled by the Teutonic Knights. In the ensuing six centuries Silesia and Pomerania were uninterruptedly German (or Austrian or Swedish) while the Corridor was temporarily taken back by Poland and for a period the Teutonic Knights became vassals of the Polish crown. All these Polish gains, principally in the fifteenth century, when Poland was a vigorous and aggressive European Power, were nullified by a series of unsuccessful wars in the eighteenth century which wiped Poland off the map. Yet, all German gains at the expense of Poland during the eighteenth century were restored to Poland in 1919 at the Treaty of Versailles, which drew Poland's western frontier at the old German boundary of the period before the first Polish partition of 1772, although thereby over 2 million Germans were left as a minority under Polish rule. By contrast, the Soviet Union at Versailles and later at Potsdam was even allowed to improve on what the tsars had taken away from Poland in the eighteenth century. Not only did the Soviet Union keep the lands which Catherine the Great had robbed Poland of in the partitions of 1772, 1793 and 1795, but it was permitted to add Lvov (Lemberg) and Galicia, which, largely Polish, had belonged to the Austrian Monarchy until the First World War.

Old Polish lands? Old Polish cities? The history of Polish territorial expansion shows that Polish conquerors had not only been in the West but had also gone very far to the East. Kiev, for instance, had been Lithuanian from 1362 to 1569 and Polish from 1569 to 1654, at a time when Breslau and Stettin had long ceased to be Polish. Smolensk had also been under Polish-Lithuanian rule until 1667.[58] Why didn't the Polish provisional government raise a historical claim to these Russian cities at the end of the Second World War? The hapless government was not even able to secure its own Lvov and Wilno! Instead, Polish scholars were sent to the world to propagate the word that Silesia and Pomerania, Breslau and Stettin were actually Poland's cradle. This message was even taken to universities in the United States and Great Britain, where it was received with considerable resistance.

On 19 April 1947 *The Economist* commented in an editorial:[59]

> The exhibition of Poland's western territories being held at the School of Slavonic Studies and opened by a member of its Council, is part of an official Polish attempt to deny the plain fact that the Oder-Neisse frontier was given to Poland only as a compensation for the Soviet annexation of the eastern provinces and to put across entirely untenable ethnic claims. The Polish Government has the right to conduct any publicity it pleases in this country through its own agencies, but it is extremely undesirable that academic institutions here should be identified with this kind of propaganda, which can only serve to discredit them as homes of serious and disinterested study.

On 3 May 1947 *The Economist* observed in an editorial entitled '1157 and all that':[60]

There must be some statute of limitations applicable to claims arising out of past conquests and migrations; ethnographically, it is only the very recent past which can reasonably be taken into account. The Poles would be well advised in their own interest to drop the talk about old medieval Slav Szczecin (still Stettin to most English-speaking people) and rest their case, such as it is, on the deal which was actually made in political bargaining among the Great Powers in 1945, and which was as innocent of ethnography as it was of historic, or any other sort, of justice. It would be best of all if they would make some material concessions on the lines of Mr. Marshall's proposals. . . .

Of course, the Poles were not free to make any concessions on the lines of the proposals made by Secretary Marshall and Foreign Minister Bevin at the Moscow Conference. Because of this, the failure of the next meeting of the Council of Foreign Ministers was thoroughly predictable. At the London meeting in November and December 1947, Secretary Marshall again proposed that there be created a boundary commission to study all frontier problems, including the Saar and Upper Silesian questions.

Again, Molotov blocked every move by Marshall and the Conference proved to be a complete fiasco. In a statement broadcast by Secretary Marshall on 19 December 1947, he summarized:[61]

On this vital matter of frontiers, three delegations agreed to the establishment of a frontier commission or commissions to make an expert study of any proposed changes from the prewar frontiers. Mr. Molotov refused to agree. It was impossible for me to reconcile his urgent insistence upon the necessity of expediting the preparation for a German treaty with his categoric refusal to agree to the appointment of boundary commissions, which three delegations considered to be an absolutely essential first step in any serious preparation for a future German peace settlement.

The Soviet bloc, however, had clearly thrown the gauntlet down before the Western Powers. They assembled a rival Foreign Minister Conference which met at Warsaw. On 24 June 1948 the Foreign Ministers of the USSR, Albania, Bulgaria,

Czechoslovakia, Yugoslavia, Poland, Romania and Hungary made a declaration blaming the West for the failure of the London Conference and stating in part:[62]

> The policy of the occupying powers in the Western zones of Germany encourages the German revisionist elements. The latter are campaigning against the agreements concluded at the Yalta and Potsdam conferences regarding the democratic reconstruction and demilitarization of Germany and her obligation to compensate for damages caused by German aggression, and against the decisions regarding the settlement of German populations, whom they are endeavouring to utilize for purposes hostile to neighbouring states.
> In particular, the German revisionist elements are campaigning against the Polish-German frontier on the Oder and the Western Neisse, which is an inviolable frontier – a frontier of peace.

After this declaration it was unequivocal that the Soviet Union would not budge on the issue of the Oder-Neisse frontier. What Molotov plainly meant but did not say in so many words was: 'Look, we don't care a hoot about what we said at Yalta or at Potsdam. The fact is that we *have* Poland now and that we have fixed her western frontier at the Oder-Neisse. You capitalists have nothing to say about this, and it is time that you realized it.'

Thus, for the Western Allies only the question of recognition or non-recognition of the Oder-Neisse remained open.

FROM 1948 TO THE PRESENT

Two decades of cold war followed during which recognition of the patently illegal frontier was out of the question. In a sense, this cold war manifestation was not unlike a poker player's refusal to play with a partner who has cheated. Everyone remembers that back in 1938 Hitler cheated at Munich and that after this painful experience no one favoured appeasing him any more. With Stalin it was somewhat different, because he had been a comrade at arms. But after Stalin so flagrantly abused the good will of his allies at Yalta and at Potsdam, no one wanted to deal with him either. Of course, no one wanted another hot war in 1945 or in 1946 or in 1947! For this reason, a 'cold war' developed, and while no one accepted the legal finality of the Oder-Neisse frontier – or for that matter of the Russian annexation of Estonia, Latvia and Lithuania – no one dared do anything about it.

In the early years of the cold war the Western Powers concentrated on salvaging those countries in Europe that had not already been subjugated by the Soviet Union. It soon became obvious that Germany would be indispensable to any defence system. Accordingly, the Western zones were allowed to merge into the Federal Republic of Germany and the Western Powers gave their moral and political support to the German wish for reunification and for a peace treaty that would effect a reasonable delimitation of Germany's eastern boundary. In the 'Convention on Relations Between the Three Powers and the Federal Republic of Germany' signed in Paris on 26 May 1952; this commitment was written into Article 7:[63]

> 1. The Three Powers and the Federal Republic are agreed
> that an essential aim of their common policy is a peace
> settlement for the whole of Germany, freely negotiated
> between Germany and her former enemies, which should lay
> the foundation for a lasting peace. They further agree that the
> final determination of the boundaries of Germany must await
> such a settlement. . . .

The political power constellation in Europe, however, has not favoured a settlement of the German question in conformity with the wishes of the Western Powers. Meanwhile, other trouble spots in the world have shifted the attention of the Western Powers away from the relatively quiescent German frontier and reunification problem. Korea, Vietnam, Algeria and the Middle East are but a few of the acute crisis areas that have relegated the solution of the German problem to a low priority in the eyes of the Western Powers. The result has been that the Federal Republic of Germany has had to shape a new and independent foreign policy *vis-a-vis* her neighbours in the East.

In an attempt to get out of the apparent dead-end of cold war politics, Chancellor Brandt decided to negotiate a new *modus vivendi* with Poland, Czechoslovakia and the Soviet Union. Détente with the Soviet bloc would be given a chance, even though the price was the political recognition of the Oder-Neisse frontier and of the partition of Germany. Of course, the Federal Republic of Germany did not possess the legal competence to make final determinations in these areas, but the Western Powers generally welcomed Brandt's *Ostpolitik* as a means of reducing world tensions;[64] moreover, *Ostpolitik* did not infringe upon Allied rights. In a report to the Congress entitled 'U.S. Policy for the 1970's: Building for Peace', President Nixon reaffirmed the traditional American position, stating further that 'it is clearly established that allied responsibilities and rights are not affected by the terms' of the recently concluded treaties between the Federal Republic of Germany and the USSR and between the Federal Republic and Poland.[65]

The most recent development on the question of the German-Polish frontier was the signing on 1 August 1975 of the Helsinki Declaration, which closed the European Conference on Security and Co-operation. This Declaration, which was signed by thirty-five nations including the Federal Republic of Germany, Poland, the United States and the Soviet Union, provides in part: 'The participating states regard as inviolable all one anothers' frontiers as well as the frontiers of all states in Europe and therefore they refrain now and in the future from assaulting these frontiers.'[66] This declaration is but a repetition of prior policy and wholly consistent with the goals of the Federal Republic of Germany. Indeed, if there is to be any revision of the Oder-Neisse frontier, everyone agrees that it can be achieved solely through peaceful means. To provide for this possibility the signatories of the Helsinki Declaration set forth: 'They consider that their frontiers can be changed, in accordance with international law, by peaceful means and by agreement.'[67] On this basis, it remains entirely legitimate for the Western Democracies to support the Federal Republic's bid for the reunification of Germany and for an eventual revision of the Oder-Neisse frontier in conformity with the principle of self-determination. Whether the Western Democracies should give a higher priority to the realization of these goals at the present time is, of course, a separate question. In any case, the governments of the United States, Great Britain and France have retained their rights with respect to a German peace treaty, which is the only legal and final way of settling the question of Germany's frontiers.

The Oder-Neisse controversy illustrates the fact that some provisional territorial arrangements made at the conclusion of the Second World War have attained a degree of permanence never contemplated at the Potsdam Conference. As shown in this chapter, this development constitutes a usurpation that might some day endanger the peace of the world. And although usurpation is certainly no *novum* in European politics, there is also ample precedent for the more enlightened policy of voluntarily terminating the occupation of foreign territories when doing so serves the cause of peace and upholds the right of self-determination as embodied in the United Nations Charter. Thus, the post-war quasi-annexation of the German Saar was terminated by France in 1955 when this territory was allowed, by plebiscite, to return to Germany and become part of the Federal Republic.[68] Similarly, the provisional American administration of Okinawa ended in 1972 when the United States returned this and other islands to Japan.[69] The provisional Polish administration of the German provinces east of the Oder-Neisse, however, will probably continue indefinitely, in spite of the Potsdam Agreement and notwithstanding the lack of formal recognition by the Western Powers. It remains, as it was in 1945, a matter of power politics.

CHAPTER TEN

TOWARDS THE FUTURE

The provisions of the Helsinki declaration represent
political as well as moral, not legal, commitments. U.S. policy
supports . . . the aspirations for freedom and national
independence of peoples everywhere. The results of this
European Security Conference will be a step in that
direction. The outcome of this Helsinki Conference remains
to be tested; but whether it is a long stride or a short step,
it is at least a forward step for freedom.

President Ford on 26 July 1975. Department of State,
Bulletin, vol. 73, 1 September 1975, p. 289.

Since the end of the Second World War Europe and the Europeans
have changed in many ways. A new generation has been born
and with it new hopes and goals have replaced the unfulfilled
aspirations of the war generation. Still, old problems have been
handed down, for which there are no satisfactory solutions at
present. An uneasy peace has endured for over thirty years. Will
it endure another thirty?

To the great relief of most Europeans, the so-called 'German
Problem' has become relatively quiescent; few, however, would
say that it has been solved in a way that promises permanence and
stability. Germany's division reflects the division of Europe.
The iron curtain that went down after the war has not been
overcome. No peace treaty formally ending the war with Germany
has been signed and none will be signed in the foreseeable future.
On the other hand, some recent developments in Europe and in
the world indicate that the *status quo* is congealing and that the
danger of armed confrontation has declined. The Federal Republic
of Germany and the German Democratic Republic have been
admitted to membership in the United Nations and have thereby
lost the last vestiges of their former 'enemy' status,[1] while at the
same time acquiring a measure of international recognition as

separate and sovereign States. Reunification, however, remains very much a cardinal goal of the Federal Republic,[2] even if it appears unlikely that it will be achieved in the near future. Surely it cannot be said that reunification is entirely beyond the limits of possibility. The world recently witnessed the reunification of another divided country, Vietnam, achieved through the military subjugation of one half by the other. The price was over 1 million war casualties, the devastation of the country and a marked decline in the political and civil liberties of the subjugated half.[3] Of course, this kind of violent reunification is not being contemplated by either German State. If achieved at all, it will be by a slow process of peaceful negotiations. Thus, for the time being, co-existence will continue, because there are no viable alternatives.

THE CONFERENCE ON SECURITY AND CO-OPERATION IN EUROPE

The principle of co-existence in Europe was recently strengthened by the Conference on Security and Co-operation in Europe (CSCE), which opened at Helsinki on 3 July 1973 and continued at Geneva from 18 September 1973 to 21 July 1975.[4] The conference was concluded at Helsinki on 1 August 1975, by the High Representatives of the United States, Great Britain, France, the Soviet Union and thirty-one other nations. Some observers have already called it a second Potsdam and even an 'ersatz' peace settlement; actually, it fell far short of being either. Still, the final protocol signed at Helsinki does represent a hard-sought general agreement to commit the nations involved 'to make détente a continuing and an increasingly viable and comprehensive process, universal in scope. . . .'[5] But what is the meaning of détente? The Soviet Union's insistence on the slogan-like formula of the 'irreversibility of détente'[6] was to prove unacceptable to the Western delegations, which regarded and regard the process of détente as one requiring practical manifestations and not mere slogans. As President Ford said on 1 August 1975 in his address at Helsinki:[7]

> Peace is not a piece of paper . . . détente is an evolutionary
> process, not a static condition . . . there must be an
> acceptance of mutual obligation. Détente, as I have often
> said, must be a two-way street. Tensions cannot be eased by

one side alone. Both sides must want détente and work to achieve it. Both sides must benefit from it.

What relevance does the Helsinki Declaration have for the German Problem and in particular for the hopes of millions of German expellees and their children? Although lacking the finality of a peace treaty, the recommendations of this conference may be said to ratify the *status quo* in Europe, including the partition of Germany and the present location of the German-Polish and German-Czechoslovak frontiers. Thus, the prospects of a policy aimed at the reunification of Germany or at the revision of the Oder-Neisse frontier have been indubitably diminished.

In Chapter 9 of this study certain passages of 'Basket 1' (political principles of security) of the Helsinki Declaration were quoted, including the provision that 'the participating states regard as inviolable all one another's frontiers as well as the frontiers of all states in Europe and therefore they refrain now and in the future from assaulting these frontiers.'[8] Although there is nothing new in the reaffirmation of such basic principles of relations between States, a certain ambiguity does become apparent as to the precise meaning of an 'assault' upon the frontiers of another State. Does the frequently expressed desire of the Federal Republic of Germany to achieve a peaceful re-unification constitute a verbal 'assault' upon the territorial integrity of the German Democratic Republic? It is not altogether improbable that the party leaders of the GDR will press this argument in an attempt to thwart the Federal Republic's policy of keeping the reunification question internationally open. The same strategy may be followed by the governments of Czechoslovakia and Poland with respect to any statement by the Federal Republic which broaches the mere possibility of frontier revisions, even though the Helsinki Declaration expressly provided for the possibility of change by peaceful means.[9]

In any case, while not forgetting its long-term goals, the Federal Republic is fully involved in the détente process and will continue to co-operate with the democratic West in working toward the realization of short-term objectives. West German politicians recognized long ago that the solution to Germany's fundamental problems does not lie in their hands but solely in the hands of the two Super-Powers. For this reason they will continue to pursue a policy of negotiating for modest improvements in intra-German relations, equal rights for the German minorities now living under Polish, Czechoslovak, Hungarian and Romanian rule, and for the issuance of exit permits to tens of thousands of these Germans who want to emigrate to the Federal Republic to rejoin their relatives and friends.

While Basket 1 of the Helsinki Declaration basically gave the Soviet Union all it wanted in the way of confirmation of its gains in Eastern Europe, Basket 3 (co-operation in humanitarian and other fields) turned out to be more of a disappointment than a source of satisfaction for Moscow, for it produced a document containing commitments to Western civil liberties and strengthened the hopes of many Germans that the Soviet Union and the East European countries could be influenced toward a measure of relaxation in their sphere. Basket 3 provides for intensified contacts and regular meetings across borders on the basis of family ties, reunification of families by way of emigration, marriage between citizens of different states, travel for personal or professional reasons, improvement of the circulation of and access to information, co-operation and exchanges in the fields of culture, education, etc. The declaration also provides with respect to national minorities that[10]

> The participating States, recognizing the contribution that national minorities or regional cultures can make to co-operation among them in various fields of education, intend, when such minorities or cultures exist within their territory, to facilitate this contribution, taking into account the legitimate interests of their members.

But even Basket 1 contains language intended to safeguard the human rights of Europeans on both sides of the iron curtain. One paragraph provides significantly:[11]

> The participating States on whose territory national minorities exist will respect the right of persons belonging to such minorities to equality before the law, will afford them the full opportunity for the actual enjoyment of human rights and fundamental freedoms and will, in this manner, protect their legitimate interests in this sphere.

Another,[12]

> In the field of human rights and fundamental freedoms, the participating States will act in conformity with the purposes

and principles of the Charter of the United Nations and with the Universal Declaration of Human Rights.

Of particular relevance to the problem of German minorities in Eastern Europe would be, of course, Article 13 of the Universal Declaration of Human Rights, which provides that 'Everyone has the right to leave any country, including his own, and to return to his country.' But, as experience has shown, these principles of human dignity are more frequently honoured by the breach than by the observance in Eastern Europe. It was no accident that the only countries abstaining from the unanimous General Assembly Resolution of 10 December 1948 were the Soviet-bloc countries.[13] In a sense, the Helsinki declaration has now bound them to the observance of fundamental human rights in their own countries, but realistically speaking, there is little hope that a mere declaration of intent will change the pattern of totalitarian denial of human rights which has unfortunately characterized the domestic scene and in particular the minority rights policies of the Eastern European countries.

It is estimated that over 1 million Germans, *Reichsdeutsche* and *Volksdeutsche* alike, live today under Polish rule.[14] Most of these Germans live in the former German provinces east of the Oder-Neisse, where they enjoy no minority rights and are subjected to strong polonizing pressures. By affirming the inviolability of the Oder-Neisse frontier in the 1970 Warsaw Treaty and again in the Helsinki Declaration, the Federal Republic of Germany did not intend to turn its back on these Germans left behind. In the Treaty the Federal Republic gave Poland an assurance that Poland had sought since the end of the war. In exchange for this assurance the negotiators of the Federal Republic attempted to obtain the release of those Germans being held back, many of whom had close family members in the West. Poland's negotiators, however, did not let themselves be nailed down and only made general statements to the effect that Poland would permit the emigration of a large number of Germans. Yet, contrary to these representations, the number of Germans allowed to leave Poland declined every year since 1971, although according to figures of the German Red Cross there were at least 300,000 desirous of emigrating to the Federal Republic. These were being held back by Poland in expectation of exchanging them for two or three billion Marks of economic aid. A further manifestation of bad faith, amounting to a violation of the spirit if not also of the letter of Article III of the Warsaw Treaty, was the ruthless implementation of unfair employment practices and other discriminatory measures against Germans who had applied or were planning to apply for emigration permits to the Federal Republic.[15] These actions were surely not guided by the purposes and principles embodied in the Charter of the United Nations, nor were they designed to broaden co-operation and understanding between the German and Polish peoples as provided for in the Treaty. The result of these disappointments was that the Federal Republic had to negotiate a new treaty with Poland, signed in October 1975, and ratified by the German parliament in March 1976, whereby 2·3 billion Marks of economic aid would be made available to Poland in exchange for the release of 120,000 Germans. Presumably, a new treaty will have to be negotiated over the remaining 180,000 who still desire to emigrate out of Poland.

Similar difficulties are being endured today by German minorities living in other East European countries.[16] To a greater or lesser extent, these Germans have very limited enjoyment of minority rights and can rarely obtain the alternatively strived-for exit visa. Thus, they are condemned to the gradual loss of their cultural heritage.

If this pattern of violations of human rights continues, diplomatic protests could be lodged based upon the language of the Helsinki declaration, and when the Conference reconvenes at the ambassadorial level in Belgrade in 1977 (if it ever does), all parties guilty of violations should be called to account.

THE BERLIN QUESTION AND DETENTE

For the average non-German, Berlin remains the symbol of the so-called 'German-Problem'. Everyone remembers the erection of the Berlin Wall in 1961 and the many victims who perished there while attempting to flee to the West. Mine-fields, automatic shooting devices and marksmen of the army of the GDR have made it practically impossible for East Germans to escape to freedom. Legal emigration presents enormous difficulties except for retired senior citizens.

On 3 September 1971 the governments of the United States, the Soviet Union, Great Britain and France signed a quadripartite agreement on Berlin,[17] which reaffirmed the international status of the occupied city as well as the special relationship of East Berlin to the GDR and of West Berlin to the Federal Republic. This important agreement was followed by the *Grundvertrag* or Basic Treaty, which representatives of the Federal Republic and the GDR signed on 21 December 1972. The *Grundvertrag* was designed to normalize inter-German relations and to encourage a more humane approach to individual rights in the GDR. Unfortunately, the shootings at the Berlin Wall and along the entire length of the frontier between the GDR and the Federal Republic have not ceased.

It was recalling the history of East-West confrontations over Berlin that President Ford stated at Helsinki on 1 August 1975, how much he hoped that Berlin might provide an example of peaceful settlement in the future. He continued:[18]

> The United States regards it as a test of détente and of the principles of this Conference. We welcome the fact that, subject to Four-Power rights and responsibilities, the results of CSCE apply to Berlin, as they do throughout Europe.

It is to be hoped that the GDR will reassess its policy on the Berlin Wall and make it conform with the spirit and the letter of the Helsinki Declaration. Corpses of refugees do not speak for détente.

THE GERMAN EXPELLEES TODAY

While the government of the Federal Republic of Germany has changed its priorities with time, the German expellees have not abandoned the hope of one day recovering at least part of their lost homeland. Some people ask whether there is a danger to the peace of Europe arising out of the activities of these groups in the Federal Republic of Germany? Thirty years after the expulsion from their homelands east of the Oder-Neisse and in the Sudetenland, these millions and their children remain conscious of their origin and frequently meet for cultural and political events. In the year 1975 the fairs of the East Prussians, Pomeranians, Silesians and Sudeten Germans, to name but a few, were attended by several hundred thousand expellees. Their leaders spoke of a right to the homeland and of maintaining their legal claim alive. Their language was clearly revisionist, but their commitment to exclusively peaceful means was equally emphasized. Twenty-five years after the issuance of the Charter of the Expellees in Stuttgart in 1950,[19] the same principles of peaceful change were reaffirmed in 1975.

At this point it would not be unprofitable to call attention to the memorable speech given by Albert Schweitzer in Oslo on 4 November 1954 upon receiving the Nobel Peace Prize. It was a strong appeal to the conscience of mankind to repudiate the enormity of the crime of mass expulsions:[20]

> The most grievous violation of the right based on historical evolution and of any human right in general is to deprive populations of their right to occupy the country where they live by compelling them to settle elsewhere. The fact that the victorious powers decided at the end of World War II to impose this fate on hundreds of thousands of human beings and, what is more, in a most cruel manner, shows how little they were aware of the challenge facing them, namely, to re-establish prosperity and, as far as possible, the rule of law.

More than two decades have elapsed since Schweitzer's appeal. In this time the Federal Republic of Germany has successfully integrated nearly 11 million expellees (the GDR some 3·5 million) providing for them a new home in a liberal society, an achievement which historians in the coming decades will not fail to acknowledge. Indeed, European history would have been quite different if the German expellees like the Palestinian Arabs had turned to international terrorism to compel the return of their homeland. The Germans, however, learned an important lesson in the Second World War. After suffering civilian and military losses numbering over 7 million, post-war Germans have rightly decided against the shedding of any more blood over the location of national frontiers in Central Europe. Taking to the pen rather than to the sword, Germans are making their plea to world public opinion by producing a formidable body of literature on the legal and moral foundation of the 'right to the homeland', that same right which Albert Schweitzer had defended in his Oslo speech.

The majority of the German expellees realize, of course, that they shall never be able to go back to the lands where they were born. They also realize that the new generation of Poles growing up in East Prussia, Pomerania and Silesia, the new generation of

Czechs who now people the Sudetenland, also have a right to their new homelands. No one would propose a reverse expulsion of Poles and Czechs from the German territories which the governments of Poland and Czechoslovakia annexed at the end of the Second World War. On the other hand, it would be unreasonable to expect the German expellees simply to forget and write off what happened to them. There is hardly an expellee who did not lose a mother or a sister in the course of the expulsion. Indeed, 2 million never survived their displacement. In this sense, although the expellees have established new homes in the West and renounced any and all forms of violence to recover what was taken from them, they do at least want a measure of recognition for their not insignificant sacrifice. The more idealistic among them also hope that their experience may serve as an example, so that other peoples may be spared the tragedy of being uprooted from the homeland. But, in order for the experience of the German expellees to serve as a case study and warning against future population expulsions, the facts will have to become more generally known.

ANGLO-AMERICAN ATTITUDES

Although not officially tabu in America or in Great Britain, the facts of the German expulsion were never given adequate coverage in the Press. As a consequence, most Americans and Britons do not even know that there was an expulsion at all, much less that Western authorization of the principle of compulsory population transfers made the American and British governments accomplices in one of the most inhuman enterprises in the history of Western civilization. Admittedly, the responsibility of the Western Powers is not as great as that of the expelling States, but it was undoubtedly Anglo-American adherence to the principle of population transfers that made the catastrophe of 1945–8 possible.

Thirty years after the Second World War is not too early to reassess certain aspects of it. The Yalta and Potsdam decisions with respect to the populations of East Prussia, Pomerania, Silesia and the Sudetenland well deserve such reassessment. Of course, the draconic measures meted upon the Eastern Germans can only be understood as retribution for unspeakable Nazi crimes in the East, but this retribution was not only practised on *Parteibonzen*, but 'on women and children, the poor, the infirm',[21] indeed, on an entire population without any regard for individual guilt or innocence.

A commitment to humanism requires the repudiation of all criminal conduct, whether exhibited in aggression or in the course of indiscriminate revenge. It is up to the free peoples of the world, and in particular to the Western democracies, to preserve those values of liberal humanism for which they ostensibly stand, by truly practising those values and not merely by paying lip service to them.

What can the Western democracies do today? Obviously, they cannot undo the damage inflicted at Potsdam, but they can and should at least acknowledge the mistakes committed there and reflect upon the causes of those failures which so completely negated the principles of the Atlantic Charter, for which the war had been fought. A better understanding of these failures should help the Western democracies to make the best of today's very complex world order (or rather, disorder) and give them reason for increased vigilance with respect to the promises and commitments made at Helsinki. History will judge the Conference on Security and Co-operation in Europe, as it will judge the Potsdam Conference, by the measure of good and evil that ensues for future generations.

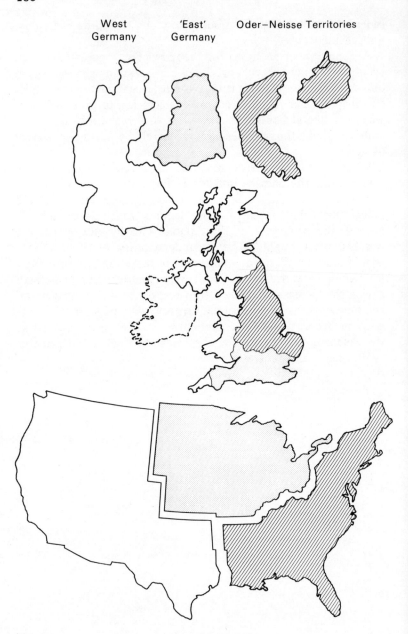

West
Germany

'East'
Germany

Oder–Neisse Territories

Map 7. The partition of Germany as applied to Great Britain and the United States

NOTES

INTRODUCTION

1 The Swiss Red Cross gives a figure of 18·1 million, or four times
the population of Switzerland in 1945. *Das Schweizerische Rote
Kreuz*, September 1949, p. 35. German statistics usually give the
figure of 17·7 million Germans in the areas of the expulsion, of
whom 1·1 million perished during the war and 2·11 millions
perished as a result of the flight from the Red Army
and subsequent expulsions. See tables in Statistisches
Bundesamt, *Die deutschen Vertreibungsverluste*, 1958, pp. 38,
45 and 46.

2 India has a population density of 434 persons per square mile,
China of 213 and the United States 58 persons per square mile.
See *Information Please Almanac*, 1973, pp. 184, 218, 686.

3 B. Oded, paper given at the Rencontre Assyriologique 1975 in
Göttingen. Compare also *Encyclopaedia Judaica*, vol. 6, pp. 1034ff.,
1971. Also F. Veale, *Advance to Barbarism*, 1968, pp. 66–67.

4 R. Billington, *Westward Expansion*, 1949, pp. 312–17. Also M.
Starkey, *The Cherokee Nation*, 1946.

5 Treaty of Lausanne, *League of Nations Treaty Series*, vol. 32,
pp. 76ff., signed on 30 January 1923.

6 E. Kulischer, *Europe on the Move*, 1948. Also Wachenheim,
'Hitler's Transfers of Population in Eastern Europe', *Foreign
Affairs*, 1942, vol. 20, pp. 705ff.

7 See V. Gollancz, *Our Threatened Values*, 1946, passim, especially
pp. 104–5.

8 The author has studied thousands of expulsion reports contained
in the Ost-Dokumente collection of the German Federal Archives
at Koblenz. The author was able to confirm a number of these
affidavits by personally interviewing the deposed expellees and
others who had undergone similar experiences.

9 Including Belgian and French prisoners of war liberated by the
Soviet Army in East Prussia and who witnessed the beginning
of the expulsions.

10 Referring to the Oder-Neisse frontier Churchill noted: 'For the
future peace of Europe here was a wrong beside which Alsace-
Lorraine and the Danzig Corridor were but trifles. One day the
Germans would want their territory back and the Poles would
not be able to stop them.' *Triumph and Tragedy*, 1953,
p. 648.

CHAPTER ONE   THE PRINCIPLE OF POPULATION TRANSFERS

1 The Germans of the Baltic States, for instance, loyally served the Tsars and even fought in the First World War in the Russian Army against Germany.

2 The principle of nationality had gained wide acceptance during the nineteenth century, when most of the Italian ethnic groups were able to join in the new Italian State, under the leadership of Cavour and Garibaldi. Similarly most of the German principalities were fused into Bismarck's Reich. Only the Slavs had not yet achieved national self-determination.

3 S. Wambaugh, *Plebiscites Since the World War*, 1933, vol. I, pp. 150–2; also Wambaugh, *Recueil des Cours*, 1927, vol. 3, pp. 199–200. Whereas in Upper-Silesia a majority vote for Germany led to partition, in the plebiscite of Sopron (Oedenburg), where a majority voted for Hungary and a minority for Austria, the entire district without partition was awarded to Hungary. The reason for the partition of Upper Silesia was that a Polish armed revolt followed the plebiscite and the League of Nations had to intervene to prevent a general Polish-German confrontation. On 19 October 1921 the League of Nations apportioned the industrial south-eastern part of Upper Silesia to Poland, including the cities of Kattowitz and Königshütte (Chorzow), which had voted 85·4 per cent and 74·7 per cent respectively in favour of remaining in Germany. See also *Rapport Général du CICR sur son activité de 1921 à 1923*, pp. 15–19.

4 Louis de Jong, *The German Fifth Column in the Second World War*, 1956. See also Inis Claude, *National Minorities*, 1955, pp. 44–7; *Expellees and Refugees of German Ethnic Origin. Report of a Special Subcommittee of the Committee on the Judiciary House of Representatives*, March 1950, hereafter Walter Report, p. 7; Radomir Luza, *The Transfer of the Sudeten Germans*, 1964, pp. 51, 154, 321; Boleslav Wiewiora, *The Polish-German Frontier*, 1959, pp. 118–21.

5 An entirely different question, of course, is whether a State should have the right of collective punishment against an entire group without a determination of individual guilt.

6 A memorandum by the Committee on Post-War Programs of the United States State Department justified its approval of a restricted transfer of German minorities as follows:
'These German minorities became the advance guard of National Socialist penetration, and the states which they helped to deliver to Hitler have a well-founded grievance against them. Their transfer to Germany would probably contribute to the tranquility of the countries concerned.' *Foreign Relations of the United States*, 1944, vol. I, p. 310.

7 I. Claude, *National Minorities*, 1955, p. 31. The author has also studied many of the petitions at the archives of the League of Nations in Geneva.

8 Text of Opinion: Publications of the Court, Series B, no. 6.
Acts and Documents relating thereto: Series C, no. 3, 3rd session,
vol. 3, parts I and II. See also *Survey of International Affairs*,
1925 Supplement, Royal Institute of International Affairs, p. 118.

9 *British Yearbook of International Law*, 1924, vol. 5, pp. 207-8.
Also Lauterpacht, *Annual Digest of Public International Law Cases*,
vol. 2, cases 167, 168.

10 Compare the Chorzow (Königshütte) Factory Case, Judgment
No. 9 delivered 26 July 1927, Permanent Court of International
Justice. *British Yearbook*, 1928, vol. 9, pp. 135ff. Also Judgment
No. 13, delivered 13 September 1928, Lauterpacht, op. cit.,
vol. 4, pp. 268ff., 499ff. Compare also the many cases before the
Upper Silesian Arbitral Tribunal.

11 See the cases digested by Lauterpacht, op. cit., among others
vol. 3, case 239.

12 Long before Hitler the government of the Weimar Republic had
taken an active interest in securing the minority rights of former
German citizens under Polish rule. See Lauterpacht, op. cit.,
vol. 2, case 123, vol. 3, case 238, etc.

13 E. Benes, 'The New Order in Europe', *Nineteenth Century and
After*, 1941, vol. 130, p. 154.

14 E. Benes, 'The Organization of Postwar Europe', *Foreign Affairs*,
1942, vol. 20, pp. 226-42, at p. 238.

15 Letter by British Foreign Office to Rudolf Storch (German Social
Democrat leader in London exile), *Der Sudetendeutsche*, 29 October
1955, p. 1; also R. Luza, op. cit., p. 236.

16 Benes, *Memoirs*, 1954, p. 207.

17 ibid., p. 222.

18 ibid., pp. 195, 223.

19 ibid., p. 195.

20 *Foreign Relations of the United States*, 1943, vol. 3, p. 15.

21 ibid.; also Sherwood, *Roosevelt and Hopkins*, 1948, p. 710.

22 *Parliamentary Debates*, House of Lords, vol. 130, col. 1128,
8 March 1944.

23 Discussing the conclusions of the Yalta Conference, Clement
Attlee said in the House of Commons on 1 March 1945: 'The
shifting of population at the present time may be very, very
painful, but it may be far better than a long drawn out sore of
populations under peoples whom they hate', *Parliamentary
Debates*, House of Commons, vol. 408, col. 1617.

24 Arthur Lane, *I saw Poland Betrayed*, 1948, p. 64; also cited in
Congressional Record, 5 April 1949, p. 3898.

25 Department of State, *Bulletin*, vol. 11, p. 836, 24 December 1944.
Documents on American Foreign Relations, 1944-5, vol. 7, p. 898.
Lane, op. cit., p. 70.

26 Churchill, *Triumph and Tragedy*, 1953, passim.

27 Société des Nations, *Recueil des Traités*, vol. 32, pp. 76ff.
Convention Concernant l'Echange des Populations Grecques et
Turques, et Protocole, Signés à Lausanne le 30 Janvier 1923.

For a discussion of the legal issues, see Séfériadès, 'L'Echange des populations', *Recueil des Cours*, 1928, vol. 24, pp. 311ff., Academie de Droit International. See also *American Journal of International Law*, vol. 18, 1924, Supp., pp. 84–90; Toynbee, *Survey of International Affairs*, 1925, vol. 2, Royal Institute of International Affairs, pp. 257–79.

28 *Parliamentary Debates*, House of Commons, 15 December 1944, vol. 406, col. 1484.

29 Quoted in G. Streit, *Der Lausanner Vertrag*, 1929, p. 24; also quoted by Lord Noel-Buxton in *Parliamentary Debates*, House of Lords, vol. 130, col. 1120, 8 March 1944.

30 *Parliamentary Debates*, House of Lords, vol. 139, col. 68, 30 January 1946.

31 *Foreign Relations of the United States*, 1945, vol. 2, pp. 1234–5.

32 ibid., 1944, vol. 1, p. 310. Also 1945, vol. 2, pp. 1321–2, for British compensation plans.

33 ibid., 1945, vol. 2, pp. 1291–2 where Robert Murphy cabled the State Department:

> As helpless as the United States may be to arrest a cruel and inhuman process which is continuing, it would seem that our Government could and should make its attitude as expressed at Potsdam unmistakably clear. It would be most unfortunate were the record to indicate that we are *particeps* to methods we have often condemned in other instances.

34 At the conclusion of the Casablanca Conference on 24 January 1943, President Roosevelt announced his and Churchill's determination to accept 'nothing less than unconditional surrender of Germany'. This unwise formula simply put the iron of desperate resistance into the Germans. In his vehement 'total war' speech in the Sportspalast in Berlin on 18 February 1943, Goebbels asked an audience of loyal party members whether they were prepared to fight to the end. In unmistakable rejection of the 'unconditional surrender' formula, they affirmed their commitment to total war. See A. Speer, *Inside the Third Reich*, 1970, p. 305; Robert Murphy, *Diplomat Among Warriors*, 1964, p. 295; R. Sherwood, *The White House Papers of Harry L. Hopkins*, 1948–9, p. 690.

35 A memorandum by the Committee on Post-War Programs of the United States State Department observed: 'Hitler himself has set an example by numerous forced migrations of the peoples of this region of Europe', *Foreign Relations of the United States*, 1944, vol. 1, p. 310. See also A. de Zayas, 'International Law and Mass Population Transfers', *Harvard International Law Journal*, 1975, vol. 16, pp. 207–58, esp. 213ff.

36 See address of Prime Minister Churchill on 27 February 1945, *Parliamentary Debates*, House of Commons, vol. 408, cols 1267ff. See Lord Vansittart's speech in the House of Lords on 23 October 1945, vol. 137, cols 412–26; President Roosevelt's

address of 1 March 1945, *Congressional Record*, vol. 91, part 2, esp. p. 1620; also letter of college history professor to Congressman Hugh de Lacy in appendix to *Congressional Record*, 8 May 1945, p. A–2141.

37 C. Hull, *Memoirs*, 1948, vol. 2, p. 1603.

38 H. Rothfels, *The German Opposition to Hitler*, 1947. See especially the new enlarged edition published 1961. The author has also visited Professor Rothfels several times at his home in Tübingen, where he is Professor Emeritus and co-publisher of the *Vierteljahreshefte für Zeitgeschichte*. A German-Jewish scholar, Professor Rothfels emigrated to the United States to escape Nazi persecution and returned to Germany after the war. See also Allen Dulles, *Germany's Underground*, 1947, and for personal recollections on the leaders of the German Opposition to Hitler see Lutz Graf Schwerin von Krosigk, *Es Geschah in Deutschland*, 1951, esp. pp. 326–63. The author has interviewed Count Schwerin v. Krosigk twice at his home in Essen.

39 Hans and Sophie Scholl belonged to the secret organization Weisse Rose (White Rose), which was led by philosophy professor Kurt Huber executed in 1943 after discovery of the organization by the Gestapo.

40 J. Neuhäusler, *Kreuz und Hakenkreuz*. Also personal interview with Bishop Neuhäusler in Munich. Bishop Neuhäusler expressed considered criticism of the 'collective guilt' thesis as expounded by Karl Jaspers, existentialist philosopher, in his widely known essay, *The Question of German Guilt*.

41 Pastor Niemöller was the head of the Lutheran 'Bekennende Kirche'. See also Bishop Hugo Hahn, *Kämpfe Wider Willen*, 1969.

42 *The Times*, 18 June 1943. Richard Stokes, MP, led the opposition to this resolution.

43 *Statistisches Jahrbuch für das Deutsche Reich*, p. 539.

44 Mr Raikes in the House of Commons on 15 December 1944, vol. 406, cols 1496–7, Mr Petherick, cols 1546–7; Mr Rhys-Davis on 1 March 1945, vol. 408, cols 1622–5, Mr Strauss, col. 1655, Mr Pethick-Laurence, cols 1656–63; Mr Wheeler and Mr Lucas in the US Senate, *Congressional Record*, 15 January 1945, pp. 251–4, etc.

45 *Time*, 21 May 1945, p. 19.

46 *Parliamentary Debates*, House of Lords, vol. 130, col. 1134, 8 March 1944.

47 ibid., House of Commons, vol. 408, col. 1617, 1 March 1945.

48 Heinrich Brüning, leader of the Zentrum (Center) Party, German Chancellor from March 1930 to June 1932. Persecuted by the National Socialists, Brüning fled Germany in May 1934 and sought exile in Great Britain, later in the United States, where he became an American citizen and was Professor at Harvard University. See Brüning, *Memoiren*, 1970, and *Briefe und Gespräche*, 1974.

CHAPTER TWO   THE GERMANS OF CZECHOSLOVAKIA

1 The 'Sudeten' is actually only that mountainous region in
  Northern Bohemia contiguous to Prussian Silesia. The term has
  been coined since the turn of the century to refer to all the
  Germans of Bohemia and Moravia, and later even to include the
  entire German population of Czechoslovakia.

2 See Wilson's speeches of 8 January 1918 (fourteen points)
  11 February 1918 (four particulars) and the famous Mount
  Vernon speech of 4 July 1918. *Foreign Relations of the United
  States,* 1918, supp. 1, vol. 1, pp. 12ff., pp. 108ff., pp. 268ff.

3 Up to 1917 Czech volunteers fought side by side with the Allies
  in the trenches of France. In 1917 a Czech Legion was organized
  in Russia which contributed more substantially to the war effort.
  See J. Bradley, *Czechoslovakia: A Short History,* 1971, pp. 144–7.
  Also D. Perman, *The Shaping of the Czechoslovak State,* 1962,
  p. 40.

4 *Congressional Record,* 8 January 1918, p. 681.

5 *Dokumentensammlung zur Sudetenfrage,* 2nd ed., 1961, p. 45.

6 ibid., p. 46.

7 ibid., p. 47.

8 Joseph Hofbauer and Emil Strauss, *Josef Seliger, ein Lebensbild,*
  1930, pp. 125ff. at p. 147. Seliger was the leading Sudeten German
  Social Democrat at the time of the Paris Peace Conference.

9 The Republic of German-Austria was formed on 12 November
  1918 and declared itself to be part of the German-Weimar
  Republic. Article 80 of the Treaty of Versailles and Article 88 of
  the Treaty of St Germain prevented this union.

10 *Papers Relating to the Foreign Relations of the United States, The
   Paris Peace Conference,* 1919, vol. 2, p. 379.

11 ibid., 1919, vol. 12, p. 273. Quaere: If Mexico were
   awarded the State of Texas, would the American population
   of Texas adjust to Mexican rule, or would they agitate for union
   with the contiguous United States?

12 ibid., p. 274. Nineteen years later the Munich Agreement
   implemented much of the Coolidge Plan. See Laurence Thompson,
   The Greatest Treason, 1968, p. 14.

13 *American Journal of International Law,* 1920, vol. 14, Supp., p. 30.

14 *Stenographische Protokolle über die Sitzungen der Konstituierenden
   Nationalversammlung der Republik Osterreich,* 1919, vol. 1,
   pp. 765ff. at p. 770. See also Hermann Raschhofer, *Die
   Sudetenfrage,* 1953, p. 133.

15 Philip Brown, 'Self-Determination in Central Europe', *American
   Journal of International Law,* 1920, vol. 14, pp. 235–9 at p. 237.

16 The Sudeten German case further gains in persuasiveness when
   considered that the Sudeten-German national group was more
   numerous than the Norwegians at the time of the Paris Peace
   Conference (less than 3 million) and nearly as numerous as the
   Danes or the Finns (4 million).

17 Unlike the Germans of Posen and West Prussia, who emigrated in large numbers to Western Germany in order to avoid polonization, relatively few Sudetens emigrated. In the period from 1919 to 1926 over a million Germans of Posen and Pomerellen, who had been placed without a plebiscite within the frontiers of the new Polish State, left for Germany, while others who had wanted to stay were evicted from their homes and their lands were confiscated. At the archives of the League of Nations in Geneva there are some twenty boxes containing files on protests and petitions by evicted Germans from Poland.

18 *Stenographische Protokolle der Sitzungen des Abgeordnetenhauses der Nationalversammlung der Tschechoslowakischen Republik*, 1920, Band I, pp. 28ff.

19 Wenzel Jaksch, *Europa's Weg nach Potsdam*, 1967, pp. 209ff.; see also Kurt Rabl, *Das Selbstbestimmungsrecht der Völker*, 1973, pp. 103ff.; also Radomir Luza, *The Transfer of the Sudeten Germans*, 1964, p. 34. The author has a list of the names and occupations of the 54 dead of 4 March 1919, including an old man of 80, women and several students aged 11, 13 and 14.

20 *Parliamentary Debates*, House of Lords, 30 January 1946, vol. 139, col. 89.

21 Inis Claude, *National Minorities*, 1955, p. 40.

22 Luza, op. cit., p. 42; Thompson, op. cit., p. 16.

23 C. Macartney, *National States and National Minorities*, 1968, pp. 414–15.

24 *The Economist*, 10 July 1937, p. 72.

25 *Akten zur deutschen Auswärtigen Politik*, Serie D (1937–45), vol. 2, *Deutschland und die Tschechoslowakei*, p. 192. For a Czech view on the Carlsbad Programme see R. Luza, op. cit., pp. 121–5. See also H. Ripka, *Munich before and After*, 1939, pp. 20, 27–8, 37, 40. Also Benes, *Memoirs*, 1954.

26 *Documents on British Foreign Policy, 1919–1939*, 3rd series, vol. 2, p. 50; also Thompson, op. cit. pp. 98–9; Luza, op. cit., pp. 135–8.

27 *Documents on British Foreign Policy, 1919–1939*, 3rd series, vol. 2, pp. 675–7; also Luza, op. cit., n. 165 on p. 145.

28 *Foreign Relations of the United States*, 1938, vol. I, p. 595.

29 ibid., p. 596.

30 ibid., p. 622.

31 A. Toynbee, 'A Turning Point in History', *Foreign Affairs*, January 1939, p. 316. See also *The Times*, 2 June 1938 for a similar opinion expressed by the Dean of St Paul's, also *The Times* editorial of 4 June 1938, suggesting that Czechoslovakia grant plebiscites to her minorities.

32 Toynbee, op. cit., p. 314.

33 At the same time between 675,000 and 743,000 Czechs were subjected to German rule. It is estimated, however, that as many as 500,000 Czechs may have left the Sudetenland and moved to the Czech heartland of Bohemia and Moravia, while thousands of Germans who had been left outside the new Reich frontiers started migrating to the annexed Sudeten territories. Those

Czechs who voluntarily migrated out of the Sudetenland were permitted to take all their property with them. See Schieder, *Documents on the Expulsion*, 1960, vol. 4, p. 12. See also Luza, op. cit., p. 158; E. Wiskemann, 'Czechs and Germans after Munich', *Foreign Affairs*, 1939, vol. 17, no. 2, p. 293.

34 *Foreign Relations of the United States*, 1938, vol. 1, pp. 708–10.

35 Slezsky Sbornik, *Acta Silesiaca*, 1969, p. 7.

36 Charles Maurice de Talleyrand (1754–1838) characterized Napoleon's kidnapping and executing of the Duke of Enghien (1804) on a weak suspicion of treason as 'plus qu'un crime—une sottise'.

37 Eduard Taborsky, *The Czechoslovak Cause*, 1944, pp. 56–8.

38 Indeed, such a proposal had already been aired at the Peace Conference in Paris in 1919, by the French sociologist Lavergne. See E. Benes, 'The Organization of Postwar Europe', *Foreign Affairs*, 1942, vol. 20, pp. 228–42.

39 Holborn, *War and Peace Aims of the United Nations*, vol. 2, p. 1036.

40 ibid.

41 ibid., p. 446.

42 E. Benes, *The Annals*, March 1944, p. 166. Compare J. W. Brügel, *Tschechen und Deutschen, 1939–1946*, 1974.

43 H. Ripka, *Munich Before and After*, 1939, p. 196.

44 Holborn, op. cit., vol. 1, p. 253; UK Command Papers, 6379 (1942), Czechoslovakia; Benes, *Memoirs*, p. 207. For the American consent to the reversal of the Munich Agreement, *Foreign Relations of the United States*, 1943, vol. 3, p. 529.

45 Letter by British Foreign Office to Rudolf Storch, *Der Sudeten-deutsche*, 29 October 1955, p. 1; Luza, op. cit., p. 236.

46 Benes, *Memoirs*, p. 207.

47 ibid., pp. 222–3.

48 E. Franzel, *Die Vertreibung Sudetenland 1945–1946*, 1967, pp. 214–19. Reinhard Heydrich was wounded when his car was thrown a bomb by Czech terrorists on 27 May 1942, and died several days later of complications. The assassins were reported to have been sheltered in Lidice after being parachuted from an English plane. But not only the victims of Lidice suffered as a result of Heydrich's death; Nazi terror claimed the lives of some 2,500 Czechs throughout the Protectorate until the assassins were found on 16 June 1942. Compare Luza, op. cit., pp. 210–12. Bradley, op. cit., pp. 164–6.

49 Luza, op. cit., pp. 260–1.

50 ibid., p. 262.

51 *Facts about Czechoslovakia*, 1958, p. 10.

52 *Time*, 22 October 1945, p. 35.

53 ibid., 5 November 1945, p. 30.

54 *Parliamentary Debates*, House of Commons, vol. 414, 26 October 1945, col. 2376.

55 *Parliamentary Debates*, House of Lords, vol. 139, col. 89, 30 January 1946.

56 Axel de Gadolin, *The Solution of the Karelian Refugee Problem in Finland*, 1952.

57 For decades historians have propagated the generalization of the German as a congenital bully. Modern historiography would do better by testing the thesis of the German as 'underdog'. Certainly the Sudeten Germans from 1919 to 1938 were underdogs in Czechoslovakia. That they tried to improve their condition is only natural. A French aphorism would seem to explain the whole situation pungently: 'Cet animal est très mèchant, quand on l'attaque il se défend.' In this sense the Sudeten German demand for equal rights cannot be termed a heinous crime, and their separation from the Czechs by the Munich Agreement should be seen as a belated vindication of the recommendations of the Coolidge Commission in 1919. But after the débâcle of the Second World War and Hitler's exit from the scene only the 'disloyal' German minorities remained in Czechoslovakia and in the Sudetenland to suffer as scapegoats for the crimes and excesses of the Nazi occupation.

CHAPTER THREE   THE GENESIS OF THE ODER-NEISSE LINE:
THE CONFERENCES OF TEHRAN AND YALTA

1 Hans Grimm, *Volk Ohne Raum*, a 1926 novel in which Grimm contrasted the lack of space in Germany with the open spaces in colonial Africa. The title of his novel became a National Socialist propaganda slogan and was misused to demand *Lebensraum* in Eastern Europe at the expense of the Slavic nations.

2 Mr Stokes quoted this statement to Prime Minister Churchill in the course of the debate in the House of Commons on 23 February 1944, *Parliamentary Debates*, House of Commons, vol. 397, cols 901–2.

3 Text in L. Holborn, *War and Peace Aims of the United Nations*, 1943, p. 2. See also Appendix, pp. 228–9.

4 *Parliamentary Debates*, House of Commons, vol. 397, col. 902.

5 H. Rothfels, 'Frontiers and Mass Migrations in Eastern-Central Europe', *Review of Politics*, 1946, p. 59.

6 *Parliamentary Debates*, House of Commons, vol. 400, col. 784, 24 May 1944.

7 After it had been decided at Tehran that Poland would receive East Prussia, Prime Minister Mikolajczyk visited the United States and in a statement to the Press in Washington on 14 June 1944, he said, 'Poland wanted Eastern Prussia after the war, because, as it stood before, it was always a knife pointed at Poland's heart.' Polish Information News, London XXI, p. 536; also dissertation, University of Geneva, 1952, 'The Division and Dismemberment of Germany', by Harold Strauss, p. 86.

8 Churchill, *The Grand Alliance*, 1953, p. 558, where Eden reports on a conversation with Stalin on 16 December 1941.

9 *Foreign Relations of the United States*, 1943, vol. 3, p. 15; also Sherwood, *Roosevelt and Hopkins*, 1948, p. 710.

10 *Foreign Relations of the United States*, 1943, vol. 3, p. 25; Sherwood, op. cit., p. 713.

11 Text of German-Soviet Treaty of Non-Aggression and Secret Additional Protocol, signed in Moscow on 23 August 1939, in *Documents on International Affairs 1939–46*, vol. 1, pp. 408–10, The Royal Institute of International Affairs, London. The Ribbentrop-Molotov frontier was even more unfavourable to Poland than the Curzon Line, which had been proposed by Lord Curzon at the end of the First World War as the eastern Polish frontier. The Poles, however, rebelled against this frontier and by force of arms established a more favourable Polish-Russian frontier which lasted through 17 September 1939.

12 On 17 November 1943, a memorandum by Stanislav Mikolajczyk, Prime Minister of the Polish government-in-exile, was transmitted to President Roosevelt. This memorandum vigorously protested against the Soviet proposal and continued:

> The attribution to Poland of Eastern Prussia, Danzig, Opole Silesia and the straightening and shortening of the Polish Western frontier are in any case dictated by the need to provide for the stability of future peace, the disarmament of Germany and the security of Poland and other countries of Central Europe. The transfer to Poland of these territories cannot therefore be treated fairly as an object of compensation for the cession to the U.S.S.R. of Eastern Poland. . . .

> *Foreign Relations of the United States*, 1943, vol. 3, p. 482. In a conversation with Elbridge Durbrow on 6 January 1943 in the State Department, Mr Arlet, the Counsellor of the Polish Embassy in Washington, had already expressed the desire that Poland should be given 'East Prussia, part of Pomerania as well as Upper Silesia'. Early Polish demands were based on economic and strategic considerations; later in the war the argument of compensating Poland at the expense of Germany for her substantial territorial losses in the East became central. ibid., p. 322.

13 Churchill, *Closing the Ring*, 1953, p. 362.

14 ibid.

15 ibid.

16 France would later express her fear of an overcrowded Germany and propose mass emigration of Germans after the war as solution.

17 Isaiah Bowman, American Geographer, President of Johns Hopkins University, participant at the Paris Peace Conference of 1919 and later at San Francisco in 1945, wrote one of the most perceptive articles on the planning of the peace, where he noted,

> There is a profound psychological difference between a transfer of territory and a change in a trade treaty or pact of international

cooperation. Territory is near and plain and evokes personal feelings and group sentiments. To a people conscious of its individuality, 'how sweet the silent backward tracings.' Such people endow the land itself with a mystical quality, hearing revered ancestors, the authors of past grandeurs and the doers of heroic deeds, speak from their graves in its soil. To all classes, landscape is an essential part of home. Enshrined in every national literature are the changing moods and compositions of river, mountain, plain, forest and shore. All the familiar techniques of living are involved in the complex of feeling, remembered experiences and imagination surrounding place and home.

It is title to sentiments like these, and not merely to so-and-so many square miles of land, that is transferred when there is a change of boundaries and rule.

Bowman, 'The Strategy of Territorial Decisions', *Foreign Affairs*, 1946, vol. 24, pp. 177–94, at p. 177.

18 Arthur Lane, *I saw Poland Betrayed*, 1948, p. 260. See also letter of Ambassador Lane to Secretary of State Marshall, dated 13 January 1947, *Foreign Relations of the United States*, 1947, vol. 2, p. 177.

19 Churchill, *Closing the Ring*, p. 396.

20 *Foreign Relations of the United States*, 1918, vol. 1, Supp. 1, p. 112.

21 The frontier at the Neisse River had not been suggested by anyone yet.

22 Churchill, *Closing the Ring*, p. 403; Feis, *Churchill-Roosevelt-Stalin*, 1957, p. 287.

23 *Foreign Relations of the United States*, 1944, vol. 1, pp. 302–3.

24 Churchill, *Closing the Ring*, p. 452; Benes, *Memoirs*, 1954, p. 149.

25 A 'Select Committee to Conduct an Investigation of the Facts, Evidence and Circumstances of the Katyn Forest Massacre' was unanimously authorized under House Resolution 390, 82nd Congress, 1st Session, 18 September 1951. The text of the hearings, with accompanying documents, entitled *The Katyn Forest Massacre*, was published in 7 parts (2362 pages). See also Edward Rozek, *Allied Wartime Diplomacy*, 1958, pp. 123–7; also Jozef Czapski, *What Happened in Katyn*, 1950; also Gen. Wladyslaw Anders, *Katyn*, 1948. Personal observations were given to the author by Dr Ernesto Giménez Caballero, the Spanish envoy to the international Katyn investigation of 1943.

26 *Foreign Relations of the United States*, 1943, vol. 3, pp. 376ff.; Rozek, op. cit., p. 128.

27 Kennan, *Memoirs*, 1967, vol. 1, pp. 200ff.; Rozek, op. cit., pp. 132ff.

28 Sikorski died in a plane accident near Gibraltar on 4 July 1943 and was succeeded by Mikolajczyk as Prime Minister of the exile government; see also David Irving, *Churchill and Sikorski, a Tragic Alliance*, 1969.

29 Benes, *Memoirs*, p. 266; Rozek, op. cit., p. 171.
30 Rozek, op. cit., pp. 277ff.; Mikolajczyk, *The Rape of Poland*, 1948, pp. 97-9; Churchill, *Triumph and Tragedy*, p. 235.
31 Rozek, op. cit., p. 283.
32 ibid., p. 285.
33 Churchill, *Triumph and Tragedy*, p. 370; Lane, op. cit., p. 70. From the outset Stalin meant an extension to the western or Lusatian Neisse River. However, since there was another Neisse River which flowed by the town of Neisse in Upper Silesia, a dispute later developed between the Western Allies and the Soviet Union as to which of the two Neisses should build the frontier. At Yalta and Potsdam the Western Allies would argue for the Eastern or Glatzer Neisse, whereby most of Lower Silesia would have remained in post-war Germany.
34 Kennan, op. cit., vol. 1, p. 214. In his celebrated *Memoirs*, which appeared over twenty years after the fateful decisions at Yalta and Potsdam, Kennan summed up:

> A border so unnatural as the Oder-Neisse could be maintained and defended, in the long run, only by armed force – and armed force on a scale greater than Poland itself could be expected to muster. Nor could the Poles be expected to place reliance, for the defense of such a border, on the Western Powers. This had all been gone through once before, in 1938 and 1939. Even at that time, the Western powers had proved a weak reed. In the face of the Oder-Neisse border a future Germany would obviously have irredentist claims far stronger and more reasonable than those that Hitler was able to put forward in 1939 (and even these, as the Western powers realized, had something to be said for them.*) A Poland carved out of a good portion of Germany would be simply obliged, in the interests of its own defense, to assure itself at all times of Russian support, and to accept it pretty much on Russia's terms. In these circumstances it made little sense to go on arguing with Stalin and Molotov about the composition of a future Polish government, as though there were a real chance of genuine Polish independence. This was simply an attempt, and an unpromising one at that, to lock the stable door after the horse was stolen (p. 215).

35 Department of State, *Bulletin*, vol. 11, p. 836, 24 December 1944. Instead of pursuing a far sighted programme, the United States in September 1944 dashed off after the will-o'-the-wisp of the Morgenthau 'Plan'. For six months it indulged in a policy of 'no

---

* Referring to the Oder-Neisse Line Churchill observed in his war recollections: 'For the future peace of Europe here was a wrong beside which Alsace-Lorraine and the Danzig Corridor were trifles', *Triumph and Tragedy*, p. 648.

policy' towards Germany. On 20 October Mr Roosevelt wrote to
Mr Hull – 'I dislike making detailed plans for a country which
we do not yet occupy.' See Hull, *Memoirs*, vol. 2, p. 1621. Also
Philip Mosely, 'The Occupation of Germany', *Foreign Affairs*,
1949–50, vol. 28, p. 596. Also R. Murphy, *Diplomat Among
Warriors*, 1964, p. 281.

36 *Foreign Relations of the United States, The Conferences at Malta
and Yalta*, p. 189.

37 ibid., p. 509.

38 ibid., p. 510.

39 ibid., p. 680.

40 ibid., p. 716 (Bohlen minutes).

41 ibid., p. 717 (Bohlen minutes), p. 720 (Matthew minutes); also
Churchill, *Triumph and Tragedy*, p. 374.

42 *Foreign Relations of the United States, The Conferences at Malta
and Yalta*, p. 717, same in Matthew minutes, p. 720, p. 726
(Hiss notes).

43 ibid., pp. 717, 720, 725; Churchill, *Triumph and Tragedy*, p. 374.

44 *Foreign Relations of the United States, The Conferences at Malta
and Yalta*, p. 792; Churchill, *Triumph and Tragedy*, p. 377.

45 *Foreign Relations of the United States, The Conferences at Malta
and Yalta*, p. 869.

46 ibid., p. 907, Churchill, *Triumph and Tragedy*, p. 374.

47 *Foreign Relations of the United States, The Conferences at Malta
and Yalta*, pp. 905 and 938.

48 *Congressional Record*, House of Representatives, vol. 91, part 2,
1 March 1945, pp. 1621–2.

49 *Parliamentary Debates*, House of Commons, 27 February 1945,
vol. 408, col. 1267.

50 ibid., col. 1277.

51 ibid.

52 ibid., 1 March 1945, col. 1623.

53 ibid., col. 1655.

54 ibid., col. 1625.

55 *Rocznik Statystyczny*, 1947, p. 29.

56 *Time*, 15 October 1945, vol. 46, p. 24.

CHAPTER FOUR   THE FLIGHT: PRELUDE TO THE EXPULSIONS

1 E. Kulischer, *Europe on the Move*, 1948, pp. 256–9; J. Schechtman,
European Population Transfers, 1946, pp. 66–225. Also Alfred de
Zayas, 'International Law and Mass Population Transfers',
Harvard International Law Journal, 1975, vol. 16, pp. 246–9.
Also D. Loeber, *Diktierte Option*, 1973.

2 Theodor Schieder, *Dokumentation der Vertreibung*, vol. I/1,
pp. 63 E, 101, 266, 274, 432, 479.

3 The author has interviewed General Hossbach three times in
order to clarify and confirm the extensive documentation in the
German archives at Koblenz and Freiburg. A good summary of
the events in East Prussia is found in Schieder, *Dokumentation der*

Vertreibung, vol. I/1, pp. 9E–41E. For the military situation see Hossbach, *Die Schlacht um Ostpreussen*, 1951.

4 See Rudolf Grenz, *Stadt und Kreis Gumbinnen*, 1971, pp. 632–6 and 811–35, unofficially known as the 'Heimatbuch' of Gumbinnen.

5 General Dethleffsen in a personal interview confirmed the contents of his 1946 deposition. This affidavit can be seen today in the Federal German Archives in Koblenz under Ost-Dok. 2, Nr. 13, pp. 31–3, and at the Peace Palace in the Hague in the Nuremberg Documents, High Command Defense, Affidavit Nr. 1608. It is also cited in E. G. Lass, *Die Flucht-Ostpreussen, 1944–45*, 1964, pp. 46–7. The author has also read contemporary reports on the Nemmersdorf massacre at the Politisches Archiv des Auswärtigen Amtes in Bonn in the collection Völkerrecht/ Kriegsrecht, vol. 82/8, no. 22. This volume also contains reports on massacres in Goldap, Tutteln and Girnen. See also *Le Courrier*, Geneva, 7 November 1944, no. 306, p. 1.

6 Ost-Dok. 2, no. 13, pp. 9–10; Schieder, *Dokumentation der Vertreibung*, vol. I/1, p. 7 footnote. Also Lass, op. cit., pp. 45–6. Stories of German civilians, mostly women, being nailed to barndoors are encountered time and again in the voluminous collection of affidavits in the Ost-Dokumente. The occurrence of this particular crime has been confirmed to the author in interviews with German refugees from East Prussia and Silesia and also by Belgians who had been prisoners of war in East Prussia and witnessed such scenes after liberation by the Red Army in 1945.

7 Schieder, *Dokumentation der Vertreibung*, vol I/1, pp. 7–8; Ost-Dok. 2, No. 21, pp. 715–16; Lass, op. cit., pp. 44–5.

8 The report of the international medical commission as well as the records of the Fourth Army after August 1944 have been lost, presumably fallen in Soviet hands or destroyed by the Germans themselves. General Dethleffsen, however, confirmed to me that a medical commission had been there and that a report had been made. A preliminary report on the state of the corpses, dated 26 October 1944, and prepared by Captain Fricke (Abt. Ic A.O. Abw. III) may be seen at the military archives in Freiburg in the Kriegstagebuch of Infantry Division 559. Events in near-by Goldap were investigated by an international commission in Berlin, the members of which, according to information from the Staatsarchiv in Nürnberg were: Chairman, Dr Hjalmar Mäe of Estonia (the author has corresponded with Dr Mäe, who now lives in Graz, Austria), Professor Dr Puentes Rojo (Spain), Hendrichs de Lestrieur (Holland), Petro Anvancini (Italy), M. Calais (Sweden), Hermansen (Denmark), Madjenovic (Serbia), Strandmais (Latvia).

9 Ost-Dok. 2 No. 8, p. 107; Lass, op. cit., p. 47. The author has corresponded with Captain Herminghaus, who specifically confirmed the authenticity of the quoted affidavit and gave the author leads for further investigation. Compare report in *Le Courrier*, Geneva, 7 November 1944, no. 306, p. 1.

10 Frau Margot Grimm died in 1969. The author has corresponded with her son Herr Johannes Grimm, who lives today in Stuttgart. The affidavit in Frau Grimm's handwriting may be found in the German Federal Archives in Koblenz: Ost-Dok. 2, No. 13, pp. 49–50. The affidavit is quoted *in toto* in Lass, op. cit., pp. 47–8 and corroborated by the affidavit of Frau Erika Feller, Ost-Dok. 2, No. 13, pp. 33–6, cited also in Lass, op. cit. p. 48.

11 Julius Streicher, Gauleiter of Franconia and publisher of the notorious Jew-baiting newspaper *Der Stuermer*. He was convicted on a charge of incitement to murder and hanged at Nuremberg on 16 October 1946. In the light of the Nuremberg Principles, it would, indeed, be difficult to conclude that Ehrenburg's propaganda did not constitute a crime against humanity, *a fortiori* when the number of victims climbed into the hundreds of thousands.

12 Translated from a propaganda leaflet distributed to Red Army soldiers at the time of the East Prussian offensive. Lieutenant Colonel Bruno Kerwin, who participated in the negotiations for the surrender of Königsberg, confirmed having seen the Russian leaflet, which had been found in the possession of a prisoner of war. General Erich Dethleffsen, Chief of Staff of the Fourth Army, also recalls having seen the Russian original. A German translation is quoted in the memoirs of Admiral Karl Dönitz, *Zehn Jahre und Zwanzig Tage*, 1967, p. 424; also in Hans-Edgar Jahn, *Pommersche Passion*, 1964, pp. 12, 23. Years after the war Ilya Ehrenburg disclaimed authorship of this particular leaflet, but samples of similar statements can be found in *Pravda* and *Red Star* and are quoted in Alexander Werth, *Russia at War*, New York, pp. 965, 414. Compare Ehrenburg's denial in vol. 5 of his memoirs, *Men, Years-Life*, Ehrenburg, *The War 1941–45*, 1964, pp. 32–3.

13 Ilya Ehrenburg, *Война* 1942, pp. 22–3. On 14 April 1945 Ehrenburg's hate propaganda was strongly criticized in an article by G. F. Alexandrow in *Pravda*. See Alexander Werth, op. cit., p. 966. Also Albert Seaton, *The Russo-German War 1941–45*, 1971, pp. 543–4.

14 F. K. Grau, *Silesian Inferno*, 1970, p. 176.

15 Werth, op. cit., p. 965.

16 Werth, op. cit., p. 964.

17 Kennan, op. cit., vol. 1, p. 265. Confirmed and elaborated in a personal interview with Mr Kennan.

18 Ost-Dokumente in the German Federal Archives in Koblenz and personal interviews with ten French and Belgian prisoners of war who were liberated by the Red Army in 1944–5. M. Georges Hautecler of the Centre de Recherches et d'Etudes Historiques de la Seconde Guerre Mondiale of the Belgian Ministry of Education informed me that 209 Belgian prisoners of war died or disappeared in the months between January and May 1945.

Among these, seventy definitely died as a result of acts of war, including bombardment by Russian planes, shelling and several cases of unprovoked killing by Soviet soldiers. On 11 March 1945 Alphonse Adnet was killed on the road from Stolp to Lauenburg by a drunken Russian soldier. On 8 April 1945 at 1.45 p.m. René Urbain was killed by a drunken Russian soldier 'because he did not have a watch'.

19 'Werewolf' was the name of the planned German partisan or guerilla organization that was supposed to continue the Nazi struggle against the Allies. The Werewolf never materialized except in Romania under Andreas Schmidt, who was parachuted with other Rumanian-German volunteers to do sabotage against the Red Army. Theodor Schieder, *Documents on the Expulsion*, vol. 3, p. 79. There is no question of organized or disorganized resistance by civilians to the Soviet Army in East Prussia or Silesia. No partisan groups ever operated there, nor were there acts of sabotage. There was only numbing fear. After Hitler's suicide the Dönitz government gave strict orders against the planned Werewolf and transmitted these orders by radio from Plön and Flensburg. This information was given to the author by Graf Schwerin von Krosigk, Foreign Minister and Finance Minister in the Dönitz government. See also Eisenhower, *Crusade in Europe*, 1948, p. 397.

20 See Lev Kopelev, *Aufbewahren für alle Zeit*, 1976, p. 127.

21 *Congressional Record*, Senate, 4 December 1945, p. 11374.

22 Solzhenitsyn, *Gulag Archipelago*, vol. 1, p. 21 (Harper & Row paperback). For an interesting verse rendition of events of the Russian occupation of East Prussia see Solzhenitsyn's 40-page poem 'Ostpreussische Nächte', 1976. It seems, however, that Russian soldiers did not behave very chivalrously either toward the recently liberated Eastern Europeans. Molovan Djilas, who was head of the Yugoslav Military Mission in Moscow during the war, writes in his book *Conversations with Stalin*, 1962, p. 95, that he complained to the Soviet Dictator about atrocities committed by Red Army troops in Yugoslavia. Stalin allegedly replied: 'Can't you understand it if a soldier who has crossed thousands of kilometers through blood and fire has fun with a woman or takes a trifle?' Also quoted in C. Ryan, *The Last Battle*, 1966, p. 493, which describes the widespread raping in conquered Berlin. See also *Congressional Record*, House of Representatives, 1 November 1945, p. 10202 for the entry of the Red Army in Bulgaria: 'After a few disastrous incidents, the farmers learned it was best to let the soldiers take what they wanted.' Also F. Voigt, 'Orderly and Humane' in *Nineteenth Century and After*, November 1945, especially on rapings in conquered Danzig, pp. 193ff.

23 See page-long article on Lev Kopelev, Major of the Red Army and today Soviet dissident in Moscow, by Marion Gräfin Dönhoff, in *Die Zeit*, 6 February 1976, p. 3.

24 Lev Kopelev, op. cit., the English-language translation is entitled *No Jail for Thought*, published by Secker & Warburg, 1976.

25 Kopelev (German edn), p. 94.

26 ibid., p. 117.

27 ibid., p. 122.

28 ibid., p. 127.

29 Werth, op. cit., p. 964.

30 F. Keating, 'The Soviet Army's Behaviour in Victory and Occupation – The First Phase', in Liddel-Hart (ed.), *The Soviet Army*, 1956, esp. pp. 185ff.

31 Schieder, *Documents on the Expulsion*, vol. 1, pp. 62–8 at p. 65; Alfred Bohmann, *Menschen und Grenzen*, vol. 1, p. 271. See also Kurt Böhme, *Gesucht Wird*, the story of the search work of the German Red Cross, pp. 261 and 275. Nearly 1 million ethnic Germans were deported to the Soviet Union, but this number included hundreds of thousands of Germans from Romania, Yugoslavia and Hungary as well as some 300,000 ethnic Germans from the Soviet Union who had fled to the West with the retreating German Army in 1944 and were repatriated by force in 1945 after the German unconditional surrender. These Russian-Germans were not returned to their villages in the area of the Black Sea but were deported to labour camps throughout the Soviet Union. See Karl Stumpp, *The German-Russians*, 1971. See also letter quoted in Appendix to the *Congressional Record*, Senate, 2 August 1946, p. A–4774.

32 The author has gone through hundreds of original accounts of the deportations. These reports are contained in the German Federal Archives at Koblenz. Among the most tragic examples are those in the Ost-Dokumente collection under catalogue numbers: Ost Dok. 2, No. 68, pp. 184, 249, 477; No. 139, pp. 41, 88, 151; No. 140, pp. 453, 521, 524.

33 For an American opinion partial to the Soviet deportations of German civilians to forced labour see John Fried, 'Transfer of Civilian Manpower From Occupied Territory', *American Journal of International Law*, 1946, vol. 40, esp. pp. 328–9. Albert Speer, Reich Minister of Arms and Munitions, wrote in his Nuremberg diary on 28 March 1947: 'Deportation of labour is unquestionably an international crime. I do not reject my sentence, even though other nations are now doing the same thing we did', *Inside the Third Reich*, 1970, p. 674. Speer served twenty years at Spandau for the crime of using forced labour recruited principally in Poland and the Ukraine. Alfred Rosenberg, Reich Minister for the Occupied Eastern Territories, signed the decree of 19 December 1941 which provided for the recruitment of 'East Workers' and at Nuremberg was convicted of the crime of enslaving people and was hanged on 16 October 1946. Compare Oppenheim-Lauterpacht, *International Law*, 1955, vol. 2, pp. 441ff.

34 *Foreign Relations of the United States, The Conferences at Malta and Yalta*, Protocol on German Reparation, pp. 982–3; see also

pp. 158, 196 and 937 for pre-conference documents and working drafts.

35 ibid., 1945, vol. 2, pp. 1238–45.

36 Schieder, *Documents on the Expulsion*, vol. 1, p. 68; the overall figure for the mortality of both Volksdeutsche and Reichsdeutsche deportees is estimated at 350,000. See K. Böhme, op. cit., p. 275.

37 Schimitzek, *Truth or Conjecture*, 1966, p. 266.

38 ibid., p. 249.

39 ibid., p. 262; Elisabeth Wiskeman, *Germany's Eastern Neighbours*, 1956, p. 87; G. Paikert, *The German Exodus*, 1962, p. 6.

40 Report of Byron Price to President Truman, 9 November 1945 in *Documents on American Foreign Policy*, vol. 8, p. 258. See also Radomir Luza, *The Transfer of the Sudeten Germans*, 1964, p. 268. For the search of the 'contrite heart' see F. A. Voigt, 'Eastern Germany', *The Nineteenth Century and After*, March 1946, pp. 97–101 at p. 97. See also excerpt of speech of Mr Paul Bellamy, in *Congressional Record*, 2 August 1946, p. A-4776. 'The Germans that I talked to . . . exhibited with few exceptions very little regret over their course of action.'

41 In many cases the American lines remained closed to the German refugees, who sometimes had fled over hundreds of miles, only to fall into the hands of the Russians at the last minute, right across from the American lines. See Schieder, *Dokumentation der Vertreibung*, vol. I/1; also Franzel, *Die Vertreibung Sudetenland 1945–1946*, 1967, pp. 305–6.

42 Montgomery, *Memoirs*, 1958, p. 356.

43 Personal accounts given to the author by French and Belgian ex-prisoners of war. See also the accounts compiled by Professor K. O. Kurth, *Documents of Humanity*, 1954, with a foreword by Albert Schweitzer.

44 Schieder, *Dokumentation der Vertreibung*, vol. I/1, pp. 36 E–37 E; G. Lass, op. cit., pp. 246–66.

45 Schieder, *Dokumentation der Vertreibung*, vol. I/1, p. 82.

46 ibid., p. 68.

47 ibid., 37 E, pp. 69, 79, etc.

48 ibid. Also personal information from many refugees and interviews with Admiral Adalbert v. Blanc, chief of the 10 Sicherungs Division and Kpt.z. See Hugo Heydel, chief of the 9 Sicherungs Division.

49 Brustat-Naval, *Unternehmen Rettung*, 1970, p. 240; also personal information from Admiral Konrad Engelhardt in two interviews in 1972 and research into the conferences of Grand Admiral Dönitz with Hitler, especially conference of 31 January 1945 after the sinking of the *Wilhelm Gustloff* and on 18 April 1945 after the sinking of the *Goya*. 'Seekriegsleitung Besprechungen beim Führer', Institut für Zeitgeschichte, Munich, microfilm MA-10(4), pp. 144, 176.

NOTES TO PAGES 74-8 205

50 Brustat-Naval, op. cit., pp. 39–45. The *Wilhelm Gustloff* was a large KdF (Kraft durch Freude) liner which had operated as a hospital ship during 1939 and 1940, but was taken out of hospital service in 1941 and not officially brought back into service as hospital ship. See Toland, *The Last 100 Days*, 1966, pp. 32–6.

51 Brustat-Naval, op. cit., pp. 145ff.; John Toland, op. cit., pp. 447–9. Even the defeat of the Spanish Armada in July and August 1588 only claimed about 4,000 lives. The real catastrophe followed on the return trip to Spain, when the Armada attempted to round Scotland and Ireland and was smashed by the September storms; in all, the Armada lost some 60 ships and nearly 14,000 men. G. Mattingly, *The Armada*, 1959; M. A. Lewis, *The Spanish Armada*, 1960.

52 Colin Simpson, *The Truth About the 'Lusitania'*, 1972.

53 Brustat-Naval, op. cit., pp. 48, 56.

54 A submarine, being a small vessel, can rescue only a handful of people. Moreover, submarines always leave the scene of a sinking ship with maximum celerity to avoid being discovered; once discovered Second World War submarines frequently could not get away due to slow speed.

55 IMT, vol. 40, pp. 50–1; Dönitz Document 35.

56 The chief medical officer of the hospital ship *Alexander von Humboldt*, confirmed to the author in a personal interview, that the Humboldt was repeatedly bombarded by the Soviets. See also affidavit in Militärarchiv–Freiburg under catalogue number RW 2 v. 234, pp. 33ff.

57 Brustat-Naval, op. cit., pp. 240–1. It should be noted, however, that not all of these vessels were sunk by Soviet torpedoes. Some of them, like the large hospital ship *Berlin* merely ran into mines, while others were sunk during air bombardment of harbours, where it would have been nearly impossible to exempt them from attack, since they were in the midst of legitimate military targets. The *Humboldt*, for instance, was sunk during an English air raid on the port of Gotenhafen (Gdingen).

58 Bustat-Naval, op. cit., p. 217.

59 ibid., pp. 224–8.

60 The last large group of soldiers and civilians was repatriated in 1955 after the successful negotiations conducted by the late Chancellor Konrad Adenauer in Moscow.

61 David Irving in his book *The Destruction of Dresden*, 1963, gives the figure of 135,000. The International Committee of the Red Cross estimated some 270,000. Other estimates range from 25,000 to 400,000. *Report of the Joint Relief Commission 1941–46*, p. 104. See also Schieder, *Dokumentation der Vertreibung*, vol. I/1, pp. 57 E, 159 E, 462; also Thorwald, *Es begann an der Weichsel*, 1950, p. 126.

62 International Commission of Jurists, *The Events in East Pakistan*, *1971*, 1972; Niall MacDermot, 'Crimes Against Humanity in Bangladesh', *International Lawyer*, vol. 7, no. 2, pp. 476–84;

also Edward Kennedy, 'Biafra, Bengal and Beyond', *American Society of International Law Proceedings*, 1972, vol. 66, pp. 89–108.
63 Schieder, *Dokumentation der Vertreibung*, vol. I/1, pp. 446ff.; vol. I/2, pp. 688ff. Also G. Paikert, op. cit., p. 7.

CHAPTER FIVE   ANGLO–AMERICAN PLAN OF LIMITED TRANSFERS

1 Churchill, *Triumph and Tragedy*, 1953, p. 661; also quoted in Byrnes, *Speaking Frankly*, 1947, p. 81.
2 *Foreign Relations of the United States*, 1944, vol. 1, pp. 302–3.
3 I. Claude, *National Minorities*, 1955, pp. 98, 230.
4 *Foreign Relations of the United States, The Conferences at Malta and Yalta*, p. 179.
5 ibid., p. 190.
6 *Parliamentary Debates*, House of Commons, vol. 406, 15 December 1944, col. 1484.
7 B. Wiewiora, *The Polish-German Frontier*, 1959, pp. 159–60; M. Lachs, *Die Westgrenze Polens*, 1967, p. 12; J. Kokot, *The Logic of the Oder-Neisse Frontier*, 1959, p. 8.
8 *Foreign Relations of the United States, The Conferences at Malta and Yalta*, 1945, pp. 505 and 509.
9 ibid., p. 509.
10 ibid.
11 *Foreign Relations of the United States*, 1945, *The Conferences at Malta and Yalta*, p. 717 (Bohlen minutes), p. 720 (Matthew minutes). Also Churchill, op. cit., p. 374.
12 *Foreign Relations of the United States*, 1945, *The Conferences at Malta and Yalta*, p. 717.
13 There is a hidden fallacy in this argument, because if 6 million die and 6 million arrive in their place, then no territorial amputations can be undertaken without thereby increasing the density of population and decreasing the self-sufficiency of the country suffering the amputations. What Churchill was trying to postulate was a reduction of Germany's land and population, which would leave it with about the same ratio of men to food and mineral supply. This, however, did not happen, because while on the one hand Germany lost some 50,000 square miles of territory, it replenished its war population losses by the deportation into post-war Germany of over 6 million Volksdeutsche from Poland, Czechoslovakia, Hungary and Rumania, who had been living outside the Reich in its frontiers of 1937. In addition to this large immigration into a reduced Reich, the 10 million native Germans of the amputated provinces of East Prussia, Pomerania, East Brandenburg, Upper and Lower Silesia and the Free City of Danzig were then crowded into the truncated torso of the Reich.
14 ibid., p. 907; also Churchill, op. cit., p. 374.
15 *Foreign Relations of the United States, The Conference of Berlin*, vol. 2, p. 210; Truman, *Memoirs*, 1955, vol. 1, p. 369; Leahy, *I was There*, 1950, pp. 406–7; Churchill, op. cit., pp. 655–6.

16 Byrnes, op. cit., p. 80; Feis, *Between War and Peace*, 1960, p. 270; Churchill, op. cit., p. 662. *Foreign Relations of the United States, The Conference of Berlin*, vol. 2, p. 382.

17 Four months after the start of the Potsdam Conference it was determined by the Allied Control Council for Germany that the 3·5 million Germans still remaining in Poland and in the Polish-administered territories should be transferred according to a certain timetable. It should be considered that Polish authorities were expelling Germans all during the summer and autumn months of 1945, so that if there were an estimated 3·5 million left on 20 November 1945, there were probably more than 4 million on 21 July 1945, the date of the fifth session.

18 Bohmann, *Menschen und Grenzen*, 1969, vol. 1, p. 272.

19 In a cable dated 4 June 1945, Churchill observed to Truman: 'I view with profound misgivings . . . the descent of an iron curtain between us and everything to the eastward.' Churchill, op. cit., p. 603.

20 Professor Boleslaw Wiewiora opposes this view in *The Polish-German Frontier*, 1959, p. 158.

21 Churchill, op. cit., p. 656; *Foreign Relations of the United States, The Conference of Berlin*, vol. 2, p. 212.

22 Churchill, op. cit., p. 658; *Foreign Relations of the United States, The Conference of Berlin*, vol. 2, p. 248 (Thompson Notes), p. 268 (Cohen notes).

23 ibid., p. 1495. *Documents on American Foreign Relations, 1945–46*, vol. 8, p. 935; Holborn, *War and Peace Aims of the United Nations*, vol. 2, p. 53.

24 It is interesting to note that throughout the discussions on the question of transfers, Stalin did not seem to perceive the Western objections. The Poles and the Czechs wanted to get rid of the Germans, and that sufficed for him. Well, Hitler had also wanted to get rid of the Jews – and it is because of this chronic wanting of illegal things that it became necessary to destroy Hitler. If the Czechs and the Poles wanted to get rid of the Germans and take vengeance on them, the only answer was – sorry, you cannot do it, and if you do it, you commit a crime.

25 *Foreign Relations of the United States, The Conferences at Malta and Yalta*, p. 189.

26 ibid., 1945, vol. 2, p. 1261.

27 *Parliamentary Debates*, House of Commons, vol. 403, col. 1726, 11 October 1944, vol. 407, col. 675; *Parliamentary Debates*, House of Lords, vol. 130, col. 1097–134, 8 March 1944; Ripka, *The Future of the Czechoslovak Germans*, 1944, p. 20, where he extended the number to 'possibly' 1 million. Also *Foreign Relations of the United States*, 1945, vol. 2, pp. 1231, 1237.

28 *Expellees and Refugees of German Ethnic Origin. Report of a Special Subcommittee of the Committee on the Judiciary House of Representatives*, March 1950, hereafter Walter Report, p. 11.

29 *Foreign Relations of the United States*, 1945, vol. 2, p. 1294.

30 Churchill, *The Sinews of Peace*, 1948, pp. 100–1.
31 Compare Walter Report, op. cit., pp. 4–7.
32 *New York Times*, 13 November 1946, p. 26, col. 5, in an article by the distinguished American journalist Anne O'Hare McCormmick.
33 *Parliamentary Debates*, House of Lords, 8 March 1944, vol. 130, col. 1132.
34 *Foreign Relations of the United States*, 1945, vol. 2, pp. 1274, 1275, passim.
35 ibid., pp. 1231, 1260.
36 ibid., p. 1228.
37 ibid., p. 1247.
38 ibid., p. 1248.
39 ibid., p. 1249.
40 ibid., p. 1256.
41 ibid., p. 1258.
42 ibid., p. 1263.
43 F. Voigt, 'Orderly and Humane', *Nineteenth Century and After*, November 1945, p. 201. On 11 July the Czechoslovak Prime Minister, Fierlinger, praised the Russian government for offering 'full help' in transferring the Germans. On 28 July the Czechoslovak Minister of Information, Kopecky, said at a speech in Liberec, 'Marshal Stalin himself has the greatest possible understanding for our endeavors to get rid of the Germans.'
44 *Foreign Relations of the United States*, 1945, vol. 2, p. 1262.
45 ibid., p. 1264.
46 ibid., *The Conference of Berlin*, vol. 2, pp. 536–7.
47 ibid., pp. 1495–96. *Documents on American Foreign Relations*, *1945–46*, vol. 8, pp. 935–6; Holborn, op. cit., vol. 2, p. 53.
48 Minority Rights Group, *The Crimean Tatars, Volga Germans and Meskhetians*, 1973. The Crimean Tatars were precipitously deported on 18 May 1944 and it is estimated that 45 per cent of their number died on the journey or during the first eighteen months after deportation. Compare Alexander Werth, *Russia at War*, 1964, p. 840.
49 Alexander Solzhenitsyn, *The Gulag Archipelago* (Harper & Row paperback), pp. 565, 78–9.
50 *Foreign Relations of the United States, The Conference of Berlin*, vol. 2, pp. 87, 383; Whiteman, *Digest of International Law*, vol. 3, p. 331; Walter Report, op. cit., p. 6; Herbert Feis, *Between War and Peace*, 1960, p. 270.
51 *Foreign Relations of the United States*, 1945, vol. 2, telegrams of the US Ambassador at Warsaw, 1279, 1280, 1319, 1321, 1323 and at Prague, p. 1284.
52 *Congressional Record*, vol. 91, September 19, 1945, A3950–51, 1 November 1945, 10292–94; 4 December 1945, 11371–82; 11 December 1945, A5417–18; 13 December 1945, A5709–11; 18 December 1945, 11287. Also International Committee of the Red Cross, *Report on its Activities During the Second World War*,

vol. 3, pp. 387–9, 424–35. V. Gollancz, *In Darkest Germany*, 1947, passim.

53 *Foreign Relations of the United States*, 1945, vol. 2, p. 1266.
54 ibid., p. 1267.
55 ibid., 1266; Arthur Lane, *I saw Poland Betrayed*, 1948, p. 153.
56 *Foreign Relations of the United States*, 1945, vol. 2, pp. 1272–3.
57 ibid., p. 1274.
58 ibid., pp. 1274–5.
59 ibid., pp. 1288, 1297, 1302.
60 Schieder, *Documents on the Expulsion*, vol. 4, Czechoslovakia, p. 315, Minutes of the talks held between representatives of the CSR on 8 and 9 January 1946, concerning ways and means of carrying out the expulsion of Sudeten Germans and their reception in the American Zone of Occupation in Germany.
61 *Foreign Relations of the United States*, 1945, vol. 2, p. 1280. For reports on the physical abuse of the Germans of the Sudetenland, see Murphy's telegrams of 9 October 1945, ibid., p. 1286, and memorandum of 12 October, 1945, p. 1291.
62 Schieder, *Documents on the Expulsion*, vol. 4, p. 68. See report of a former official of the Czech Administrative Commission in Aussig, ibid., pp. 430–2. See also W. Jaksch, *Europa's Weg nach Potsdam*, 1967, pp. 438–9. Wenzel Jaksch was the leader of the exiled Sudeten Social Democrats in London.
63 Holborn, op. cit., vol. 2, p. 1048.
64 On 28 July 1945 M. Kopecky, the Czechoslovak Minister of Information, made a speech in Liberec (Reichenberg), in which he said: 'We shall expel all the Germans, we shall confiscate their property, we shall de-germanise not only the town but the whole area . . . so that the victorious spirit of Slavdom shall permeate the country from the frontier ranges to the interior.' V. Gollancz, *Our Threatened Values*, 1946, p. 43.
65 *The Economist*, 15 September 1945, p. 369. *The Economist* again demanded a halt in the expulsions of 13 October 1945: 'The first priority in any policy for Germany is thus to persuade the Russians, Czechs and Poles to stop the expulsions', p. 514.
66 *Parliamentary Debates*, House of Commons, 10 October 1945, vol. 414, col. 241.
67 ibid., 22 October 1945, col. 1816.
68 *The Times*, 26 October 1945, p. 4.
69 *Parliamentary Debates*, House of Commons, 26 October 1945, vol. 414, col. 2351.
70 ibid., col. 2360. *The Times*, 27 October, 1945, p. 4.
71 *The Economist*, 10 November 1945, p. 671. Compare, for instance, the Associated Press report on the expulsion of the Germans from Breslau:

> The Polish authorities in Breslau to-day demolished one of the few remaining German monuments in the city, that of Kaiser Wilhelm I, and announced that the 200,000 Germans still in

Breslau would be forced to move into one of the occupied zones
of Germany. The city president, M. Stainislaw Gosniej,
declared in a speech before the monument that 4,000 Germans
were leaving the city every week, and within six months
Wroclaw (Breslau) will be the second city of all Poland. . . .
The Times, 27 October 1945, p. 3.

72 *Foreign Relations of the United States*, 1945, vol. 2, p. 1301.
Telegram of Secretary Byrnes to Robert Murphy, 26 October 1945.

73 *Documents on American Foreign Relations, 1945–46*, vol. 8,
pp. 256–7; Department of State, *Bulletin*, vol. 13, p. 937; Walter
Report, p. 8; Foreign Minister Bevin's speech in the House of
Commons, *Parliamentary Debates*, 23 Nov. 1945, vol. 417, col. 764.

74 *Foreign Relations of the United States*, 1945, vol. 2, pp. 1316–17;
also *Parliamentary Debates*, House of Commons, 19 December
1945, vol. 417, col. 1471.

75 V. Gollancz, *Our Threatened Values*, 1946, p. 7; ICRC, *Report on
its Activities during the Second World War*, vol. 1, p. 425.

76 V. Gollancz, *In Darkest Germany*, 1947, passim.

77 *Time*, 24 December 1945, p. 32.

78 ICRC, *Report on its Activities During the Second World War*,
vol. 1, p. 673.

79 The report of the ICRC further noted with regret the 'apathy and
lack of interest in the deported minorities on the part of peoples
who had themselves been too long oppressed and persecuted.'
p. 674.

CHAPTER SIX 'ORDERLY AND HUMANE' TRANSFERS

1 *Foreign Relations of the United States*, 1945, vol. 2, p. 1321,
Ripka Memorandum, pp. 1234–5.

2 *Parliamentary Debates*, House of Lords, vol. 130, col. 1097–134.
Also, US Post-War Planning Committee Paper, 22 November
1944 in *Foreign Relations of the United States*, 1944, vol. 1, p. 310.

3 *Expellees and Refugees of German Ethnic Origin. Report of a Special
Subcommittee of the Committee on the Judiciary House of
Representatives*, March 1950, hereafter Walter, Report, p. 7:
'American military records reveal that considerable numbers of
expellees began to enter the United States zone of occupation
in Germany long before the official transfer began on 25 January
1946'. See also Monthly Report of the Military Governor,
OMGUS, no. 19, 1 December 1946–31 January 1947.

4 In the summer of 1945 a group of American Senators visited
Europe in order to study conditions there. Senator Eastland
reported to the Senate on 4 December 1945 on his visit:

> We were unable to go into eastern Germany because of the policies
> of the Russian Government, but from authentic reports received,
> both in person and through the press, conditions there, due to the
> policies of the Soviet Government and the conduct of the Soviet

armies, are horrible beyond human comprehension. In fact, by eyewitness accounts, loot, pillage, pestilence, rape, wholesale murder and human suffering form one of the most terrible chapters in human history. Words are incapable of adequately picturing conditions there. The virtue of womanhood and the value of human life are civilized man's most sacred possessions, yet they are the very cheapest thing in Russian-occupied Germany today. . . .

Thousands of people have been murdered, thousands of women violated, and conditions horrible beyond civilized human comprehension prevail. *Congressional Record*, Senate, 4 December 1945, pp. 11372-3.

5 *Daily Mail*, 6 August 1945, quoted in Gollancz, *Our Threatened Values*, 1946, pp. 96-7.

6 F. A. Voigt, 'Orderly and Humane', *The Nineteenth Century and After*, November 1945, pp. 203-4.

7 *Report of the Joint Relief Commission of the International Red Cross, 1941-1946*, pp. 103-4. See also Norman Clark (writing from Berlin) in an article in *News Chronicle*, 12 September 1945 for a similar story about the survivors of a Stettin orphanage. See also *Time*, 12 November 1945, p. 27, for a report on German orphans expelled from an orphanage in Danzig, illustrated with a picture of the starving children. Also V. Gollancz, *Our Threatened Values*, 1946, p. 102.

8 *Parliamentary Debates*, House of Commons, 16 August 1945, vol. 414, col. 83-4; also quoted in *Time*, 27 August 1945, p. 34.

9 *The Times*, Tuesday, 23 October 1945, p. 5; T. S. Eliot echoed Lord Russell's letter in *The Times* of 30 October 1945, p. 5.

10 *Congressional Record*, Senate, 5 February 1946, pp. 878-9.

11 In *Congressional Record*, House of Representatives, Friday, 1 February 1946, A-397, the British major is quoted as saying: 'The greatest horror in modern history is taking place in eastern Germany. Many millions of German people have been ejected onto the roads . . . are dying by the thousands on the roads from starvation, dysentery, and exhaustion. Even a cursory visit to the hospitals in Berlin is an experience which would make the concentration camps appear normal.'

12 Quoted in V. Gollancz, op. cit., pp. 97-9.

13 ibid., pp. 101-2.

14 Voigt, op. cit. p. 200; also cited in *Congressional Record*, Senate, 29 March 1946, p. 2806.

15 Voigt, op. cit., p. 203.

16 Also cited in *Congressional Record*, Senate, 4 December 1945, pp. 11373-4. For other expulsion reports see *Congressional Record*, Senate, 11 December 1945, Appendix, A-5417-18; House of Representatives, 1 February 1946, Appendix, A-397, 398; Senate, 5 February 1946, pp. 878-9, 894-5, 900-1; 29 March 1946, pp. 2805-6; 29 July 1946, A-4772.

17 *Parliamentary Debates*, House of Commons, 26 October 1945, vol. 414, col. 2382; also cited in *The Times*, 27 October 1945, p. 4, in the US *Congressional Record*, 11 December 1945, p. A-5417 and again on 29 January 1946, p. 511.
18 *Foreign Relations of the United States*, 1945, vol. 2, pp. 1290-2.
19 ibid., p. 1301.
20 ibid., p. 1312.
21 ibid., p. 1317.
22 ibid., pp. 1318-19.
23 ibid., p. 1321.
24 ibid., p. 1322.
25 ibid., p. 1323. Admiral Nelson broke up the armed neutrality of Denmark in 1801 by bombarding Copenhagen – without a declaration of war. Lord Nelson had lost vision in one eye during the battle of Calvi (Corsica) in 1794.
26 Arthur Lane, *I Saw Poland Betrayed*, 1948, p. 153.
27 *Foreign Relations of the United States*, 1945, vol. 2, p. 1325. According to the Polish Yearbook of 1947, a total of 1,485,603 Poles from the area east of the Curzon Line had been transferred to Western Poland. *Rocznik Statystyczny*, 1947, p. 29.
28 *Foreign Relations of the United States*, 1945, vol. 2, p. 1325.
29 ibid., pp. 1275, 1278.
30 ibid., p. 1280.
31 Ost-Dokumente, Bundesarchiv-Koblenz; see also Schieder, *Dokumentation der Vertreibung*, vol. 4.
32 *Foreign Relations of the United States*, 1945, vol. 2, p. 1283.
33 ibid., p. 1286.
34 ibid., pp. 1286, 1291.
35 K. Kurth, *Documents of Humanity*, 1954, with a foreword by Albert Schweitzer, pp. 18-23.
36 *Parliamentary Debates*, House of Lords, 30 January 1946, vol. 139, col. 85.
37 ibid., col. 84.
38 The ICRC's delegation in Slovakia received early authority to operate in camps of German internees. Czech authorities, however, required special application to be made for each visit. *ICRC Report on its Activities during the Second World War* (hereafter *ICRC Report*), vol. 1, p. 676.
39 *Revue International de la Croix Rouge*, November 1945, pp. 898-9.
40 Lucius Clay, *Decision in Germany*, 1950, pp. 313-14.
41 Gollancz, *Our Threatened Values*, pp. 104-5.
42 *New York Times*, Monday, 4 February 1946, 'Abroad: As UNO Prepares to Settle in this Neighborhood'.
43 ibid., Wednesday, 23 October 1946, 'Abroad: Wiesbaden Plans Portentous Exhibition'.
44 Clay, op. cit., p. 314; also M. Proudfoot, *European Refugees*, 1957, p. 375.
45 *ICRC Report*, vol. 1, p. 677.
46 A. Bohmann, *Das Sudetendeutschtum in Zahlen*, 1959. There are

lists of the 1946 and 1947 transports going into the American zones. No lists were prepared for the Germans sent into the Soviet zone. It should be noted, however, that while the train-transport itself may have been 'orderly', the many months of internment that usually preceded the transfers claimed a very high toll of lives and left many so weak that they died soon after arrival in the Soviet or American zones.

47 Personal interviews with survivors of camps in Poland and Czechoslovakia. Tape recordings in author's library. Original affidavits of survivors in the Ost-Dokumente collection of the German Federal Archives in Koblenz. Also in various reports published in Schieder, *Dokumentation der Vertreibung*.

48 *ICRC Report*, vol. 1, p. 334. Also personal research in the archives of the ICRC in Geneva.

49 ibid., p. 675.

50 ibid., p. 676.

51 H. G. Alder, *Theresienstadt 1941–1945 – Das Antlitz einer Zwangsgemeinschaft*, 1955, p. 214. See also Schieder, *Documents on the Expulsion*, vol. 4, p. 76. Also personal interview with a German survivor.

52 M. Littman, 'The Bible of Pan-Slavism', *Nineteenth Century and After*, December 1945, pp. 261–3.

53 H. Esser, *Lamsdorf, Dokumentation über ein Polnisches Vernichtungslager*, 1971, p. 98. Compare Schieder, *Dokumentation der Vertreibung*, vol. 1/2, pp. 423ff. See also questions of CDU Abgeordneter Milz to Bundesinnenminister Maihofer about the Lamsdorf documents. Bundestag Drucksache 7/2642, 7. Wahlperiode, questions 11 and 12.

54 *ICRC Report*, vol. 1, p. 677. For an interesting report on conditions in Polish camps see 'Evacuation and Concentration Camps in Silesia', *Congressional Record*, Senate, 2 August 1946, Appendix A-4778/79.

55 *ICRC Report*, vol. 1, p. 677.

56 In the year 1948 the ICRC was able to visit Kalawsk and the assembly centres of Wroclaw and Lodz, but was not given permission to visit other civilian internee camps. *ICRC Report* for 1948, p. 65.

57 *ICRC Report*, vol. 1, p. 678.

58 ibid.

59 ibid.

60 ibid.

61 United States Court, Allied High Commission for Germany, Fifth District, President Leo M. Goodman, *In re Hrnecek*, Matter Number Crim 52-A-5-486, of 26 May 1954. Also cited in H. Schoenberg, *Germans from the East*, p. 19, n. 10.

62 *Isvestija*, 3 March 1975; *Radio Moskau* (transmission in German), 2 August 1974; *Rude Pravo*, 2 August 1974, p. 7, article by Kubin entitled 'Unparalleled cynicism; ibid., 5 August 1974, p. 5, article by Karel Doudera entitled 'A legend that twists history'; ibid.,

2 February 1975, p. 7, article by Doudera 'Cui Bono'; *Trybunu Ludu*, 7 February 1975, 13 February 1975, long article by R. Wojna, 17 February 1975; *Neues Deutschland*, 31 July 1974, 6 August 1974, etc.

63 In his book *The Polish-German Frontier*, 1959, Professor Wiewiora writes, for instance, 'It is not difficult to see that Laun follows the Hitlerite line of thought', p. 156.

64 Wiewiora, op. cit., p. 132.

65 L. Gelberg, 'Poland's Western Border and Transfer of German Population', *American Journal of International Law*, 1965, vol. 59, p. 590. See also M. Lachs, *Poland's Western Frontier*, 1965.

66 Churchill, *Triumph and Tragedy*, 1953, pp. 374, 648, 658, 672, Truman, *Mèmoirs*, 1955, vol. 1, p. 370, Byrnes, *Speaking Frankly*, 1947, p. 80.

67 von Braun, 'Germany's Eastern Border and Mass Expulsions', *American Journal of International Law*, 1964, vol. 58, p. 749.

68 Gelberg, op. cit., p. 591.

69 Speaking in the House of Commons on 22 August 1945, Mr Evans reported

at the present time 200,000 old people, women and children are pouring into Berlin each week from the east. They are homeless and possess nothing but that in which they stand up. One woman brought six children in two perambulators 90 miles . . . Is this what those gallant souls, who will not come back, those who will not grow old as we shall grow old, fought and died for? *Parliamentary Debates*, House of Commons, vol. 413, col. 743. See Stanislaw Schimitzek, *Truth or Conjecture*, 1966.

70 Benes, *Memoirs*, 1954, p. 222.

71 ibid., p. 237, n. 9. Compare report in *Neue Zürcher Zeitung*, 23 August 1945, p. 1, col. 7.

72 Statistisches Bundesamt, *Vertreibungsverluste*, 1958, p. 325.

73 R. Luza, *The Transfer of the Sudeten Germans*, 1964, p. 269.

74 ibid., p. 272, n. 26. Compare Schieder, *Documents on the Expulsion*, vol. 4, pp. 201-2. See also Gollancz, *Our Threatened Values*, pp. 96-7 and report of Rhona Churchill in *Daily Mail*, 6 August 1945.

75 Luza, op. cit., p. 272; Schieder, op. cit., pp. 68, 430-2; also Jaksch, *Der Weg Nach Potsdam*, 1958, p. 438-9, Ernst Paul, *Es gibt nicht nur ein Lidice*. n.d. Jaksch and Paul were both Sudeten Social Democrats who went into exile in London in 1938 after the Munich Agreement.

76 Luza, op. cit., pp. 272-3.

77 ibid., p. 273, n. 29.

78 ibid., p. 321.

79 Walter Report, op. cit., p. 11; also Proudfoot, op. cit., p. 375.

80 The American Congressman Caroll Reece argued in the House of Representatives that the expulsion of the Germans involved the crime of genocide (*Congressional Record*, 16 May 1957, p. 7118). Whilst the UN Convention on the Prevention and Punishment of

genocide does not include transfers of population as a form of
genocide, transfers that degenerate into expulsions and result in
millions of deaths would certainly fall in the category of genocide.
See also the articles of Ann O'Hare McCormick in the *New York
Times*, 4 February 1946 and 23 October 1946.

81 Alfred de Zayas, 'International Law and Mass Population
Transfers', *Harvard International Law Journal*, 1975, vol. 16,
pp. 207ff.

CHAPTER SEVEN   FROM MORGENTHAU PLAN TO MARSHALL PLAN

1 *Documents on American Foreign Relations*, vol. 7, 1944-5, p. 189.
H. Morgenthau, *Germany is Our Problem*, 1945; reviewed in
Time, 15 October 1945, p. 23. The English counterpart of
Secretary Morgenthau was Lord Vansittart, who advocated a hard
peace in his books, *Bones of Contention*, 1943, *Black Record*, 1941,
and *Lessons of My Life*. See review in *Time*, 16 July 1945, p. 27.

2 The American Secretary of State Cordell Hull remained in
Washington where the Dumbarton Oaks Conference was still in
progress. Hull, *Memoirs*, vol. 2, p. 1602.

3 L. Clay, *Decision in Germany*, 1950, p. 11.

4 See Senator Eastland's critique of the plan in *Congressional Record*,
Senate, 4 December 1945, pp. 11372-5; also Sen. Langer,
18 April 1946, pp. 3962-70.

5 *Documents on American Foreign Relations*, vol. 7 pp. 196, 202; also
Herbert Feis, *Between War and Peace*, 1960, p. 336.

6 In a memorandum to Secretary of War Stimson dated 26 August
1944, President Roosevelt objected to the *Handbook* drawn up by
the War Department for the guidance of military government
officials in Germany. 'It gives the impression,' Roosevelt
complained, 'that Germany is to be restored just as much as the
Netherlands or Belgium, and the people of Germany brought
back as quickly as possible to their prewar estate.' *Foreign
Relations of the United States*, 1944, vol. 1, p. 544. See also Hull,
Memoirs, p. 1602. In a memorandum to the President written by
Hull on 29 September 1944 'It is of the highest importance that
the standard of living of the German people in the early years be
such as to bring home to them that they have lost the war . . .'
*Foreign Relations of the United States, The Conferences at Malta
and Yalta*, p. 158.

7 *Report of the International Committee of the Red Cross on its
activities during the Second World War*, vol. 3, pp. 288-9.

8 *Foreign Relations of the United States, The Conference of Berlin*,
vol. 2, p. 1504; also *American Journal of International Law*, 1945,
vol. 39, Supp., p. 250.

9 ibid., p. 250.

10 ibid.

11 ICRC Report, vol. 3, pp. 427-8.

12 ibid., pp. 388, 431.

13 ibid., p. 431.
14 ibid., pp. 433-4.
15 *Congressional Record*, Senate, 29 January 1946, p. 512.
16 In his *Memoirs*, 1955, President Truman recalls a conversation
   with Secretary of War Henry L. Stimson:
   I made it clear that I was opposed to what was then loosely
   called the Morgenthau Plan – that is, the reduction of Germany
   to a wholly agrarian economy. I had never been for that plan
   even when I was in the Senate, and since reaching the White
   House I had come to feel even more strongly about it. I thought
   it was proper to disarm Germany, to dismantle her military
   might, to punish the war criminals, and to put her under an
   overall Allied control until we could restore the peace. But I
   did not approve of reducing Germany to an agrarian state.
   Such a program could starve Germany to death . . . (vol. 1,
   p. 235).
17 ibid., p. 327.
   When he found out I was going to Potsdam in July, Secretary
   Morgenthau came in to ask if he could go with me. I told
   him I thought the Secretary of the Treasury was badly needed
   in the United States – much more so than in Potsdam. He
   replied that it was necessary for him to go and that if he could
   not he would have to quit.
      'All right,' I replied, 'if that is the way you feel, I'll accept
   your resignation right now.' And I did. That was the end of
   the conversation and the end of the Morgenthau Plan.
18 See Morgenthau's defence of his plan in *Congressional Record*,
   21 March 1946, pp. A-2150-1 (Appendix). For a lively report on
   the foibles of the Morgenthau Plan as implemented by Joint
   Chiefs of Staff Memorandum No. 1067/6, see David M. Nichol,
   'The Hard Peace', in Arthur Settel (ed.), *This is Germany*,
   1950, pp. 226-48.
19 *Congressional Record*, Senate, 15 May 1946, p. 5039.
20 Morgenthau, op. cit., annexed memorandum for the Quebec
   Conference. See also map on p. 160 of Morgenthau, op. cit.
21 On the other hand, the Morgenthau Plan had envisioned the
   permanent cession of the industrial province of the Saar to
   France. The Potsdam Agreement only awarded to France
   certain limited rights over the Saar, far less than France might
   have been able to obtain if it had been allowed to participate as
   equal partner at Potsdam. Subsequently the French
   Government tried to correct this matter, especially at the
   meetings of the Council of Foreign Ministers. The German
   population of the Saar was also offered attractive economic
   privileges in order to induce them to embrace French
   nationality, but in the plebiscite of 1955 the Saar population
   decided to return to Germany. See L. Cowan, *France and the
   Saar*, 1950; P. Fischer, *Die Saar zwischen Deutschland und
   Frankreich*, 1959.

22 In 1971 Holland had a population density of 932·8. *Information Please Almanac*, 1973, p. 249.

23 In 1971 Belgium had a population density of 825·9, ibid., p. 170.

24 In 1970 West Germany had a population density of 620·2, ibid., p. 207. By comparison, France has a density of 242·7, p. 202, Great Britain 587·2, p. 286 and Poland 270·1, p. 259.

25 In 1914 Germany occupied an area of 208,830 square miles. Compare with the area of the State of Texas, 262,134 with a population density of 42·7, ibid., p. 639.

26 Matthias Kramer, 'Agriculture in Eastern Germany', in *The German East*, 1954, p. 135. See also G. C. Paikert, *The German Exodus*, 1962, Table XI in the Appendix.

27 Kramer, op. cit.

28 ibid.

29 Kennan, *Memoirs*, 1967, vol. I, pp. 415–48.

30 Jonathan Swift, *A Modest Proposal for Preventing the Children of Ireland from being a Burden to their Parents or Country*, 1724.

31 Department of State, *Bulletin*, vol. 5, p. 125; *Documents on American Foreign Relations*, vol. 4, p. 209. It was in this spirit that wartime public opinion in America had favoured the idea of helping to rebuild Europe, including a non-Nazi Germany. In July 1944, for instance, the National Opinion Research Center of Denver University polling the forty-eight States on the subjects of whether Americans should help to put Germany back on her industrial feet, even at the cost of continued rationing at home, reported that 64 per cent or nearly a two-thirds majority of the American people advocated this course. See the remarks of Senator Wheeler on the floor of the Senate on 15 January 1945, *Congressional Record*, vol. 91, p. 253. The Morgenthau Plan never really became popular in America; even early in 1945, when 40 per cent of the American public favoured the dismemberment of Germany, only 13 per cent favoured the destruction of German industry. See Gallup, *The Gallup Poll 1935/71*, vol. I, 1972.

32 Kennan, op. cit., vol. I, esp. Ch. 14, 'The Marshall Plan', pp. 325–53, at p. 325.

33 Harry Price, *The Marshall Plan and its Meaning*, 1955, p. 28. In June 1948 Yugoslavia was successful in breaking away from the other communist-bloc countries. By June 1952 it had received 109 million dollars of Marshall Plan aid. ibid., pp. 86 and 91.

34 ibid., p. 29. See also Edwin Borchard, 'Intervention – The Truman Doctrine and the Marshall Plan', *American Journal of International Law*, 1947, vol. 41, p. 886.

35 See quoted report of Mr N. H. Collisson, Deputy Chief of the ECA Mission to the United States-United Kingdom Occupied Areas of Western Germany, to the Foreign Relation Committee of the US Senate, quoted in *Congressional Record*, Senate, 5 April 1949, p. 3893.

36 Herbert Mayer, *German Recovery and the Marshall Plan*, 1969, p. 1.

37 Economic Co-operation Administration, *Third Report to Congress,* 1949, p. 126. From 1938 to 1947 industrial output in the US had more than doubled. *Federal Reserve Bulletin,* November 1954, p. 1193. Price, op. cit., p. 29.

38 Gollancz, *In Darkest Germany,* 1947, passim.

39 Clay, *Decision in Germany,* 1950, p. 124; also Edward Mason, 'Has our Policy in Germany Failed?', *Foreign Affairs,* 1946, vol. 24, pp. 579-90.

40 Clay, op. cit., pp. 121-2.

41 L. Cowan, op. cit.

42 *Documents on American Foreign Relations,* 1947, vol. 9, p. 65. The US-British Zonal Merger Pact was signed on 2 Dec. 1946.

43 *Documents on American Foreign Relations,* 1948, vol. 10, p. 78 and 1949, vol. 11, p. 111. See also Borchard, op. cit., p. 887, where the author expresses a pessimistic forecast for the Marshall Plan and mentions that France continued objecting to increasing the German output.

44 *Documents on American Foreign Relations,* 1949, vol. 11, p. 109.

45 Date of entry into force of the West German Constitution. See Strupp-Schlochauer *Wörterbuch des Völkerrechts,* vol. 1, p. 354. On 21 September 1949 the Allied High Commissioners in Germany were formally advised of the formation of the Federal Republic of Germany and proclaimed on that date that the Occupation Statute was in force. Department of State, *Bulletin,* vol. 21, p. 51, 3 October 1949.

46 Price, op. cit., p. 91.

47 Eugene Davidson, *The Death and Life of Germany,* 1959, pp. 382-3. See also Paikert, op. cit., pp. 34-7.

48 Department of State, *Bulletin,* vol. 28, 1953, pp. 373, 374, 665. See also *Bundesgesetzblatt,* 1953, pp. 492ff.

49 In 1948 Senator Langer introduced section 12 of the DP Law which facilitated the immigration to the US of German expellees. See Appendix to the *Congressional Record,* 24 May 1951, p. A-3055. From 1948 to June 1950 only 10,090 visas were issued by the State Department to ethnic-German immigrants.

50 See statement by M. Bidault on the German population problem on 15 March 1947, *Documents on International Affairs 1947-8,* Royal Institute of International Affairs, pp. 422-4 at p. 423.

51 *Expellees and Refugees. Report of a special subcommittee of the Committee on the Judiciary House of Representatives,* March 1950, hereafter Walter Report, p. 87. For a German opinion opposed to emigration see the pamphlet prepared by the Göttingen Scientific Circle, 1950, *Emigration, A Means of Solving the German Problem?* The pamphlet concludes, 'Only by re-uniting the German East to Europe can the German Problem be solved and at the same time the creation of a Europe both self-supporting and united be rendered possible. Until the time has come to consider this, no purely superficial pseudo-solution by emigration should be attempted', p. 9.

52 Mayer, op. cit., p. 100.
53 E. Dittrich, 'Verlagerungen in der Industrie', in Lemberg and Edding (eds), *Die Vertriebenen in Westdeutschland*, 1959, vol. 2, pp. 296-374.
54 The Germans of Bohemia and Moravia established breweries in nearly all the towns they founded. German settlers founded Pilsen in the year 1295, and the town retained a German majority until 1860 when industry introduced large numbers of Czech labourers. The special quality of Pilsener Beer was an achievement of the Bavarian brew-master Josef Groll who headed one of the four Pilsener breweries in 1842. Similarly the town of Budweis retained its German majority until around 1900 and boasted of one of Bohemia's best-loved beers.

CHAPTER EIGHT PEACE WITHOUT A PEACE TREATY

1 Oppenheim-Lauterpacht, *International Law*, vol. 2 (7th edn), p. 597.
2 ibid., p. 600: 'Subjugation takes place only when a belligerent, after having annihilated the forces and conquered the territory of his adversary, destroys his existence by annexing the conquered territory.' In the Berlin Declaration of 5 June 1945 the Allies renounced annexation of Germany. Text in *American Journal of International Law*, 1945, vol. 39, Supp., p. 172.
3 *Documents on American Foreign Relations*, vol. 9, 1947, p. 2.
4 ibid., p. 699; Department of State, *Bulletin*, vol. 16, p. 199. For the text of the treaty with Italy, see Department of State, Treaties and Other International Acts Series 1648; The First Five Peace Treaties. Supplement: *Documents on American Foreign Relations*, vol. 8, 1945-6.
5 ibid., vol. 9, pp. 641, 696, 711.
6 ibid., vol. 12, pp. 485-6.
7 Department of State, *Bulletin*, vol. 26, no. 671, pp. 687ff. 5 May 1952. For the text of the treaty of peace with Japan, see *Bulletin* of 27 August 1951, p. 349. At the time of its coming into force, the United States, Great Britain and France had ratified the treaty, but not the Soviet Union.
8 During the Yalta Conference the zonal division of Germany drawn by the European Advisory Commission on 12 September 1944, was officially adopted. See *Foreign Relations of the United States*, 1944, vol. 1, General, pp. 150-3, 177, 231, 318; Also *The Conferences at Malta and Yalta*, pp. 138-41; also Berlin Declaration of 5 June 1945, supra. For an interesting article on how the zones were drawn, see Philip Mosely, 'The Occupation of Germany', *Foreign Affairs*, 1949, vol. 28, pp. 580-604.

It has sometimes been suggested that it was a basic error to divide Germany into zones of occupation; and that it would have been better to station Allied forces in dispersed or interlarded fashion and thus to avoid the creation of separate zones. A tentative proposal to this effect was put forward informally in late December 1943 by a member of the British Foreign Office during a reconnaissance visit to Washington. If the proposal had been adopted, the establishment of zones and the de facto partition of Germany might conceivably have been avoided (p.588).

9 The phrase 'iron curtain' was popularized by Winston Churchill in his Address at Westminster College in Fulton, Missouri on 5 March 1946. His first recorded use of the phrase was in a cable to Truman on 4 June 1945, 'I view with profound misgivings . . . the descent of an iron curtain between us and everything to the eastward', *Triumph and Tragedy*, 1953, p. 523. However, the term had already been used by Dr Goebbels in the leading article of the weekly *Das Reich*, 25 February 1945: 'Should the German people lay down its arms, the agreement between Roosevelt, Churchill and Stalin would allow the Soviets to occupy all Eastern and South-eastern Europe together with the major part of the Reich. An iron curtain would at once descend on this territory. . . .'

10 See statement on zones of occupation in Germany, Berlin Declaration of 5 June 1945, Text in *Department of State, Bulletin*, 1945, vol. 12, p. 1052.

11 *American Journal of International Law*, 1945, vol. 39, Supplement p. 247. See also President Truman's radio address of 9 August 1945, in which Truman summarized the decisions of the Potsdam Conference, which was understood by all as laying the groundwork for the peace conference. See L. Holborn, *War and Peace Aims of the United Nations*, vol. 2, pp. 340ff. Also Department of State, *Bulletin*, 1945, vol. 13, pp. 208–13.

12 *Parliamentary Debates*, House of Commons, vol. 427, 22 October 1946, col. 417.

13 ibid., col. 1519.

14 L. Clay, *Decision in Germany*, 1950, pp.134–5.

15 ibid., pp. 138–9.

16 Department of State, *Bulletin*, vol. 13, p. 964; *Documents on American Foreign Relations*, vol. 8, pp. 198–201.

17 Department of State, *Bulletin*, vol. 15, p. 49; *Documents on American Foreign Relations*, vol. 8, pp. 210–18. For a description of the reaction to the speech, see L. Clay, op. cit., pp. 78–81.

18 *Parliamentary Debates*, House of Commons, 22 October 1946, col. 1521–2.

19 Robert Murphy, *Diplomat among Warriors*, 1964, p. 376.

20 ibid.

21 Kennan, *Memoirs*, 1967, vol. 1, p. 420.

22 L. Clay, op. cit., pp. 240–1.

23 ibid., p. 444.

24 Edward Taborsky, 'Benes and the Soviets', *Foreign Affairs*, 1949, vol. 27, pp. 302–14.

25 Kennan, op. cit., p. 258.

26 In a personal conversation with a professor of international law at a university in East Germany, this Professor, who is a politically convinced Communist, expressed criticism of the Soviet Union and said with respect to the colonial status of the GDR: 'Zwanzig Jahre lang haben uns die Russen ausgepresst.'

27 Note, 'Judicial Determination of the End of the War', *Columbia Law Review*, 1947, vol. 47, pp. 255–68. Also H. Mosler and K. Doehring *Die Beendigung des Kriegszustands mit Deutchland nach dem zweiten Weltkrieg*, 1963, reviewed in *American Journal of International Law*, 1965, vol. 59, p. 696.

28 Department of State, *Bulletin*, vol. 16, 77. Also Proclamation 2714, Federal Register, XII, p. 1; also *Documents on American Foreign Relations*, vol. 8, pp. 112–3.

29 Oppenheim-Lauterpacht, op. cit., vol. 2, p. 604.

30 Proc. 2940, 16 *Fed. Reg.* 10915; Department of State, *Bulletin*, vol. 25, p. 769

31 *United Nations Treaty Series*, vol. 331, pp. 252ff.

32 ibid., pp. 327ff.

33 See Doc. No. 11, 84th Congress 1st Session (1955), Appendix A, p. 129; *American Journal of International Law*, 1955, vol. 49. Supp., p. 59.

34 United Kingdom Command Papers, 9304, p. 55 A. Toynbee, *Survey of International Affairs*, 1954, p. 146.

35 Gottfried Zieger, *Der Warschauer Pakt*, 1974. The Warsaw Pact had its genesis on 14 May 1955 and was signed by the representatives of the governments of Albania, Bulgaria, Hungary, and the Soviet Union.

36 A. Toynbee, op. cit., pp. 132ff., 1958, pp. 575–6.

37 At this time Kennan occupied a special chair known as the Eastman Professorship at the University of Oxford, and was invited by the British Broadcasting Corporation to deliver the annual series of talks known as the Reith Lectures. In previous years Arnold Toynbee, Oliver Franks, Bertrand Russell and Robert Oppenheimer had given these radio talks. The Reith Lectures were published in the volume entitled *Russia, the Atom, and the West*, 1958.

38 Kennan, op. cit., vol. 2, p. 243.

39 ibid., p. 253.

40 ibid.

CHAPTER NINE   RECOGNITION OR REVISION OF THE ODER-NEISSE LINE

1 English Text in Press and Information Office of the Federal Government of Germany, The Treaty between the Federal Republic of Germany and the People's Republic of Poland. See

also *The Times* (London), Saturday, 21 November 1970, p. 3, col. 1.

2 For a Polish view on this question see Krzysztof Skubiszewski, 'Poland's Western Frontier and the 1970 Treaties', *American Journal of International Law*, 1973, vol. 67, p. 23. For a German view see Dietrich Rauschning, 'Die Endgültigkeit der in dem Vertrag mit Polen getroffenen Gebietsregelung', in *Ostverträge*, Veröffentlichungen des Instituts für Internationales Recht an der Universität Kiel, Symposium, March 1971, pp. 164–73.

3 *United Nations Treaty Series*, vol. 319, pp. 93ff. and *Dokumente zur Aussenpolitik der Regierung der Deutschen Demkratischen Republik*, vol. 1, pp. 342ff.

4 Compare Wiewiora, *The Polish-German Frontier*, 1959, pp. 170–1. See also B. Wiewiora, 'Territorial Changes after the Second World War', *Polish Western Affairs*, vol. 5, pp. 21ff., 1964. For a moderate Polish opinion compare Krysztof Skubiszewski, 'Polish-German Frontier as a Problem of International Law', *Polish Western Affairs*, vol. 5, pp. 311–31, 1964. This was a paper delivered by Professor Skubiszewski at the Harvard International Law Club on 13 April 1964.

5 Declarations by the Soviet Minister for Foreign Affairs, 17 September 1946 and 9 April 1947. See V. Molotov, *Questions de Politique Extérieure*, 1949, pp. 244 and 429. Also cited in Krzysztof Skubiszewski, 'Poland's Western Frontier and the 1970 Treaties', *American Journal of International Law*, 1973, vol. 67, p. 23.

6 Documents on Germany 1944–70 (Committee print, Committee on Foreign Relations, US Senate, 92nd Congress, 1st Session). Also, 'US Foreign Policy for the 1970's Building for Peace', A Report to the Congress by Richard Nixon, 25 February 1971. Also Communiqué of 1 June 1972, Department of State, *Bulletin*, vol. 66, pp. 913–14.

7 Letter to the author from the British Embassy in Bonn, dated 27 June 1975, stating that 'HMG's legal position remains that to which they are committed by the terms of the Potsdam Protocol of 1945, namely that 'the final delimitation of the western frontier of Poland should await a peace settlement.' Also letter to the author from the US State Department, dated 27 May 1975, confirming that 'The position expressed in these statements is still the official United States position.'

8 The Soviet Government blocked all plans for holding free elections in Germany after the war. Among others it rejected the 1951 proposal of the Western Allies that free elections be supervised by the United Nations, *United Nations Year Book*, 1951, p. 325. UN General Assembly 6th Session, General Committee, 76th Meeting, para. 38ff. Compare H. Schneider, *Die Charter der Vereinten Nationen und das Sonderrecht für die im Zweiten Weltkrieg unterlegenen Nationen*, Bonner Rechtswissenschaftliche Abhandlungen, vol. 76, 1967, pp. 112–15. See above, Chapter 8.

9 Text in Department of State, *Bulletin*, vol. 12, 1945, p. 1052.
10 With the exception of Königsberg and the northern third of East Prussia.
11 Leahy, *I was There*, 1950, p. 406.
12 For a discussion of the difference between 'delimitation' and 'demarcation' see E. Luard, *The International Regulation of Frontier Disputes*, 1970, pp. 112ff.; C. de Visscher, *Problèmes de Confins en Droit International Public*, 1969, pp. 11ff.; P. de Lapradelle, *La Frontière*, 1928, pp. 144ff.; A. O. Cuckwurah, *The Settlement of Boundary Disputes in International Law*, 1967. For a Polish view see J. Kokot, *The Logic of the Oder-Neisse Frontier*, 1959, esp. pp. 27–37.
13 Churchill, *Triumph and Tragedy*, 1953, p. 656; Truman, *Memoirs*, 1955, vol. 1, p. 368; *Foreign Relations of the United States, The Conference of Berlin*, vol. 2, p. 212.
14 Churchill, op. cit., p. 672.
15 *Foreign Relations of the United States, The Conference of Berlin*, vol. 2, p. 534. Truman, op. cit., p. 405; Fischer, *Tehran, Jalta, Potsdam*, 1968, p. 348.
16 *Foreign Relations of the United States, The Conference of Berlin*, vol. 2, p. 519, Truman, op. cit., p. 405, Fischer, op. cit., p. 348, Leahy, op. cit., p. 423.
17 Byrnes, *Speaking Frankly*, 1947, p. 81.
18 Department of State, *Bulletin*, vol. 13, 1945, p. 211; Holborn, *War and Peace Aims of the United Nations*, vol. 2, p. 352.
19 Holborn, op. cit., p. 353, Department of State, *Bulletin*, vol. 13, 1945, p. 211.
20 Wiewiora, *The Polish-German Frontier*, 1959, pp. 142–3, 184. Manfred Lachs, *Die Westgrenze Polens*, 1967 p. 69; Drzewieniecki, *The German-Polish Frontier*, p. 69. J. Kokot, *The Logic of the Oder-Neisse Frontier*, pp. 12, 13, 53, 76.
    Molotov cited this part of Truman's speech at the Moscow Conference of Foreign Ministers in March of 1947 and was at once sharply refuted by Secretary of State Marshall. *Foreign Relations of the United States*, 1947, vol. 2, p. 322.
21 Wiewiora, op. cit., p. 143.
22 Truman, op. cit., p. 411. In a letter dated 30 July 1945 Truman complained about the difficulties of reaching any agreement with the Russians: 'You never saw such pig-headed people as are the Russians. I hope I never have to hold another conference with them – but, of course, I will' (p. 402).
23 *United Nations Treaty Series*, vol. 10, pp. 193–201 at p. 201: 'Jusqu à la solution définitive des questions territoriales lors du réglement de la paix, la partie de la frontière polono-soviétique adjacente à la mer Baltique suivra, conformément à la décision de la Conférence de Berlin, une ligne. . . ' The Soviet-Polish frontier through East Prussia was not 'finalized' until the Treaty of 8 July 1948, of course, without the consent of the Western Allies, *United Nations Treaty Series*, vol. 37, p. 25.

24 *Parliamentaty Debates*, House of Commons, vol. 414, col. 83.
See also *Time*, 27 August 1945, p. 34.
25 Wiewiora, op. cit., pp. 148, 160 note; J. Kokot, op. cit., p. 8;
Elisabeth Wiskemann, *Germany's Eastern Neighbours*, 1956,
pp. 133–4.
26 *Foreign Relations of the United States, The Conferences at Malta
and Yalta*, pp. 717, 720, 726, etc.
27 Churchill, op. cit., pp. 661–2.
28 ibid., pp. 663–4.
29 ibid., p. 664.
30 ibid., pp. 666–7. It would not be long before Churchill again
raised his voice in protest against what was happening in
Eastern Europe. In his widely known 'Sinews of Peace' address at
Westminster College in Fulton, Missouri on 5 March 1946,
Churchill deplored the excesses to which his own policy of
compensating Poland at the expense of Germany had led. The
Allies had offered Poland a finger and Poland had proceeded to
take the whole arm: 'The Russian-dominated Polish Government
has been encouraged to make enormous and wrongful inroads
upon Germany, and mass expulsions of millions of Germans on a
scale grievous and undreamed-of are now taking place.' *The
Sinews of Peace*, 1948, pp. 100–1.
31 *Parliamentary Debates*, House of Commons, vol. 414, cols 242–3,
10 October 1945.
32 Arthur Lane, *I Saw Poland Betrayed*, 1948, pp. 240, 254, 117n,
180–1, 191. Also Mikolajczyk, *The Rape of Poland*, 1948, esp.
Chs 13 and 14, pp. 161–202.
33 Lane, op. cit., p. 246; Mikolajczyk, op. cit., pp. 167–8.
34 *Parliamentary Debates*, House of Commons, 22 October 1946,
vol. 427, col. 1523.
35 Department of State, *Bulletin*, vol. 15, pp. 496ff. *Documents on
American Foreign Relations*, vol. 8, pp. 210–18 at p. 217.
Mikolajczyk learned of the speech in Copenhagen and immediately
made a declaration to the Press protesting against it. Mikolajczyk,
op. cit., pp. 171–2. Also Rozek, *Allied Wartime Diplomacy*, 1958,
pp. 423–4.
36 S. Welles, *Where are We Heading?* 1946, p. 120.
37 *Foreign Relations of the United States*, 1947, vol. 2, p. 1.
38 The government of Czechoslovakia even proposed adjustments of
her frontiers with Germany that would have given her additional
German lands in the north and the west.
39 *Foreign Relations of the United States*, 1947, vol. 2, p. 110.
40 ibid., p. 67.
41 ibid.
42 ibid., p. 65.
43 ibid., p. 63.
44 *Documents on American Foreign Relations*, 1947, vol. 9, p. 46.
Department of State, *Bulletin*, 20 April 1947, pp. 693–4; also

Documents on International Affairs, Royal Institute, 1947-8, pp. 462-5; Whiteman, *Digest of International Law*, vol. 3, p. 365.

45 Montgomery, *Memoirs*, 1958, p. 415, Gollancz, *Our Threatened Values*, 1946, p. 7, passim.

46 Europa Archiv 2/1947, pp. 719-20; also Whiteman, op. cit., p. 370.

47 Europa Archiv 2/1947, p. 720; Whiteman, op. cit., p. 371; also Royal Institute, *Documents on International Affairs*, 1947-8, pp. 476-7.

48 Wiewiora, op. cit., pp. 140-3. Lachs, op. cit., pp. 24-6 (German edn).

49 W. M. Drzenieniecki, *The German-Polish Frontier*, 1959, pp. 68-9.

50 Clay, *Decision in Germany*, 1950, p. 313.

51 *Foreign Relations of the United States*, 1945, vol. 2, p. 1301.

52 ibid., 1947, vol. 4, p. 428.

53 ibid.

54 Secretary of State Edward Stettinius recalls in his book on the Yalta Conference that the Western Allies asked Stalin for a magnanimous act in favour of the Poles, for a modification of the Curzon Line that would leave Lemberg within Poland. Stalin replied that 'he would prefer to have the war continue, in spite of the blood it would cost Russia, in order to secure land from Germany to compensate Poland.' Stettinius, *Roosevelt and the Russians*, 1950, p. 146. Stalin's statement sounds even more macabre when one considers that the Soviet Union had adhered to the Atlantic Charter, Article I of which was a renunciation of territorial aggrandizement and Article II of which provided that that the signatories 'desire to see no territorial changes that do not accord with the freely expressed wishes of the peoples concerned'.

55 *Documents on International Affairs*, 1947-8, Royal Institute on International Affairs, p. 488.

56 ibid., p. 508. Compare in this connection J. Kokot, 'The Economic Aspects of the Resettlement of German Population after the Second World War', *Polish Western Affairs*, 1964, vol. 5, pp. 92ff.

57 The Germanic Silinger tribe of the Vandal family lived in Silesia from 300 BC to about AD 350 and gave their name to the province. For a Polish view on the German settlement in Silesia and East Prussia in the Middle Ages and after see G. Labuda, 'A Historiographic Analysis of the German Drang nach Osten', *Polish Western Affairs*, 1964, vol. 5, pp. 221-65.

58 On 1 March 1945 Mr Attlee said in the House of Commons: 'I recall very well receiving a card this Christmas from one of my Polish friends. It was rather characteristic. It consisted of a map of Poland in the 17th Century. It is this tragic harking back . . . instead of looking to the future, that makes the establishment of permanent peace so difficult.' *Parliamentary Debates*, House of Commons, vol. 408, col. 1615.

59 *The Economist*, 19 April 1947, p. 578.
60 ibid., 3 May 1947, pp. 663ff.
61 *Documents on International Relations*, Royal Institute, 1947-8, pp. 532-7 at p. 533. Department of State, *Bulletin*, 28 December 1947, pp. 1244-7.
62 *Documents on International Affairs*, Royal Institute of International Affairs, 1947-8, p. 571.
63 Department of State, Publication 6096, *Termination of the Occupation Regime in the Federal Republic of Germany*, p. 142. *United Nations Treaty Series*, vol. 331, pp. 327ff., at p. 334.
64 Conversation with German expert at the Office of the Legal Adviser to the State Department in Washington, Mr David Small, on 5 January 1976.
65 'U.S. Foreign Policy for the 1970's: Building for Peace', a report to the Congress by Richard Nixon, President of the United States, 25 February 1971, p. 41.
66 Department of State, *Bulletin*, vol. 73, p. 324.
67 ibid.
68 D. Vignes, 'Le referendum sarrois', *Annuaire Français de Droit International*, 1955, p. 134; M. Merle, 'La Convention franco-allemande du 23 octobre 1954 sur la Sarre', ibid., 1955, p. 128; Marcel Merle, 'Le Réglement de la Question Sarroise et la Liquidation du Contentieux Franco-Allemand', ibid., 1956, pp. 181-203.
69 Okinawa (454 square miles) is the largest of the Ryukyu Islands (848 square miles) extending from southern Japan to Taiwan and having a population of approximately 1 million. On 15 May 1972 the Ryukyus were returned to Japanese administration under the the terms of the Okinawa Reversion Treaty of 17 June 1971. See Department of State, *Bulletin*, vol. 64, pp. 323, 381, 452, 470, 598, 798; vol. 65, pp. 8, 69, 299, 461, 514, 624, 655.

CHAPTER TEN TOWARDS THE FUTURE

1 U. Scheuner and Beate Lindemann, *Die Vereinten Nationen und die Mitarbeit der Bundesrepublik Deutschland*, 1973, especially the article written by Professor Wilhelm Kewenig.
2 Reunification is written into the German Constitution (Grundgesetz), see preamble and Article 146.
3 *Freedom at Issue*, January-February 1976, no. 34, p. 15.
4 *The Times* (London), Monday 21 July 1975, p. 1.
5 Department of State, *Bulletin*, vol. 73, 1 September 1975, pp. 323ff.
6 *The Times*, Monday 21 July 1975, p. 4.
7 Department of State, *Bulletin*, vol. 73, 1 September 1975, pp. 304-5.
8 ibid., p. 324.
9 ibid. See also President's Ford statement at p. 306.
10 ibid., p. 348.
11 ibid., p. 325.

12 ibid.
13 G. A. Res. 217 A (III), UN Doc. A/811 (1948); *American Journal of International Law*, 1949, vol. 43, Supp., p. 127. This document is a declaration only, without the legal force of a convention.
14 F. v. Loesch, *Die Deutschen in den osteuropäischen Staaten*, 1972, p. 9.
15 The author has personally interviewed German emigrants from Poland shortly after their arrival in the Friedland Reception Camp near Göttingen in West Germany. These emigrants complained of widespread abuses, loss of gainful employment and discrimination following their application for an exit visa. Most of those arriving today had submitted several unsuccessful applications before being allowed to leave. Many of the children speak German very badly, because there were no German schools for them in Poland and because the German language was not taught in most of the Polish schools.
16 F. v. Loesch, op. cit., passim. For a history of the presence of German minorities in the East see also A. Bohmann, *Menschen und Grenzen*, 1969–75.
17 Department of State, *Bulletin*, vol. 65, pp. 318ff.
18 ibid., vol. 73, p. 307. See also the Four-Power Berlin Agreement of 1971, vol. 65, Statements by President Nixon, vol. 65, pp. 191, 475, 477; Hillenbrand, p. 518.
19 See Appendix.
20 Albert Schweitzer, *Das Problem des Friedens in der heutigen Welt*, 1954, p. 6. Also cited in Raschhofer, *Eastern Germany*, pp. 91–2.
21 *Foreign Relations of the United States*, 1945, vol. 2, p. 1291.

APPENDIX

ATLANTIC CHARTER

Declaration of Principles, Known as the Atlantic Charter, by the President of the United States (Roosevelt) and the Prime Minister of the United Kingdom (Churchill) August 14, 1941

Joint declaration of the President of the United States of America and the Prime Minister, Mr. Churchill, representing His Majesty's Government in the United Kingdom, being met together, deem it right to make known certain common principles in the national policies of their respective countries on which they base their hopes for a better future for the world.

First, their countries seek no aggrandizement, territorial or other;

Second, they desire to see no territorial changes that do not accord with the freely expressed wishes of the peoples concerned;

Third, they respect the right of all peoples to choose the form of government under which they will live; and they wish to see sovereign rights and self-government restored to those who have been forcibly deprived of them;

Fourth, they will endeavor, with due respect for their existing obligations, to further the enjoyment by all States, great or small, victor or vanquished, of access, on equal terms, to the trade and to the raw materials of the world which are needed for their economic prosperity;

Fifth, they desire to bring about the fullest collaboration between all nations in the economic field with the object of securing, for all, improved labor standards, economic adjustment and social security;

Sixth, after the final destruction of the Nazi tyranny, they hope to see established a peace which will afford to all nations the means of dwelling in safety within their own boundaries, and which will afford assurance that all the men in all the lands may live out their lives in freedom from fear and want;

Seventh, such a peace should enable all men to traverse the high seas and oceans without hindrance;

Eighth, they believe that all of the nations of the world, for realistic as well as spiritual reasons, must come to the abandonment of the use of force. Since no future peace can be maintained if land, sea or air armaments continue to be employed by nations which threaten, or may threaten, aggression outside of their frontiers, they believe, pending the establishment of a wider and permanent system of general security, that the disarmament of such nations is essential. They will likewise aid and encourage all other practicable measures which will lighten for peace-loving peoples the crushing burden of armaments.

United States, Executive Agreement Series 236, p. 4; *D. S. Bul.*, V, p. 125; *D.A.F.R.*, IV, p. 209.

MORGENTHAU PLAN

Top Secret

Program to Prevent Germany from starting a World War III

1. *Demilitarization of Germany.*
It should be the aim of the Allied Forces to accomplish the complete demilitarization of Germany in the shortest possible period of time after surrender. This means completely disarming the German Army and people (including the removal or destruction of all war material), the total destruction of the whole German armament industry, and the removal or destruction of other key industries which are basic to military strength.

2. *New boundaries of Germany.*
   (a) Poland should get that part of East Prussia which doesn't go to the U.S.S.R. and the southern portion of Silesia. (See map in 12 Appendix.)
   (b) France should get the Saar and the adjacent territories bounded by the Rhine and the Moselle Rivers.
   (c) As indicated in 4 below an International Zone should be created containing the Ruhr and the surrounding industrial areas.

3. *Partitioning of New Germany.*
The remaining portion of Germany should be divided into two autonomous, independent states, (1) a South German state comprising Bavaria, Wuerttemberg, Baden and some smaller areas and (2) a North German state comprising a large part of the old state of Prussia, Saxony, Thuringia and several smaller states.

There shall be a custom union between the new South German state and Austria, which will be restored to her pre-1938 political borders.

4. *The Ruhr Area.* (The Ruhr, surrounding industrial areas, as shown on the map, including the Rhineland, the Kiel Canal, and all German territory north of the Kiel Canal.)

Here lies the heart of German industrial power. This area should not only be stripped of all presently existing industries but so weakened and controlled that it can not in the foreseeable future become an industrial area. The following steps will accomplish this:

(a) Within a short period, if possible not longer than 6 months after the cessation of hostilities, all industrial plants and equipment not destroyed by military action shall be completely dismantled and transported to Allied Nations as restitution. All equipment shall be removed from the mines and the mines closed.

(b) The area should be made an international zone to be governed by an international security organization to be established by the United Nations. In governing the area the international organization should be guided by policies designed to further the above stated objective.

5. *Restitution and Reparation.*

Reparations, in the form of future payments and deliveries, should not be demanded. Restitution and reparation shall be effected by the transfer of existing German resources and territories, e.g.,

(a) by restitution of property looted by the Germans in territories occupied by them;

(b) by transfer of German territory and German private rights in industrial property situated in such territory to invaded countries and the international organization under the program of partition;

(c) by the removal and distribution among devastated countries of industrial plants and equipment situated within the International Zone and the North and South German states delimited in the section on partition;

(d) by forced German labor outside Germany; and

(e) by confiscation of all German assets of any character whatsoever outside of Germany.

6. *Education and Propaganda.*

(a) All schools and universities will be closed until an Allied Commission of Education has formulated an effective reorganization program. It is contemplated that it may require a considerable period of time before any institutions of higher education are reopened. Meanwhile the education of German students in foreign universities will not be prohibited. Elementary schools will be reopened as quickly as appropriate teachers and textbooks are available.

(b) All German radio stations and newspapers, magazines, weeklies, etc. shall be discontinued until adequate controls are established and an appropriate program formulated.

7. *Political Decentralization.*

The military administration in Germany in the initial period should be carried out with a view toward the eventual partitioning of Germany. To facilitate partitioning and to assure its permanence the military authorities should be guided by the following principles:

(a) Dismiss all policy-making officials of the Reich government and deal primarily with local governments.

(b) Encourage the reestablishment of state governments in each of the states (Lander) corresponding to 18 states into which Germany is presently divided and in addition make the Prussian provinces separate states.

(c) Upon the partition of Germany, the various state governments should be encouraged to organize a federal government for each of the newly partitioned areas. Such new governments should be in the form of a confederation of states, with emphasis on states' rights and a large degree of local autonomy.

8. *Responsibility of Military for Local German Economy.*

The sole purpose of the military in control of the German economy shall be to facilitate military operations and military occupation. The Allied Military Government shall not assume responsibility for such economic problems as price controls, rationing, unemployment, production, reconstruction, distribution, consumption, housing, or transportation, or take any measures designed to maintain or strengthen the German economy, except those which are essential to military operations. The responsibility for sustaining the German economy and people rests with the German people with such facilities as may be available under the circumstances.

9. *Controls over Development of German Economy.*

During a period of at least twenty years after surrender adequate controls, including controls over foreign trade and tight restrictions on capital imports, shall be maintained by the United Nations designed to prevent in the newly-established states the establishment or expansion of key industries basic to the German military potential and to control other key industries.

10. *Agrarian program.*

All large estates should be broken up and divided among the peasants and the system of primogeniture and entail should be abolished.

11. *Punishment of War Crimes and Treatment of Special Groups.*

A program for the punishment of certain war crimes and for the treatment of Nazi organizations and other special groups is contained in section 11.

12. *Uniforms and Parades.*
   (a) No German shall be permitted to wear, after an appropriate period of time following the cessation of hostilities, any military uniform or any uniform of any quasi military organizations.
   (b) No military parades shall be permitted anywhere in Germany and all military bands shall be disbanded.

13. *Aircraft.*
All aircraft (including gliders), whether military or commercial, will be confiscated for later disposition. No German shall be permitted to operate or to help operate any aircraft, including those owned by foreign interests.

14. *United States Responsibility.*
Although the United States would have full military and civilian representation on whatever international commission or commissions may be established for the execution of the whole German program, the primary responsibility for the policing of Germany and for civil administration in Germany should be assumed by the military forces of Germany's continental neighbors. Specifically, these should include Russian, French, Polish, Czech, Greek, Yugoslav, Norwegian, Dutch and Belgian soldiers.
   Under this program United States troops could be withdrawn within a relatively short time.

POTSDAM PROTOCOL, ARTICLES 3, 6, 9, 13

III
Germany

The Allied armies are in occupation of the whole of Germany and the German people have begun to atone for the terrible crimes committed under the leadership of those whom, in the hour of their success, they openly approved and blindly obeyed.
   Agreement has been reached at this Conference on the political and economic principles of a coordinated Allied policy toward defeated Germany during the period of Allied control.
   The purpose of this agreement is to carry out the Crimea declaration on Germany. German militarism and Nazism will be extirpated and the Allies will take in agreement together, now and in the future, the other measures necessary to assure that Germany never again will threaten her neighbors or the peace of the world.
   It is not the intention of the Allies to destroy or enslave the German

people. It is the intention of the Allies that the German people be given the opportunity to prepare for the eventual reconstruction of their life on a democratic and peaceful basis. If their own efforts are steadily directed to this end, it will be possible for them in due course to take their place among the free and peaceful peoples of the world.

The text of the agreement is as follows:

The Political and Economic Principles to Govern the Treatment of Germany in the Initial Control Period

A. *Political Principles.*

1. In accordance with the Agreement on Control Machinery in Germany, supreme authority in Germany is exercised on instructions from the respective Governments, by the Commanders-in-Chief of the armed forces of the United States of America, the United Kingdom, the Union of Soviet Socialist Republics, and the French Republic, each in his own zone of occupation, and also jointly, in matters affecting Germany as a whole, in their capacity as members of the Control Council.

2. So far as is practicable, there shall be uniformity of treatment of the German population throughout Germany.

3. The purposes of the occupation of Germany by which the Control Council shall be guided are:

(i) The complete disarmament and demilitarization of Germany and the elimination or control of all German industry that could be used for military production. To these ends:

(*a*) All German land, naval and air forces, the S.S., S.A., S.D. and Gestapo, with all their organizations, staffs and institutions, including the General Staff, the Officers' Corps, Reserve Corps, military schools, war veterans' organizations and all other military and quasi-military organization[s], together with all clubs and associations which serve to keep alive the military tradition in Germany, shall be completely and finally abolished in such manner as permanently to prevent the revival or reorganization of German militarism and Nazism;

(*b*) All arms, ammunition and implements of war and all specialized facilities for their production shall be held at the disposal of the Allies or destroyed. The maintenance and production of all aircraft and all arms, ammunition and implements of war shall be prevented.

(ii) To convince the German people that they have suffered a total military defeat and that they cannot escape responsibility for what they have brought upon themselves, since their own ruthless warfare and the fanatical Nazi resistance have destroyed German economy and made chaos and suffering inevitable.

(iii) To destroy the National Socialist Party and its affiliated and supervised organizations, to dissolve all Nazi institutions, to ensure that they are not revived in any form, and to prevent all Nazi and militarist activity or propaganda.

(iv) To prepare for the eventual reconstruction of German political life on a democratic basis and for eventual peaceful cooperation in international life by Germany.

4. All Nazi laws which provided the basis of the Hitler regime or established discrimination on grounds of race, creed, or political opinion shall be abolished. No such discriminations, whether legal, administrative or otherwise, shall be tolerated.

5. War criminals and those who have participated in planning or carrying out Nazi enterprises involving or resulting in atrocities or war crimes shall be arrested and brought to judgment. Nazi leaders, influential Nazi supporters and high officials of Nazi organizations and institutions and any other persons dangerous to the occupation or its objectives shall be arrested and interned.

6. All members of the Nazi Party who have been more than nominal participants in its activities and all other persons hostile to Allied purposes shall be removed from public and semi-public office, and from positions of responsibility in important private undertakings. Such persons shall be replaced by persons who, by their political and moral qualities, are deemed capable of assisting in developing genuine democratic institutions in Germany.

7. German education shall be so controlled as completely to eliminate Nazi and militarist doctrines and to make possible the successful development of democratic ideas.

8. The judicial system will be recognized in accordance with the principles of democracy, of justice under law, and of equal rights for all citizens without distinction of race, nationality or religion.

9. The administration of affairs in Germany should be directed towards the decentralization of the political structure and the development of local responsibility. To this end:

(i) local self-government shall be restored throughout Germany on democratic principles and in particular through elective councils as rapidly as is consistent with military security and the purposes of military occupation;

(ii) all democratic political parties with rights of assembly and of public discussion shall be allowed and encouraged throughout Germany;

(iii) representative and elective principles shall be introduced into regional, provincial and state (Land) administration as rapidly as may be justified by the successful application of these principles in local self-government;

(iv) for the time being no central German government shall be established. Notwithstanding this, however, certain essential central German administrative departments, headed by State Secretaries, shall be established, particularly in the fields of finance, transport, communications, foreign trade and industry. Such departments will act under the direction of the Control Council.

10. Subject to the necessity for maintaining military security, freedom of speech, press and religion shall be permitted, and religious institutions shall be respected. Subject likewise to the maintenance of military security, the formation of free trade unions shall be permitted.

B. *Economic Principles.*

11. In order to eliminate Germany's war potential, the production of arms, ammunition and implements of war as well as all types of aircraft and sea-going ships shall be prohibited and prevented. Production of metals, chemicals, machinery and other items that are directly necessary to a war economy shall be rigidly controlled and restricted to Germany's approved post-war peacetime needs to meet the objectives stated in Paragraph 15. Productive capacity not needed for permitted production shall be removed in accordance with the reparations plan recommended by the Governments concerned or if not removed shall be destroyed.

12. At the earliest practicable date, the German economy shall be decentralized for the purpose of eliminating the present excessive concentration of economic power as exemplified in particular by cartels, syndicates, trusts and other monopolistic arrangements.

13. In organizing the German economy, primary emphasis shall be given to the development of agriculture and peaceful domestic industries.

14. During the period of occupation Germany shall be treated as a single economic unit. To this end common policies shall be established in regard to:

(*a*) mining and industrial production and allocation;
(*b*) agriculture, forestry and fishing;
(*c*) wages, prices and rationing;
(*d*) import and export programs for Germany as a whole;
(*e*) currency and banking, central taxation and customs;
(*f*) reparation and removal of industrial war potential;
(*g*) transportation and communications.

In applying these policies account shall be taken, where appropriate, of varying local conditions.

15. Allied controls shall be imposed upon the German economy but only to the extent necessary:

(*a*) to carry out programs of industrial disarmament and demilitarization, of reparations, and of approved exports and imports.

(*b*) to assure the production and maintenance of goods and services required to meet the needs of the occupying forces and displaced persons in Germany and essential to maintain in Germany average living standards not exceeding the average of the standards of living of European countries. (European countries means all European countries excluding the United Kingdom and the Union of Soviet Socialist Republics.)

(*c*) to ensure in the manner determined by the Control Council the equitable distribution of essential commodities between the several zones so as to produce a balanced economy throughout Germany and reduce the need for imports.

(*d*) to control German industry and all economic and financial international transactions, including exports and imports, with the aim of preventing Germany from developing a war potential [sic] and of achieving the other objectives named herein.

(*e*) to control all German public or private scientific bodies, research and experimental institutions, laboratories, et cetera, connected with economic activities.

16. In the imposition and maintenance of economic controls established by the Control Council, German administrative machinery shall be created and the German authorities shall be required to the fullest extent practicable to proclaim and assume administration of such controls. Thus it should be brought home to the German people that the responsibility for the administration of such controls and any breakdown in these controls will rest with themselves. Any German controls which may run counter to the objectives of occupation will be prohibited.

17. Measures shall be promptly taken:

(*a*) to effect essential repair of transport;
(*b*) to enlarge coal production;
(*c*) to maximize agricultural output; and
(*d*) to effect emergency repair of housing and essential utilities.

18. Appropriate steps shall be taken by the Control Council to exercise control and the power of disposition over German-owned external assets not already under the control of United Nations which have taken part in the war against Germany.

19. Payment of Reparations should leave enough resources to enable the German people to subsist without external assistance. In working out the economic balance of Germany the necessary means must be provided to pay for imports approved by the Control Councils in Germany. The proceeds of exports from current production and stocks shall be available in the first place for payment for such imports.

The above clause will not apply to the equipment and products referred to in paragraphs 4 (*a*) and 4 (*b*) of the Reparations Agreement.

VI
City of Koenigsberg and the Adjacent Area

The Conference examined a proposal by the Soviet Government that pending the final determination of territorial questions at the peace settlement, the section of the western frontier of the Union of Soviet Socialist Republics which is adjacent to the Baltic Sea should pass from a point on the eastern shore of the Bay of Danzig to the east, north of Braunsberg–Goldap, to the meeting point of the frontiers of Lithuania, the Polish Republic and East Prussia.

The Conference has agreed in principle to the proposal of the Soviet Government concerning the ultimate transfer to the Soviet Union of the City of Koenigsberg and the area adjacent to it as described above subject to expert examination of the actual frontier.

The President of the United States and the British Prime Minister have declared that they will support the proposal of the Conference at the forthcoming peace settlement.

IX*
Poland

The Conference considered questions relating to the Polish Provisional Government and the western boundary of Poland.

On the Polish Provisional Government of National Unity they defined their attitude in the following statement:

A.†—We have taken note with pleasure of the agreement reached among representative Poles from Poland and abroad which has made possible the formation, in accordance with the decisions reached at the Crimea Conference, of a Polish Provisional Government of National Unity recognized by the Three Powers. The establishment by the British and United States Governments of diplomatic relations with the Polish Provisional Government has resulted in the withdrawal of their recognition from the former Polish Government in London, which no longer exists.

The British and United States Governments have taken measures to protect the interest of the Polish Provision Government as the recognized government of the Polish State in the property belonging to the Polish State located in their territories and under their control, whatever the form of this property may be. They have further taken measures to prevent alienation to third parties of such property. All proper facilities will be given to the Polish Provisional Government for the exercise of the ordinary legal remedies for the recovery of any property

---

*This Roman numeral is a manuscript correction of the numeral 'VII' in the original typescript. The correction is initialed by George M. Elsey.

†'A—' is a manuscript addition.

belonging to the Polish State which may have been wrongfully alienated.

The Three Powers are anxious to assist the Polish Provisional Government in facilitating the return to Poland as soon as practicable of all Poles abroad who wish to go, including members of the Polish Armed Forces and the Merchant Marine. They expect that those Poles who return home shall be accorded personal and property rights on the same basis as all Polish citizens.

The Three Powers note that the Polish Provisional Government in accordance with the decisions of the Crimea Conference has agreed to the holding of free and unfettered elections as soon as possible on the basis of universal suffrage and secret ballot in which all democratic and anti-Nazi parties shall have the right to take part and to put forward candidates, and that representatives of the Allied press shall enjoy full freedom to report to the world upon developments in Poland before and during the elections.

B. The following agreement was reached on the western frontier of Poland:

In conformity with the agreement on Poland reached at the Crimea Conference the three Heads of Government have sought the opinion of the Polish Provisional Government of National Unity in regard to the accession of territory in the north and west which Poland should receive. The President of the National Council of Poland and members of the Polish Provisional Government of National Unity have been received at the Conference and have fully presented their views. The three Heads of Government reaffirm their opinion that the final delimitation of the western frontier of Poland should await the peace settlement.

The three Heads of Government agree that, pending the final determination of Poland's western frontier, the former German territories east of a line running from the Baltic Sea immediately west of Swinemunde, and thence along the Oder River to the confluence of the western Neisse River and along the western Neisse to the Czechoslovak frontier, including that portion of East Prussia not placed under the administration of the Union of Soviet Socialist Republics in accordance with the understanding reached at this conference and including the area of the former free city of Danzig, shall be under the administration of the Polish State and for such purposes should not be considered as part of the Soviet zone of occupation in Germany.

XIII
Orderly Transfer of German Populations

The Conference reached the following agreement on the removal of Germans from Poland, Czechoslovakia and Hungary:

The three Governments, having considered the question in all its aspects, recognize that the transfer to Germany of German populations, or elements thereof, remaining in Poland, Czechoslovakia and Hungary, will have to be undertaken. They agree that any transfers that take place should be effected in an orderly and humane manner.

Since the influx of a large number of Germans into Germany would increase the burden already resting on the occupying authorities, they consider that the Allied Control Council in Germany should in the first instance examine the problem with special regard to the question of the equitable distribution of these Germans among the several zones of occupation. They are accordingly instructing their respective representatives on the Control Council to report to their Governments as soon as possible the extent to which such persons have already entered Germany from Poland, Czechoslovakia and Hungary, and to submit an estimate of the time and rate at which further transfers could be carried out, having regard to the present situation in Germany.

The Czechoslovak Government, the Polish Provisional Government and the Control Council in Hungary are at the same time being informed of the above, and are being requested meanwhile to suspend further expulsions pending the examination by the Governments concerned of the report from their representatives on the Control Council.

CHARTER OF THE GERMAN EXPELLEES

[On 5 August 1950 this 'Charter of the German Expellees' was proclaimed by the unknown expellee in Stuttgart at a large rally in the presence of members of the Federal Government, of the Churches and of the Parliaments. The Charter bears the signatures of the elected spokesmen of various fellowships (Landsmann-schaften) and of the chairman of the Central Union of German Expellees and its Land Unions. It was endorsed at large rallies in all parts of Germany.]

Conscious of their responsibility before God and men,
conscious of their adherence to the Christian community of the Occident,
conscious of their German origin, and realizing the common task of all the nations of Europe,
the elected representatives of millions of expellees, having carefully deliberated and searched their conscience, have resolved to make public a Solemn Declaration to the German people and to the entire world, in which are defined both the duties and the rights which the German

expellees consider their basic law, and an absolute indispensable condition for the establishment of a free and united Europe.

1. We, the expellees, renounce all thought of revenge and retaliation. Our resolution is a solemn and sacred one, in memory of the infinite suffering brought upon mankind, particularly during the past decade.

2. We shall support with all our strength every endeavour directed towards the establishment of a united Europe, in which the nations may live in freedom from fear and coercion.

3. We shall contribute, by hard and indefatigable work, to the reconstruction of Germany and Europe.

We have lost our homeland. The homeless are strangers on the face of the earth. Almighty God himself placed men in their native land. To separate a man from his native land by force, means to kill his soul.
We have suffered and experienced this fate.
We, therefore, feel competent to demand that the right to our native land be recognized and be realized, as one of the basic rights of man, granted to him by the grace of God. We do not, however, wish to stand aside and be doomed to inactivity, as long as this right is not realized, but want, rather to strive and toll with every member of our nation in a new spirit of community life, in a manner purified by a spirit of brotherly consideration. For this reason, we claim and demand, today as in the past:

1. Equal rights as citizens, not merely before the law, but also in the hard realities of every day's life.

2. Just and reasonable repartition of the burdens of the last war among the entire German people, and an honest execution of this principle.

3. A sensible integration of all professional groups of expellees into the life of the German people.

4. An active part of the German expellees in the reconstruction of Europe.

The nations of the world shall be conscious of their share of the responsibility for the fate of the expellees, who have suffered more than all others from the hardship of our times. The nations shall act according to their Christian duty and conscience.
The nations must realize that the fate of the German expellees, just as that of all refugees, is a world problem, the solution of which calls for the highest sense of moral responsibility and the stern necessity of making a tremendous effort.
We, therefore, call upon all nations and men of good will, to join in the

mutual task of finding a way out of guilt, misfortune, suffering, poverty and misery, which will lead us all to a better future.

Stuttgart, August 5, 1950.

Dr Linus Kather
Josef Walter
Helmut Gossing
Dr Mocker
H. Eschenbach
Wilhelm Zeisberger
Dr Alfred Gille
Dr Bernhard Geisler
Erwin Engelbrecht
A. Deichmann

Roman Herlinger
Dr Rudolf Lodgman
  von Auen
Erwin Tittes
Dr Rudolf Wagner
Dr Alfred Rojek
Walter von Keudell
Dr Konrad Winkler
Axel de Vries
Franz Hamm
Erich Luft

Dr Bartunek
Dr Schreiber
Erik von Witzleben
Dr Walter Rinke
Anton Birkner
v. Bismarck
Waldemar Kraft
Dr Gottlieb Leibbrandt
Dr Kimme
Dr Kautzor

BIBLIOGRAPHY

I UNPUBLISHED DOCUMENTS

Archives of the International Committee of the Red Cross, Geneva. Papers relating to visits of Red Cross delegates to internment camps (German civilians awaiting expulsion) in Czechoslovakia and Poland. Papers relating to negotiations of the ICRC with the Four Powers with respect to relief activities in occupied Germany.

Archives of the League of Nations, Palais des Nations, Geneva. Petitions submitted on behalf of German minorities in Poland and Czechoslovakia.

Bundesarchiv, Koblenz. Ost-Dokumente (partially published in Th. Schieder, *Dokumentation der Vertreibung*). Report prepared in 1969–75 entitled 'Dokumentation der Vertreibungsverbrechen' (partially published by W. Ahrens).

Bundesarchiv-Militärarchiv, Freiburg. Files of the legal division of the Wehrmacht, OKW-Untersuchungstelle für Verletzungen des Völkerrechts.

Archives of the German Foreign Office in Bonn, especially collection Völkerrecht/Kriegsrecht, vol. 82/8, no. 22.

Centre de Recherches et d'Etudes Historiques de la Seconde Guerre Mondiale, Brussels. Commandant e.r. Georges Hauteclear on the Belgian prisoners of war in German hands.

Cour Internationale de Justice, La Haye, Palais de la Paix. Affidavits submitted as evidence to the International Military Tribunal by Dr Hans Laternser, especially affidavit of General Erich Dethleffsen, Nr. 1608.

Institute für Zeitgeschichte, Munich. Nuremberg Documents,

especially Plädoyer of Dr Alfred Seidl, defence attorney of Hans Frank, on the count of mass expulsion of Poles from the Warthegau area to the Generalgouvernement, especially pp. 34–42.

'Seekriegsleitung-Besprechungen beim Führer', microfilm MA-10 (4), especially Conference of 18 April 1945 on the evacuation of refugees from East Prussia and the sinking of *Goya*, pp. 144–6, and Conference of 31 January 1945 on the sinking of *Wilhelm Gustloff*, pp. 176–8.

US Department of State Files. US Court of the Allied High Commission for Germany *US HICOG* v. *Hernecek*, Vaclav, Aerea V Munich, Case No. 54–23, Court of Appeals. Also in the Bayerische Staatsbibliothek, Munich, Nr. 4M 57 16.

II PUBLISHED DOCUMENTS

International
Permanent Court of International Justice, The Hague, *World Court Reports*, ed. by Manley O. Hudson, 4 vols, Carnegie Endowment for International Peace, Washington, 1934–43.

International Military Tribunal, *Trial of the Major War Criminals before the International Military Tribunal, Nuremberg, 1945–6*, 42 vols, Nuremberg, 1947–9.

League of Nation Treaty Series, 205 vols, London, 1920–46.

United Nations Treaty Series, New York, 1946 to date.

Red Cross
Report of the International Committee of the Red Cross on its activities during the Second World War (September 1, 1939 to June 30 1947), Geneva, 1948: vol. 1 *General Activities*; 2 *The Central Agency for Prisoners of War*; 3 *Relief Activities*.

Report on General Activities, Geneva (annual).

Report of the Joint Relief Commission of the International Red Cross, 1941–1946, Geneva, 1948.

ICRC, *Inter Arma Caritas*. Geneva, 1947.

Revue Internationale de la Croix Rouge, Geneva (monthly).

Swiss Red Cross
Das Schweizerische Rote Kreuz – Eine Sondernummer des deutschen Flüchtlingsproblems. Nr. 11/12, Bern, September–October 1949.

Volk ohne Raum – Berichte aus deutschen Flüchtlingslagern. Bern, 1949.

Red Cross in Germany
Das Vertriebenen-Problem, Tagung 9.–14. April 1951 in Hannover. Bundesministerium für Vertriebene, Bonn, 1951.

Böhme, Kurt, *Gesucht Wird*, Munich, 1965.

Czechoslovakia
Czechoslovak Ministry of Information, *Cesky narod soudi K. H. Franka*, Prague, 1946.

Czechoslovak Ministry of the Interior, *Lidice*, Prague, 1946.

Germany
Akten zur Auswärtigen Politik, Baden-Baden; *Documents on German Foreign Policy, 1918–45* from the Archives of the German Foreign Ministry, published jointly by the British Foreign Office and the US Department of State, Series D and E (1937–45) 8 vols, Washington, USGPO, and London, HMSO.
Bundesministerium für Vertriebene, *Dokumentation der Vertreibung der Deutschen aus Ostmitteleuropa*, Bonn, 1953.
Zwanzig Jahre Lager Friedland, Bonn, 1965.
Tatsachen zum Problem der deutschen Vertriebenen und Flüchtlinge, Bonn, 1960.
Vertriebene, Flüchtlinge, Kriegsgefangene, Heimatlose Ausländer –949–52, Bonn, 1953.
Bundesverfassungsgericht. Decision of 31 July 1973 on the Grundvertrag. BVerfGE 36, 1 bis 37. Decision of 7 July 1975 on the Ost-Verträge.

Poland
Polish Statistical Office, *Rocznik Statystyczny* of 1947, 1949 and 1957, Warsaw.
Polish Ministry of Foreign Affairs, *The Polish White Book*, New York, 1942.
Polish Ministry of Information, *The German New Order in Poland*, London, 1941.

United Kingdom
Documents on British Foreign Policy, London, HMSO.
Parliamentary Debates, House of Commons, London, HMSO.
Parliamentary Debates, House of Lords, London, HMSO.
Royal Institute of International Affairs, *Documents on International Affairs 1939–46*, vols 1–2. 1947–8, etc., London, 1951, 1952, 1954.
United Kingdom Command Papers, London.

Union of Soviet Socialist Republics
Documents: The Crimea and Potsdam Conferences of the Leaders of the Three Great Powers.
International Affairs, nos 6–10, Moscow, 1965.
Soviet Documents on Foreign Policy, J. Degras (ed.), London, 1953.

United States
Congressional Record, Senate, Washington.
Congressional Record, House of Representatives, Washington.
Department of State:
The Axis in Defeat, A Collection of Documents on American Policy toward Germany and Japan, Washington, 1945.

Foreign Relations of the United States: 1918 – especially *The Conferences at Cairo and Teheran*, 1943; *The Conferences at Malta and Yalta*, 1945; *The Conference at Berlin*, 1945; also vol. 2, 1945, *General, Political and Economic Matters*.
Termination of the Occupation Regime in the Federal Republic of Germany, Pub. 6096, Washington, 1955.
Marjorie M. Whiteman, *Digest of International Law*, esp. vols 2 and 3, Department of State Publication 7737, 1964.
Documents on American Foreign Relations, Boston, 1939–54.
Documents on Germany, Senate Committee on Foreign Relations, 92nd Congress, 1st Session, Washington, 1971.
Holborn, Louise W. (ed.), *War and Peace Aims of the United Nations*, vols 1 and 2. Boston, 1943 and 1948.
House Committee on the Judiciary, Report no. 1841, 81st Congress, 2nd Session, Walter Report, Washington, 1950.
House Report, 83rd Congress, 2nd Session, no. 2684.
House, Select Committee on the Katyn Forest Massacre. Washington, 1952.
Nixon, Richard, *U.S. Foreign Policy for the 1970's: Building for Peace. A Report to the Congress by Richard Nixon, President of the United States, February 25, 1971*. Washington.
Office of Strategic Services, *Transfers of Population in Europe since 1920*, Washington, 1945.
On German Provinces East of the Oder-Neisse Line, and Economic, Historical, Legal and Political Aspects Involved, paper by Representative Carroll B. Reece. Washington, 16 May 1957.

III   MEMOIRS AND BIOGRAPHIES

Adenauer, Konrad, *Erinnerungen*, vols 1–4, Stuttgart, 1965–8.
Ball, George, *The Discipline of Power*, Boston, 1968.
Benes, Eduard, *Memoirs*, London, 1954.
Bohlen, Charles, *Witness to History*, New York, 1973.
Bonnet, Georges, *Défense de la Paix*, Geneva, 1946.
Brüning, Heinrich, *Memoiren*, Stuttgart, 1970.
Brüning, Heinrich, *Briefe und Gespräche* (Claire Nix, ed.), Stuttgart, 1974.
Byrnes, James, *Speaking Frankly*, New York, 1947.
Churchill, W. S., *The Sinews of Peace*, London, 1948.
Churchill, W. S., *The Second World War*, vols 1–6: *The Gathering Storm; Their Finest Hour; The Grand Alliance; Hinge of Fate; Closing the Ring; Triumph and Tragedy*, Boston, 1953.
Churchill, W. S., *The War Speeches*, London, 1952.
Ciechanowski, Jan, *Defeat in Victory*, Garden City, 1947.
Clay, Lucius, *Decision in Germany*, New York, 1950.
Deutscher, I., *Stalin, a Political Biography*, London, 1949.
Dilks, David (ed.), *The Diaries of Sir Alexander Cadogan 1938–45*, London, 1971.
Dönitz, Karl, *Zehn Jahre und Zwanzig Tage*, Frankfurt, 1967.

Djilas, Milovan, *Conversations with Stalin*, New York, 1962.
Eden, Anthony (Lord Avon), *The Memoirs of Anthony Eden*, Boston, 1960.
Eisenhower, Dwight D., *Crusade in Europe*, Garden City, 1948.
Gannon, Robert, *The Cardinal Spellman Story*, esp. Ch. 14 'President Roosevelt', New York, 1962.
de Gaulle, Charles, *Mémoires de guerre*, Paris, 1959.
Henlein, Konrad, *Heim ins Reich, Reden aus den Jahren 1937 und 1938*, Reichenberg, 1939.
Hull, Cordell, *The Memoirs*, London, 1948, vols 1–2.
Kennan, George, *Memoirs 1925–1950*, Boston, 1967.
Kennan, George, *Memoirs 1950–1963*, Boston, 1972.
Lane, Arthur Bliss, *I saw Poland Betrayed, An American Ambassador Reports to the American People*, Indianapolis, 1948.
Lansing, Robert, *The Big Four and Others of the Peace Conference*, Boston, 1929.
Leahy, William, *I was There*, New York, 1950.
Lipski, Josef, *Diplomat in Berlin, 1933–1939*, New York, 1968.
Masaryk, T. G., *The Making of a State*, London, 1927.
Mikolajczyk, Stanislaw, *The Rape of Poland*, New York, 1948.
Montgomery, B., *Memoirs*, London, 1958.
Molotov, V. M., *Problems of Foreign Policy. Speeches and Statements*. Moscow, 1947.
Moran, Lord, *Winston Churchill. The Struggle for Survival 1940–1965*, London, 1966.
Murphy, Robert, *Diplomat Among Warriors*, Garden City, 1964.
Roosevelt, Elliot, *As He Saw It*, New York, 1946.
Schwerin von Krosigk, Lutz Graf, *Es Geschah in Deutschland. Menschenbilder unseres Jahrhunderts*, Tübingen, 1951.
Selle, Götz von, *Ostdeutsche Biographien*, Würzburg, 1955.
Sherwood, R. E., *The White House Papers of Harry L. Hopkins*, London, 1948–9.
Sherwood, R. E., *Roosevelt and Hopkins, An Intimate History*, New York, 1948.
Speer, Albert, *Inside the Third Reich*, New York, 1970.
Stettinius, E. R., *Roosevelt and the Russians, The Yalta Conference*, New York, 1949.
Stimson, Henry and Bundy, McGeorge, *On Active Service in Peace and War*, New York, 1947.
Strang, William, *Home and Abroad*, London, 1956.
Stresemann, Gustav, *Diaries, Letters and Papers*, New York, 1935–40 vols 1–3.
Truman, Harry S., *Memoirs*, New York, 1955, vols 1–2.
Weizsäcker, Ernst von, *Erinnerungen*, Munich, 1950.

IV ENGLISH-LANGUAGE SOURCES (GENERAL)

American Friends Service Committee, *Report on Conditions in Central Europe*, 'Expellees', Philadelphia, 1946.

American Friends Service Committee, *The Problem of 12 Million German Refugees*, Boston, 1949.

American Friends Service Committee, *After Seven Years*, Philadelphia, 1952.

App, Austin J., *History's Most Terrifying Peace*, Takoma Park, Md., 1946.

Armstrong, Anne, *Unconditional Surrender: The Impact of the Casablanca Policy upon World War II*, New Brunswick, 1961.

Bedell Smith, Walter, *Moscow Mission 1946–1949*, London, 1950.

Bedell Smith, Walter, *Eisenhower's Six Great Decisions*, New York, 1956.

Blum, John Morton, *The Morgenthau Diaries. Years of War 1941–45*, Boston, 1967.

Bohlen, Charles, *The Transformation of American Foreign Policy*, London, 1970.

Bouman, P. J., G. Beijer and J. J. Oudegeest, *The Refugee Problem in Western Germany*, The Hague, 1950.

Bradley, John, *Czechoslovakia: A Short History*, Edinburgh, 1971.

Brandt, Willy, *A Peace Policy for Europe*, New York, 1969.

Clemens, Diane, *Yalta*, New York, 1970.

Committee Against Mass Expulsions, *The Land of the Dead*, New York, 1947.

Committee Against Mass Expulsions, *Tragedy of a People*, New York, 1948.

Committee Against Mass Expulsions, *Men without the Rights of Man*, New York, 1948.

Conant, James, *Germany and Freedom*, Cambridge, Mass., 1958.

Crawley, A., *The Spoils of War*, Indianapolis, 1973.

Czapski, Jozef, *What Happened in Katyn*, Newport, 1950.

Dallin, Alexander, *German Rule in Russia, 1941–45*, London, 1949.

Davidson, E., *The Death and Life of Germany*, New York, 1959.

Deane, J. R., *The Strange Alliance*, New York, 1947.

Deutsch, Karl and Edinger, Lewis, *Germany Rejoins the Powers*, Stanford, 1959.

Drzewieniecki, W. M., *The German Polish Frontier*, Polish Western Association of America, Chicago, 1959.

Dulles, Allen, *Germany's Underground*, New York, 1947.

Dulles, John Foster, *War or Peace*, New York, 1950.

Ehrenburg, Ilya, *Russia at War*, London, 1943.

Ehrenburg, Ilya, *The War 1941–1945*, Cleveland, 1964.

Erdely, Eugene, *Germany's First European Protectorate. The Fate of the Czechs and Slovaks*, London, 1941.

Erickson, J., *The Soviet High Command*, London, 1962.

Essler, F. W., *Twenty Years of Sudeten German Losses 1918–1938*, Vienna, 1938.

Feis, Herbert, *Churchill-Roosevelt-Stalin*, Princeton, 1957.

Feis, Herbert, *Between War and Peace, The Potsdam Conference*, Princeton, 1960.

Fritsch, Ludwig, *The Crime of our Age*, Chicago, 1949.

Gadolin, Axel de, *The Solution of the Karelian Refugee Problem in Finland*, The Hague, 1952.

Gayre, G. R., *Teuton and Slav on the Polish Frontier*, London, 1944.

Göttingen Research Committee, *Eastern Germany*, Würzburg, 1961.

Göttingen Research Committee, *Emigration. A means of Solving the German Problem?*, Göttingen, 1949.

Gollancz, Victor, *Our Threatened Values*, London, 1946.

Gollancz, Victor, *In Darkest Germany*, London, 1947.

Grau, K. F., *Silesian Inferno*, Cologne, 1970.

Grosser, Alfred, *Germany in Our Time. A Political History of the Postwar Years*, New York, 1971.

Halecki, O., *The Limits and Divisions of European History*, 1950.

Hankey, Lord, *Politics, Trials and Errors*, London, 1950.

Harrimann, Averell, *Peace with Russia?* New York, 1959.

Herford, T. H., *The Case of German South Tyrol Against Italy*, London, 1927.

Hermens, Ferdinand, *Potsdam or Peace*, Chicago, 1946.

Hilberg, Paul, *The Destruction of European Jews*, Chicago, 1961.

Holborn, Louise, *Refugees, A Problem of Our Time*, Metuchen, 1975.

Hollingworth, Claire, *The Three Weeks' War in Poland*, London, 1940.

Irving, David, *The Destruction of Dresden*, London, 1963.

Irving, David, *Churchill and Sikorski. A Tragic Alliance*, London, 1969.

Jasper, Karl, *The Question of German Guilt*, New York, 1961.

Jong, Louis de, *The German Fifth Column in the Second World War*, New York, 1956.

Jordan, Z., *Oder-Neisse Line*, London, 1952.

Kaps, Johannes, *The Tragedy of Silesia*, Munich, 1952.

Keeling, Ralph, *Gruesome Harvest*, Chicago, 1947.

Kennan, George F., *American Diplomacy 1900–1950*, Chicago, 1951.

Kennan, George F., *From Prague after Munich. Diplomatic Papers 1938–1940*, Princeton, 1968.

Kennan, George F., *Russia, the Atom and the West* (The Reith Lectures). London, 1958.

Kirchliche Hilfsstelle, *The Martyrdom of Silesian Priests 1945–1946*, Munich, 1950.

Kohn, Hans, *Pan-Slavism, its History and Ideology*, Notre Dame, 1953.

Kopelev, Lev, *No Jail for Thought*, London, 1976.

Kostrzewski, Joseph, *Poland East of the Oder-Neisse*, London, 1961.

Kulischer, Eugene, *Europe on the Move*, New York, 1948.

Kurth, K. (ed.), *Documents of Humanity*, New York, 1954.

Ladas, Stephen, *The Exchange of Minorities*, New York, 1932.

v. Lehndorff, Hans, *East Prussian Diary 1945–1947*, London, 1963.

Langer, William and Everett, Gleason, *The Challenge to Isolation, 1937–1940*, New York, 1952.

Layton, Sir Walter, *How to Deal with Germany*, London, 1944.

Lerner, Daniel, *Propaganda in War and Crisis*, New York, 1951.

Liddell-Hart, B. E. (ed.), *The Soviet Army*, London, 1956, esp. Keating, Frank, 'The Soviet Army's Behaviour in Victory and Occupation'.

Luza, Radomir, *The Transfer of the Sudeten Germans*, New York, 1964.

Machray, Robert, *The Polish-German Problem*, London, 1941.

Machray, Robert, *East-Prussia: Menace to Poland and Peace*, London, 1943.

Machray, Robert, *The Problem of Upper Silesia*, London, 1945.

Mackiewicz, Joseph, *The Katyn Wood Murders*, London, 1951.

McNeill, W., *America, Britain and Russia: Their Cooperation and Conflict*, New York, 1953.

Mamatey, Victor and Luza, Radomir (eds.), *A History of the Czechoslovak Republic 1918–1948*, Princeton, 1973.

Marzian, Herbert, *The German Frontier Problem*, Göttingen, 1969.

Mayer, A. J., *The Politics and Diplomacy of Peacemaking*, London, 1968.

Mayer, Herbert, *German Recovery and the Marshall Plan*, Bonn, 1969.

Mee, Charles, *Meeting and Potsdam*, New York, 1975.

Meinecke, Friedrich, *The German Catastrophe*, Boston, 1963.

Meyer, Cord, *Mitteleuropa in German Thought and Action 1815–1945*, The Hague, 1955.

Mikolajczyk, Stanislaw, *The Pattern of Soviet Domination*, London, 1948.

Minority Rights Group, *The Crimean Tartars and Volga Germans*, London, 1973.

Morgenthau, Hans (ed.), *Germany and the Future of Europe*, Chicago, 1951.

Morgenthau, Henry, *Germany is our Problem*, New York, 1945.

Morrow, Jan, *The Peace Settlement in the German Polish Borderlands*, London, 1936.

Mosely, Philip E., *Repatriation of Greeks, Turks and Bulgars after the Greco-Turkish War*, Philadelphia, 1941.

Namier, Lewis, *Facing East*, London, 1947.

Nizer, Louis, *What to do with Germany*, New York, 1944.

Pagel, Karl (ed.), *The German East*, Berlin, 1954.

Paikert, G. C., *The German Exodus*, The Hague, 1962.

Paikert, G. C., *The Danube Swabians*, The Hague, 1967.

Palmer, Alan, *The Lands Between, A History of East-Central Europe since the Congress of Vienna*, New York, 1970.

Paprocki, S. I. (ed.), *Minority Affairs and Poland*, Warsaw, 1935.

Perman, D., *The Shaping of the Czechoslovak State*, Leiden, 1962.

Pinson, Koppel, S., *Modern Germany*, New York, 1966.

Planck, Charles R., *The Changing Status of German Reunification in Western Diplomacy 1955–1966*, Baltimore, 1967.

Plischke, Elmer, *Contemporary Government of Germany*, Boston, 1961.

Pounds, Norman, *Divided Germany and Berlin*, Princeton, 1962.

Pounds, Norman, *The Economic Pattern of Modern Germany*, London, 1963.

Price, Harry, *The Marshall Plan and its Meaning*, Ithaca, 1955.

Price, Hoyt and Schorske, Carl, *The Problem of Germany*, Council on Foreign Relations, New York, 1947.

Prittie, Terence, *Germany Divided*, Boston, 1960.

Proudfoot, Malcolm J., *European Refugees*, London, 1957.
Rauschning, Hermann, *The Voice of Destruction*, New York, 1940.
Reitlinger, Gerald, *The Final Solution*, London, 1953.
Reves, E., *The Anatomy of Peace*, New York, 1946.
Rhode, Gotthold, and Wagner, Wolfgang, *The Genesis of the Oder-Neisse Line in the Diplomatic Negotiations During World War II Sources and Documents*, Stuttgart, 1959.
Ripka, H., *The Future of the Czechoslovak Germans*, London, 1944.
Ripka, H., *Munich: Before and After*, London, 1939.
Roberts, H. L., *Russia and America*, New York, 1956.
Robinson, Jacob *et al.*, *Were the Minorities Treaties a Failure?* New York, 1943.
Rothfels, Hans, *German Opposition to Hitler*, London, 1961.
Roucek, Joseph, *Central-Eastern Europe, Crucible of World Wars*, New York, 1946.
Rozek, Edward, *Allied Wartime Diplomacy*, New York, 1958.
Ryan, Cornelius, *The Last Battle*, New York, 1966.
Schechtman, J., *European Population Transfers*, New York, 1946.
Schimitzek, Stalislaw, *Truth or Conjecture – German Civilian War Losses in the East*, Warsaw, 1966.
Schlamm, William, *Germany and the East-West Crisis: The Decisive Challenge to American Policy*, New York, 1959.
Schoenberg, Hans, *Germans from the East*, The Hague, 1970.
Schwarz, Leo, *Refugees in Germany Today*, New York, 1957.
Seaton, Albert, *The Russo-German War 1941–45*, London, 1971.
Seton-Watson, Hugh, *Eastern Europe between the Wars*, Cambridge, 1946.
Settel, Arthur (ed.), *This is Germany*, New York, 1950.
Seyda, Marjan, *Poland and Germany and the Post-War Reconstruction of Europe*, New York, 1943.
Sharp, S., *Poland's White Eagle on a Red Field*, Cambridge, Mass., 1953.
Sharp, Tony, *The Wartime Alliance and the Zonal Division of Germany*, London, 1975.
Simpson, Sir John Hope, *The Refugee Problem*, London, 1939.
Snyder, Louis, *German Nationalism. The Tragedy of a People*, Harrisburg, 1952.
Snyder, L. (ed.), *Documents of German History*, New Brunswick, 1958.
Solzhenitsyn, Alexander, *The Gulag Archipelago*, New York, 1974.
Solzhenitsyn, Alexander, *One Day in the Life of Ivan Denisovich*, New York, 1963.
Speier, Hans, *Divided Berlin. The Anatomy of Soviet Political Blackmail*, New York, 1961.
Strauss, Franz Josef, *The Grand Design – A European Solution to German Reunification*, London, 1965.
Swanstrom, E., *Pilgrims of the Night. A Study of Expelled Peoples*, New York, 1950.
Szaz, Zoltan, *Germany's Eastern Territories. The Problem of the Oder-Neisse Line*, Chicago, 1960.

Taborsky, Eduard, *The Czechoslovak Cause. An Account of the Problems of International Law in Relation to Czechoslovakia*, London, 1944.

Taborsky, Eduard, *Czechoslovak Democracy at Work*, London, 1945.

Taborsky, Eduard, *Benes and Stalin. Moscow 1943 and 1945*, Springfield, Illinois, 1953–4.

Taylor, A. J. P., *The Origins of the Second World War*, London, 1961.

Taylor, A. J. P., *From Sarajevo to Potsdam*, London, 1966.

Thompson, Laurence, *The Greatest Treason*, New York, 1968.

Thomsen, D., Meyer, E., Brigge, A., *Patterns of Peacemaking*, New York, 1945.

Thorwald, Jürgen, *Flight in the Winter*, London, 1953.

Tilford, Roger (ed.), *The Ostopolitik and Political Change in Germany*, Lexington, Mass., 1975.

Toland, John, *The Last 100 Days*, New York, 1966.

Toynbee, Arnold, *The World After the Peace Conference*, London, 1926.

Utley, Freda, *The High Cost of Vengeance*, Chicago, 1949.

Vansittart, Lord Robert Gilbert, *Black Record*, London, 1941.

Vansittart, Lord Robert Gilbert, *Roots of the Trouble*, London, 1942.

Vansittart, Lord Robert Gilbert, *Bones of Contention*, London, 1943.

Vansittart, Lord Robert Gilbert, *The Mist Procession*, London, 1958.

Veale, F. J. P., *Advance to Barbarism*, New York, 1968.

Vernant, Jacques, *The Refugee in the Post-War World*, London, 1953.

Voigt, F. A., *Documents on the Expulsion of the Sudeten Germans*, Munich, 1953.

Wagner, Wolfgang, *The Genesis of the Oder-Neisse Line*, Stuttgart, 1957.

Welles, Sumner, *The World of the Four Freedoms*, New York, 1943.

Welles, Sumner, *Time for Decision*, New York, 1944.

Welles, Sumner, *Where are We Heading*, New York, 1946.

Welles, Sumner, *Seven Decisions that Shaped History*, New York, 1951.

Werth, Alexander, *Russia at War 1941–1945*, New York, 1964.

Wheeler-Bennett, John, *Munich. Prologue to Tragedy*, New York, 1948.

Wilder, J. A., *The Polish Regained Provinces*, London, 1948.

Wiskemann, Elisabeth, *Czechs and Germans*, New York, 1967.

Wiskemann, Elisabeth, *Undeclared War*, London, 1967.

Wiskemann, Elisabeth, *Germany's Eastern Neighbours*, London, 1956.

Wittlin, Thaddeus, *Time Stopped at 6:30*, Indianapolis, 1965.

Wolfe, James, *Indivisible Germany*, The Hague, 1963.

Woodward, L., *British Foreign Policy in the Second World War* (3 vols), London, 1970, 1971.

Zhukov, Marshal (ed. by Harrison Salisbury), *Marshal Zhukov's Greatest Battles*, New York, 1969.

Zimmern, Sir Alfred, *The American Road to World Peace*, New York, 1953.

Zink, Harold, *The United States in Germany, 1944–1955*, New York, 1957.

V ENGLISH-LANGUAGE SOURCES (LEGAL)

Baxter, R. R., 'Treaties and Custom', *Recueil des Cours* de l'Academie die Droit International. Leiden, 1970.
Brownlie, Ian, *Principles of Public International Law*, London, 1972.
Claude, Inis, *National Minorities. An International Problem*, Cambridge, Mass. 1955.
Cukwurah, A., *The Settlement of Boundary Disputes in International Law*, Manchester, 1967.
Friedman, Leon, *The Law of War*, New York, 1972.
Friedmann, Wolfgang, *Allied Military Government of Germany*, London, 1947.
Gruchman, Bohdan, Klafkowski, Alfons, *Polish Western Territories*, Poznan, 1959.
Jennings, R. Y., *The Acquisition of Territory in International Law*, Manchester, 1963.
Klafkowski, Alfons, *The Potsdam Agreement*, Warsaw, 1963.
Kokot, Jozèf, *The Logic of the Oder-Neisse Frontier*, Poznan, 1959.
Lachs, Manfred, *The Polish German Frontier*, Warsaw, 1964.
Lauterpacht, H., *International Law and Human Rights*, London, 1950.
Luard, E., *The International Regulation of Frontier Disputes*, New York, 1970.
Macartney, C. A., *National States and National Minorities*, London, 1934.
McNair, Lord Arnold and Watts, A. D., *Legal Effects of War*, Cambridge, 1966.
O'Connell, D. P., *The Law of State Succession*, London, 1956.
O'Connell, D. P., *International Law* (2nd edn), London, 1970.
Oppenheim, L., *International Law* (7th edn), London, 1955.
Pompe, C. A., *Aggressive War – An International Crime*, The Hague, 1953.
Stone, Julius, *Regional Guarantees of Minority Rights*, New York, 1933.
Tunkin, G. I., *Theory of International Law*, London, 1974.
Wambaugh, Sarah, *Plebiscites Since the World War, with a collection of Official Documents*, Washington, 1933.
Wambaugh, Sarah, *The Saar Plebiscite*, Cambridge, 1940.
Wiewiora, B., *The Polish-German Frontier* (2nd ed.), Poznan, 1964.
Winiewicz, Józef, *The Polish-German Frontier*, London, 1944.

VI GERMAN-LANGUAGE SOURCES (GENERAL)

Adler, H. G., *Theresienstadt 1941–1945, Das Antlitz einer Zwangsgemeinschaft*, Tübingen, 1955.
Ahrens, Wilfried (ed.), *Verbrechen an Deutschen*, Huglfing, 1975.
Aurich, Peter, *Der Deutsch-Polnische September 1939*, Munich, 1970.
Becker, Rolf, *Niederschlesien 1945. Die Flucht, die Besetzung*, Bad Nauheim, 1965.
Bekker, Cajus, *Flucht übers Meer*, Oldenburg, 1964.

Betz, H., *Flüchtlings-Schicksal auf dem Lande*, Frankfurt am Main, 1949.
Böhling, Peter, *Die Nationalpolnische Bewegung in Westpreussen, 1815–1871*, Marburg, 1973.
Bohmann, Alfred, *Menschen und Grenzen*, vols 1–4, Cologne, 1969–75.
Bohmann, Alfred, *Die Ausweisung der Sudetendeutschen*, Marburg, 1955.
Breyer, R., *Das Deutsche Reich und Polen 1932–1937*, Würzburg, 1955.
Broszat, Martin, *Zweihundert Jahre deutsche Polenpolitik*, Munich, 1963.
Broszat, Martin, *Nationalsozialistische Polenpolitik 1939–1945*, Stuttgart, 1961.
Brügel, Johann, *Die Aussiedlung der Deutschen aus der Tschechoslowakei*, Stuttgart, 1960.
Brügel, Johann, *Tschechen und Deutsche 1918–1938*, Munich, 1967.
Brügel, Johann, *Tschechen und Deutsche 1939–1946*, Munich, 1974.
Brustat-Naval, Fritz, *Unternehmen Rettung*, Herford, 1970.
Burckhardt, Carl, *Meine Danziger Mission*, Munich, 1960.
Dieckert, Major, Grossmann, General, *Der Kampf um Ostpreussen*, Munich, 1960.
Eggert, Oskar, *Geschichte Pommerns*, Hamburg, 1974.
Esser, Heinz, *Lamsdorf. Dokumentation über ein polnisches Vernichtungslager*, Bonn, 1971.
Falk, Lucy, *Ich blieb in Königsberg*, Munich, 1965.
Fechner, H., *Deutschland und Polen, 1772–1945*, Würzburg, 1964.
Fischer, Alexander (ed.), *Teheran, Jalta, Potsdam*, Cologne, 1968.
Franzel, E., *Die Vertreibung Sudetenland 1945–1946*, Bad Nauheim, 1967.
Fredmann, Ernst, *Sie kamen übers Meer*, Cologne, 1971.
Göttinger Arbeitskreis, *Das Östliche Deutschland*, Würzburg, 1959.
Göttinger Arbeitskreis, *Dokumente der Menschlichkeit*, Würzburg, 1960.
Gollancz, Victor, *Stimme aus dem Chaos*, Frankfurt, 1960.
Grimm, Hans, *Volk Ohne Raum*, Berlin, 1926.
Guz, Eugeniusz und Weseloh, Hans, *Der Kongress von Helsinki*, Stuttgart, 1975.
Hillgruber, A. (ed.), *Probleme des Zweiten Weltkrieges*, Cologne, 1967.
Hofbauer, J. and Strauss, E., *Josef Seliger – Ein Lebensbild*, Prague, 1930.
Hossbach, Friedrich, *Die Schlacht um Ostpreussen*, Überlingen, 1951.
Hubatsch, W., *Die Deutsche Frage*, Würzburg, 1961.
Jahn, Hans-Edgar, *Pommersche Passion*, Preetz, 1964.
Jaksch, Wenzel, *Der Weg nach Potsdam*, Stuttgart, 1958.
Kielczewska, Marja und Grodek, Andrzei, *Oder Neisse, die beste Grenze Polens*, Poznan, 1946.
Klepetar, Harry, *Seit 1918 . . . Eine Geschichte der tschechoslowakischen Republik*, Moravska-Ostrava, 1937.
Kopelew, Lew, *Aufbewahren für alle Zeit*, Hamburg, 1976.
Lapradelle, Geouffre de, *Verjagt, beraubt, erschlagen*, Wiesbaden, 1961.
Lange, Friedrich, *Ostland kehrt heim*, Berlin, 1940.

Lasch, Otto, *So fiel Königsberg*, Munich, 1958.
Lass, Edgar, *Die Flucht – Ostpreussen 1944–45*, Bad Nauheim, 1964.
Lemberg, Eugen and Edding, Friedrich (eds), *Die Vertriebenen in Westdeutschland*, vols 1–3, Kiel, 1959.
Loeber, Dietrich, *Diktierte Option*, Neumünster, 1974.
v. Loesch, Freda, *Die Deutschen in den osteuropäischen Staaten*, Munich, 1972.
Lüdde-Neurath, Walter, *Regierung Dönitz*, Göttingen, 1964.
Mackiewicz, Josef, *Katyn – ungesühntes Verbrechen*, Zürich, 1949.
Marzian, Herbert, *Annexion und Massenvertreibung. Festschrift für Herbert Kraus*, Würzburg, 1964.
Meisner, Boris, *Russland, die Westmächte und Deutschland*, Hamburg, 1953.
Müller-Sternberg, Robert, *Deutsche Ostsiedlung – Eine Bilanz für Europa*, Bielefeld, 1971.
Murawski, Erich, *Die Eroberung Pommerns durch die Rote Armee*, Boppard am Rhein, 1969.
Nahm, Peter, *Nach zwei Jahrzehnten: Erlebnisberichte über Flucht, Vertreibung und Eingliederung*, Bonn, 1961.
Osteuropa-Institut, *Oberschlesien und der Genfer Schiedsspruch*, Breslau, 1925.
Paul, Ernst, *Es gibt nicht nur ein Lidice*, Munich, n.d.
Pius XII, *Zum Problem der Vertreibung*, Cologne, 1953.
Plaschka, Richard and Mack, Karlheinz (eds), *Die Auflösung des Habsburgerreiches*, Munich, 1970, especially contribution by John Bradley, 'Die Teschechoslowakische Legion und die Haltung der Alliierten zur Auflösung der Habsburgermonarchie'.
Rachocki, Janusz, *Volksrepublik Polen/Bundesrepublik Deutschland. Probleme der Normalisierung gegenseitiger Beziehungen*, Poznan, 1972.
Rauschning, H., *Die Entdeutschung Posens und Westpreussens*, Berlin, 1930.
Rauschning, H., *Deutschland zwischen West und Ost.*, Stuttgart, 1950.
Rauschning, Hermann, *Ist Friede noch möglich?* Heidelberg, 1953.
Reece, Carrol, *Das Recht auf Deutschlands Osten*, Göttingen, 1957.
Reichenberger, E. J., *Ostdeutsche Passion*, Munich, 1948.
Reichenberger, E. J., *Fahrt durch besiegtes, Land*, Karlsruhe, 1950.
Rhode, Gotthold, *Die Ostgebiete des Deutschen Reiches*, Würzburg, 1955.
Rimscha, Hans von, *Die Umsiedlung der Deutschbalten aus Lettland im Jahre 1939*, Hannover, 1959.
Ritter, Gerhard, *Carl Goerdeler und die deutsche Widerstandsbewegung*, Stuttgart, 1954.
Roegele, Otto B. (ed.), *Versöhnung oder Hass? Der Schriftwechsel der Bischofe Polens und Deutschlands und seine Folgen*, Osnabrück, 1966.
v. Rosen, Hans Freiherr, *Bilanz, das deutsche Gut in Posen und Pommerellen*, Rosbach v.d.H., 1972.
Rothfels, Hans, *Bismarck, der Osten und das Reich.* Darmstadt, 1960.
Schimitzek, Stanislav, *Vertreibungsverluste? Westdeutsche Zahlenspiele*, Warsaw, 1966.

Schenck, Ernst-Günther, *Das menschliche Elend im 20. Jahrhundert*, Herford, 1960.
Schulz, Eberhard (ed.), *Leistung und Schicksal*, Cologne, 1967.
Schulz, Rudolf, *Der deutsche Bauer im Baltikum*, Berlin, 1938.
Schwarz, Wolfgang, *Die Flucht und Vertreibung – Oberschlesien*, Bad Nauheim, 1965.
Schweitzer, Albert, *Das Problem des Friedens in der heutigen Welt*, Munich, 1954.
Simon, Ellen and Möhring, Werner, *Millionen ohne Heimat*, Frankfurt am Main, 1950.
Solschenizyn, *Ostpreussische Nächte*, Darmstadt, 1976.
Steinert, Marlis, *Die 23 Tage der Regierung Dönitz*, Düsseldorf, 1967.
Thorwald, Jürgen, *Es begann an der Weichsel*, Stuttgart, 1950.
v. Tippelskirch, Kurt, *Geschichte des zweiten Weltkrieges*, Bonn, 1951.
Turnwald, Wilhelm, *Dokumente zur Austreibung der Sudetendeutschen*, Munich, 1951.
Wagner, Ruth and Stamm, Hans, *Die letzten Stunden daheim*, Cologne, 1972.
Wagner, Wolfgang, *Die Entstehung der Oder-Neisse Linie*, Stuttgart, 1953.
Wüscht, Johann, *Geschichte der Deutschen in Jugoslawien*, Kehl, 1966.
Ziemer, Gerhard, *Deutscher Exodus*, Stuttgart, 1973.
Zöllner, Erich, *Geschichte Österreichs*, Vienna, 1961.

VII GERMAN-LANGUAGE SOURCES (LEGAL)

Blumenwitz, Dieter, *Die Grundlagen eines Friedensvertrages mit Deutschland. Ein völkerrechtlicher Beitrag zur künftigen Deutschlandpolotik*, Berlin, 1966.
Decker, Günther, *Das Selbstbestimmungsrecht der Nationen*, Göttingen, 1955.
du Buy, F. H., *Das Recht auf die Heimat im historischpolitischen Prozess*, Euskirchen, 1974.
Faust, Fritz, *Das Potsdamer Abkommen und seine völkerrechtliche Bedeutung*, Berlin, 1964.
Heinze, Kurt und Schilling, Karl, *Die Rechtsprechung der Nürnberger Militärtribunale*, Bonn, 1952.
Kimminich, Otto, *Menschenrechte, Versagen und Hoffnung*, Munich, 1973.
Kimminich, Otto, *Das Münchener Abkommen in der tschechoslowakischen wissenschaftlichen Literatur*, Munich, 1968.
Klafkowski, Alfons, *Die Rechtsgrundlage der Oder-Neisse Linie auf Grund von Jalta und Potsdam*, Poznan, 1947.
Kloss, Heinz (ed.), *Beiträge zu einem System des Selbstbestimmungsrechts*, Band 2. Völkerrechtliche Abhandlungen. Vienna, 1970.
Kraus, Herbert, *Massenaustreibung und Völkermord*, Kitzingen, 1953.
Kraus, Herbert, *Die Oder-Neisse Linie, eine völkerrechtliche Studie*, Cologne Braunsfeld, 1954.

Kraus, Herbert, *Der völkerrechtliche Status der deutschen Ostgebiete innerhalb der Reichsgrenzen nach dem Stande vom 31.12.1937*, Göttingen, 1966.

Kraus, Herbert and Kurth, Karl, *Deutschlands Ostproblem*, Würzburg, 1958.

Krülle, Sigrid, *Die völkerrechtlichen Aspekte des Oder-Neisse Problems*, Berlin, 1970.

Lachs, M., *Die Westgrenze Polens*, Warsaw, 1967.

Laun, Rudolf, *Das Recht auf die Heimat*, Hannover, 1951.

Maurach, Reinhart, *Handbuch der Sowjetverfassung*, Munich, 1955.

Menzel, Eberhard, *Das Annexionsverbot des modernen Völkerrechts in das östliche Deutschland*, Würzburg, 1959.

Meyer-Lindenberg, Hermann, *Deutschlands Grenzen, Die politische Meinung*, Cologne, 1962.

Mosler, Hermann and Doehring, Karl, *Die Beendigung des Kriesszustands mit Deutschland nach dem zweiten Weltkrieg*, Cologne, 1963.

Mosler, Hermann (ed.), *Fontes Juris Gentium*, Cologne and Berlin.

Parplies, Hans Günther, *Deutschland nach den Verträgen*, Hamburg, 1975.

Pieper, Helmut, *Die Minderheitenfrage und das Deutsche Reich, 1919–1934*, Hamburg, 1974.

Rabl, Kurt, *Das Selbstbestimmungsrecht der Völker*, Cologne, 1973.

Rabl, Kurt, *Das Recht auf die Heimat*, 4 vols, Munich, 1960.

Raschhofer, Hermann, *Die Sudetenfrage: Ihre völkerrechtliche Entwicklung vom Ersten Weltkrieg bis zur Gegenwart*, Munich, 1953.

Rauschning, Dietrich (ed.), *Die Gesamtverfassung Deutschlands*, Frankfurt, 1962.

Rauschning, Dietrich (ed.), *Verträge und andere Akten zur Rechtsstellung Deutschlands*, Munich, 1975.

Schätzel, Walter and Veiter, Theodor, *Handbuch des internationalen Flüchtlingsrechts*, Vienna, 1959.

Scheuner, J. and Lindemann, B. (eds), *Die Vereinten Nationen und die Mitarbeit der Bundesrepublik Deutschland*, Munich, 1973.

Seidl-Hohenfeldern, Ignaz, *Das Münchener Abkommen im Lichte des Prager Vertrages von 1973. In Recht im Dienst des Friedens, Festschrift für Eberhard Menzel*, Berlin, 1975.

Seidl-Hohenfeldern, Ignaz, *Völkerrecht* (2nd edn), Cologne, 1969.

v. Stedingk, Ivonne, *Die Organisation des Flüchtlingswesens in Österreich seit dem Zweiten Weltkrieg*, Vienna, 1970.

Stöder, Rolf, *Deutschlands Rechtslage*, Hamburg, 1948.

Streit, G., *Der Lausanner Vertrag und der griechischtürkische Bevölkerungsaustausch*, Berlin, 1929.

Thomas, Fritz, *Das Recht der Vertriebenen*, Dortmund, 1950.

Truhart, H. v., *Völkerbund und Minderheiten Petitionen*, Vienna, 1931.

Tunkin, Gregorij, *Das Völkerrecht der Gegenwart*, E. Berlin, 1963.

Urbanek, Kurt, *Das Heimkehrrecht der deutschen Ausgetriebenen: ein Anspruch des positiven Völkerrechts*, Dortmund, 1959.

Veiter, Theodor (ed.), *System eines internationalen Volksgruppenrechts*, Vienna, 1970.

Veiter, Theodor and Klein, Friedrich (ed.), *Die Menschenrechte*, Vienna, 1966.

Verdross, Alfred, *Völkerrecht*, vols 1–3 (5th edn), Vienna, 1964.

Wiewiora, Boleslaw, *Die Anerkennung territorialer Erwerbungen im Völkerrecht*. Poznan, 1961. Translated by Göttinger Research Committee, Göttingen, 1962.

Zayas, Alfred de, 'Massenumsiedlungen und das Völkerrecht', *Abhandlungen zu Flüchtlingsfragen*, vol. 10, Vienna, 1975.

Zieger, Gottfried, *Die Atlantik Charter*, Hannover, 1963.

Zieger, Gottfried, *Alliierte Kriegskonferenzen 1941–43*, Hannover, 1964.

Zieger, Gottfried, *Die Teheran Konferenz*, Hannover, 1967.

Zieger, Gottfried, *Der Warschauer Pakt*, Hannover, 1974.

VIII   FRENCH-LANGUAGE SOURCES (INCLUDING SOME IMPORTANT ARTICLES)

Academie de Droit International, *Recueil des Cours*, 1923, vol. 1; 1927, vol. 3; 1928, vol. 4; 1957, vol. 2. The Hague.

Annuaire de l'Institut de Droit International, vol. 44, 1952; vol. 46, 1956. Geneva.

Anders, Wladislaw, *Katyn*, Paris, 1949.

Aron, R., *Paix et Guerre entre les Nations*, Paris, 1962.

Barraclough, G., *Une Voix dans le désert*, Cahiers Pologne-Allemagne, Paris, no. 3, 1963.

Carzou, Jean Marie, *Un genocide exemplaire. Arménie 1915*, Paris, 1975.

George, Bernard, *Les Russes Arrivent*, Paris, 1966.

George, Pierre, *Le Problème allemand en Tchécoslovaquie (1919–1946)*, Paris, 1947.

d'Harcourt, R., *Visage de l'Allemagne actuelle*, Paris, 1949.

Institut National de la Statistique et des études économiques, *Les minorités ethiques en Europe centrale et balkanique*, Paris, 1946.

Institut National de la Statistique et des études économiques, *Les transferts internationaux de populations*, Paris, 1946.

La Pradelle, Paul de, *La Frontière*, Paris, 1928.

La Pradelle, Raymond de Geouffre de, *Le Problème de la Silésie et le Droit*, Paris, 1958.

Laun, Rudolf, 'Le droit des peoples à disposer d'eux mêmes', *Annuaire de l'Association des Auditeurs de l'Académie de Droit International de la Haye*, The Hague, 1958.

Mordal, Jacques, *La Guerre a Commencé en Pologne*, Paris, 1968.

Noel, Léon, *L'agression allemande contre la Pologne*, Paris, 1946.

Pange, Jean de, 'Les Populations expulsées de l'Allemagne Orientale', *Revue des Deux Mondes*, Paris, June 1952.

Pictet, Jean, *La Convention de Genève Relative à la Protection des Personnes Civiles en Temps de Guerre*, Geneva, 1958.

Pictet, Jean, *Les principes du Droit international humanitaire*, Geneva, 1966.

Pinon, René, 'La Destin de la Pologne', *Revue des Deux Mondes*, Paris, September 1952.

Pinto, R., 'Les thèses "juridiques" du cercle de Göttingen sur la frontière polono-allemande', *Cahiers Pologne-Allemagne*, Paris, no. 4, 1963.

Visscher, Charles de, *Problèmes de Confins en Droit International Public*, Paris, 1969.

Visscher, Charles de, *Les Effectivités du Droit International Public*, Paris, 1967.

IX   DISSERTATIONS

Binzberger, Peter, 'Die Ausweisung der Volksdeutschen aus den Donau-Karpaten Raum', Tübingen, 1952.

Bötzer, Brigitte, 'Das Vertriebenenproblem in der Münchener Tagespresse, 1945–1953', Munich, 1957.

Braumühl, Gerold von, 'Austreibungsverbot und Rücksiedlungsanspruch im geltenden Völkerrecht', Mainz, 1963.

Brown, MacAlister, 'Expulsion of German Minorities from Eastern Europe: The Decision at Potsdam and its Background', Harvard, 1953.

Fischer, Diether, 'Die Aussichten für die Positivierung eines Menschenrechts auf die Heimat', Würzburg, 1966.

Fukas, Dieter, 'Gibt es im positiven Völkerrecht eine Norm des Inhalts, dass der Mensch in der Heimat leben und nicht aus ihr vertrieben werden darf?', Erlangen, 1960.

Gawenda, Jerzy, 'Le Plébiscite en droit international', University of Fribourg, Switzerland, 1946.

Habel, Fritz Peter, 'Historische, politische und soziale Voraussetzungen des Zusammentreffens zwischen Bayern und Sudetendeutschen nach 1945', Munich, 1966.

Hilf, Rudolf, 'Die Presse der Sudetendeutschen nach 1945 und ihre Stellungnahme zum Schicksal der vertriebenen Volksgruppe', Munich, 1951.

Jessen, Jacob, 'Rechtsfragen der deutschen Umsiedlung nach dem 2. Weltkrieg', Kiel, 1951.

Oberkesch, Valentin, 'Völkerrechtliche Betrachtungen zum Problem der deutschen Heimatvertriebenen', Graz, 1952.

Schmidt, Manfred, 'The East German Landsmannschaften in the German Federal Republic. Their Organization and Influence', Ann Arbor: University of Michigan, 1959.

Strauss, Harold, 'The Division and Dismemberment of Germany', University of Geneva, 1952.

Tichy, Karl, 'Die Massenausweisungen nach dem 2. Weltkrieg und das öffentliche Recht', Tübingen, 1949.

Wetz, Wolfgang, 'Selbstbestimmungsrecht der Völker und völkerrechtlicher Schutz nationaler Minderheiten in den Friedensverträgen von Versailles und St. Germain en Laye', University of Freiburg, 1929.

X PERSONAL INTERVIEWS

Partial list of interviews and conversations that contributed to the making of this book (protocols and tape-recordings in author's files).

Hon. George F. Kennan, Princeton
Hon. Robert D. Murphy, New York
David Small, Office of the Legal Adviser to the State Department

Professor Dr Hans Booms, Dr Johannes Hopf, Budesarchiv Koblenz
Professor Walter Mertineit, German UNESCO Commission, head of German Delegation to German-Polish Schoolbook Conference
Kurt Boehme, German Red Cross, Bonn
Professor Hans Rothfels, Tübingen
Bishop Johann Neuhäusler, Munich
Professor Józef Kokot, Silesian Institute (Instytut Slaski, Opole)
Director Roman Wionczek, Warsaw
Dr Jiri Toman, Institut Henry-Dunant, Geneva

Belgian and French Prisoners of War:
Arthur Keppenne, Pierre Pirotte, Charles Boyen, Clodomir Richard

German military and political leaders involved in evacuation, flight, capitulation, etc.:
Grand Admiral Karl Dönitz, Aumühle
Count Lutz Schwerin von Krosigk, Essen
General Friedrich Hossbach (defence of East Prussia)
General Erich Dethleffsen (defence of East Prussia)
General Ernst König (defence of East Prussia)
Oberstleutnant Bruno Kerwin (capitulation of Königsberg)
Admiral Konrad Engelhardt (Baltic evacuation)
Admiral Adalbert v. Blanc (Baltic evacuation)
Kpt. z.See Hans Meckel (Baltic evacuation)
Korvettenkapitän Hugo Heyel (Baltic evacuation)

Expellee accounts, expellee organizations (more than 300 interviews):
Joachim and Freda von Loesch, Bonn
Hans Freiherr von Rosen, Rossbach
Count Hans von Lehndorff, Bonn
Count Carl Elimar zu Eulenburg, Göttingen

Members of West-German Parliament:
Minister a.D. Heinz-Joachim v. Merkatz
Minister a.D. Theodor Oberländer
Minister a.D. Heinz Starke
Minister a.D. Heinrich Windelen
Dr. Walter Becher, Dr Philip v. Bismarck, Dr Herbert Czaja, Dr Herbert Hupka, Dr Hans Edgar Jahn, Manfred Schmidt, Count Franz v. Stauffenberg, Karl Friedrich Storm.

INDEX

Numbers in **bold type** indicate more important references

A graduate of the Harvard Law School and a member of the New York and Florida Bar, Alfred de Zayas worked for 2 years as an attorney on Wall Street. A Fulbright Graduate Fellowship in Germany led to an appointment at the University of Göttingen, where he is at present head of a research team at the Institute of Public International Law. Upon conclusion of a new book on human rights law Mr de Zayas plans to return to the United States.